ALLIED DUNBAR

RETIREMENT PLANNING HANDBOOK

7th edition

edited by

David Bertram

CPG
CLAYFIELD PROFESSIONAL GUIDANCE LTD

PEARSON EDUCATION LIMITED

London Office:
128 Long Acre, London WC2E 9AN
Tel: +44 (0)171 447 2000
Fax: +44 (0)171 240 5771
Website : www.pearsoned-ema.com

First published in Great Britain in 1999

ISBN 0 273 64173 5

British Library Cataloguing in Publication Data
A CIP catalogue record for this book can be obtained from the British Library

Typeset by M Rules
Printed and bound in Great Britain by
Biddles Ltd, Guildford, Surrey

The Publishers' policy is to use paper manufactured from sustainable forests.

CONTENTS

PREFACE

We all want a long life and a merry one. But while your allotted life span is in the lap of the gods, your lifestyle in retirement is very much down to you. Money will not necessarily make you merry, but the lack of it is guaranteed to bring misery.

If you have not yet started to plan seriously for retirement, consider this. Early retirement – often compulsory following a corporate 'downsizing' exercise – is endemic in the UK. Despite your best laid plans, you may yet be one of the thousands who each year are forced to accept a longer than expected retirement on a lower than expected pension.

Moreover, as a nation we are blessed with increased longevity. Yet the experience of our parents and elderly relatives has taught us that a long life is not always a healthy one, let alone merry. The number of frail elderly people entering residential care and nursing homes is rising rapidly – as are the costs. If you planned to live comfortably in retirement and to leave behind a tidy sum you may find that nursing home fees at £15,000 to £20,000 a year will quickly decimate your children's inheritance.

In a changing world, one thing is certain. The state will not provide. The Labour Government, like the Conservative Government before it, aims to help people to help themselves. The cradle to grave welfare state is truly a thing of the past and retirement after the Millennium will be a private affair. Private, that is, because for most people it will be virtually entirely financed from private means.

Good financial planning to a large extent depends on a stable environment for our investments. Unfortunately, what we face is a period of great change and uncertainty. The Government plans to completely overhaul the state pension and many aspects of the private pension system. This is likely to encourage those who do not presently save, to do so. However, higher earners and those with substantial pension funds may find the tax and contribution rules less attractive.

Good independent advice and a practical, flexible retirement plan are essential. Your first priority will be your pension. You may also decide to take out some insurance to cover your long-term care needs – or trust to luck and a healthy bank balance. Protecting your loved ones should you die clearly is essential and need not be expensive. You may also have the means to invest to provide a boost to your income or to fund capital projects such as that world cruise you always promised yourself or the cottage by the sea.

Whichever options you select, armed with the increased financial knowledge this book offers, you will have the courage and confidence to make well informed choices.

1

INTRODUCTION TO FINANCIAL PLANNING FOR RETIREMENT

This opening chapter outlines the importance of financial planning in the context of your retirement. It also explains how this book can help you understand what you need to know about your retirement income – whether this is derived solely from pensions or from a mixture of pensions and other investments – and how taxation affects all your financial arrangements.

1.1 THE STRUCTURE OF THE BOOK

The book is broadly divided into three sections. The first section (Chapters 2–6) concentrates mainly on pension planning, which is likely to form the foundation of your retirement income. However, many people are not able or do not wish to derive all their retirement income from pensions and so this section also examines other suitable investments for long-term income and growth.

The second section (Chapters 7–12) looks at the wider aspects of financial planning – for example protection insurances, taxation and how to make a will. There is also a chapter on retiring abroad.

The third section (Chapters 13–15) focuses on the problems of later retirement when, unfortunately, physical and mental frailty may influence or even determine your lifestyle. With an increase in both the number of employees who take early retirement and their longevity, it is no longer unusual to have two retired generations in the same family. This means that the problem of looking after frail elderly parents in the light of welfare cuts is likely to coincide with your own retirement planning and concern about long-term care.

Finally, Appendix 1 provides a bluffer's guide to all the financial terms you are likely to come across, while Appendix 2 provides further sources of information and useful contact addresses.

1.2 THE IMPORTANCE OF GOOD PLANNING

Few people have the confidence and expertise to plan all their investments and insurances themselves. There is no shortage of help. The UK has over 22,000 independent financial advisers, several thousand professional advisers (chartered accountants and solicitors, for example) and a further 60,000 company representatives. If you need help your problem will not be how to find an adviser, but how to find a good one.

Appendix 2 lists some useful organisations which can get you started. Our comments here are confined to the more general considerations you make when selecting a firm.

Above all it is essential that your adviser considers all your financial requirements and not, say, just your pension plan or long-term care insurance in isolation. A good plan, therefore, is likely to incorporate the following topics and will be updated, preferably annually, to take account of developments:

- Protection insurance
- General savings and investments
- Retirement provision (state, occupational and private)
- Investing to pay specific bills or debts – for example, repayment of the mortgage or regular contributions to school fees for grandchildren
- Income and capital gains tax planning
- Estate planning, including inheritance tax (IHT) and making a will

Your adviser should have access to a wide range of technical expertise. This does not mean you have to go to a large and expensive firm. However, if the firm is too small to cater for all the above categories it should have close contacts with other professional firms which can supply the missing elements.

Finally on this point, in order to provide the best financial plan, firms must be able to draw on every available good quality insurance product, savings scheme and taxation arrangement – they should not be restricted in their choice, nor should they be influenced by the amount of sales commission offered by the product providers.

1.3 AUTHORISATION AND REGULATION

The 1986 Financial Services Act (FSA) set up a system of self-regulation for financial services in the UK. Under this system each firm or company is regulated by a self-regulatory organisation (SRO) or, in the case of the professionals bodies, by a recognised professional body (RPB).

If you use an unauthorised firm or you invest in a scheme which itself is unauthorised you are taking an unnecessary risk and you will not be entitled to compensation if things go wrong. You can check authorisation by making a quick phone call to the Securities and Investments Board which runs a comprehensive database. Details are provided in Appendix 2.

Under the FSA, advisers are split into two broad categories: company or appointed representatives, and independent financial advisers. The important point to remember is that company representatives are employed by, and work solely for, just one company. They can only sell the products of the company they represent and through which they are authorised. Appointed representatives are companies which have a contract with a financial institution to sell one or more of their products in return for commission. So, here again, your choice will be very limited.

Independent financial advisers (IFAs), as their name suggests, are not tied to one company. Their job is to examine your needs and to select the product that offers the best value in terms of performance, charges, and contract flexibility, among other factors.

In theory at least, you stand a better chance of coming away with the right insurances and investments than if you go to a company or appointed representative. However, IFAs vary considerably in their level of competence. Ultimately your choice of adviser will be dictated partly by your pocket and partly by your requirements. However, there are certain guidelines to remember.

1.4 QUALIFICATIONS

Qualifications are becoming increasingly important in the financial services sector and are a good indication of a firm's commitment to high standards. Stockbrokers, for example, are regulated by the Securities and Futures Authority and in order to give you advice they must first pass the SFA's 'Registered Persons Examinations'.

A committed investment adviser is also likely to be a member of The Securities Institute. To become a full member the adviser needs to pass the Institute's Diploma, which is a professional level qualification for practitioners who have already gained experience in such areas as securities, derivatives, corporate finance and investment management.

For more general investment advice you can go to a firm of independent financial advisers or financial planners. This category includes an increasing number of chartered accountants and solicitors who specialise in this area.

All advisers should have achieved a 'benchmark' or basic qualification. There are several of these but you are most likely to come across the Financial Planning Certificate (FPC). This is examined by the Chartered Insurance Institute (CII). The Securities Institute also runs a benchmark examination for independent advisers – the Investment Advice Certificate. Accountants and bankers have their own benchmark regulatory qualifications.

The next stage up from the FPC is the Advanced Financial Planning Certificate (AFPC), which includes a personal investment planning syllabus. The AFPC allows advisers to become full members of the Society of Financial Advisers (SOFA), the financial services arm of the CII. SOFA has launched associate and fellowship qualifications.

The AFPC also allows advisers to become associate members of the Institute of Financial Planning. Through the Institute, members can take the CFP – the Certified Financial Planner which is recognised in six countries: the UK, the US, Canada, Japan, Australia and New Zealand.

1.5 RESEARCH AND TECHNOLOGY

Technology is no substitute for experience and expertise but there are some first class systems designed to help an adviser eliminate the companies which are financially weak, have a poor performance track record, high charges, and/or inflexible contract conditions (for example exit penalties if you stop the plan early). Ask about the systems the firm uses and find out whether they offer comprehensive coverage of the investment and insurance market.

1.6 PAYING FOR ADVICE

Professional advisers (eg accountants and solicitors) are fee based and any sales commission would be rebated to you or reinvested in your plan. The broader band of independent financial advisers (IFAs) may operate on a fee basis or accept commission. Some do both.

Fee based advisers charge anything from around £50–250 per hour depending on whether you go to a local high street adviser or a leading firm of consulting actuaries or chartered accountants. As a rough guide, however, for good advice you can expect to pay at least £80–130 per hour.

One of the particularly daft aspects of the tax system is that you pay fees out of your taxed income, on top of which you have to pay VAT. If you pay through the commission route not only do you avoid VAT but in the case of pension plans, effectively you get tax relief at your highest rate on the payment. This is because the commission is deducted from your pension contributions, which themselves benefit from full tax relief.

1.7 PRE-SALE 'KEY FEATURES' DOCUMENT

Since January 1995 life assurance companies have been required by the financial services regulators to disclose all their charges in full, including sales commission, in a pre-sale 'key features' document. Similar rules came into force in May 1997 for unit trusts and regular savings investment trusts.

Commission rates vary depending on the size of premium and the term of the contract. As a rough guide you can assume that on a 'single premium' or one-off payment to a pension or life assurance investment plan the sales commission will be 4–6 per cent of your investment. For a 25-year 'regular premium' plan, where you agree to pay a certain amount each month or each year, the commission it is likely to be worth about 70 per cent of the value of your first year's contributions. If this is deducted and paid out during the early years you will get very little back if you have to stop your policy during this period.

So, if you do buy commission based products, your best bet may be to ask for single premiums or 'recurring' single premium terms. Under this system each contribution is treated as a one-off and only the commission related to that amount is paid to the adviser.

Your key features document will show what your fund might be worth at retirement assuming various rates of return. This is a rather pointless exercise since none of these rates is guaranteed, nor does it take account of inflation.

A more useful set of figures is provided in the little table which shows the impact of charges assuming a growth rate of 9 per cent per annum. This can be used to compare different companies' charges to check if you are getting good value for money. As a quick guide, refer to the 'reduction in growth' figure which shows by how much the charges would reduce the annual yield of 9 per cent.

One point to watch though. A low reduction in growth figure for one level of contribution does not indicate that charges are low across the board. Of course changes are just one consideration when you choose an investment. Equally important are the investment performance, the financial strengths of the institution and the flexibility of the plan. Cheapest is not necessarily best.

1.8 PLANNING YOUR PENSION AND INVESTMENT INCOME

Armed with this book and, preferably, a good adviser, you should be able to embark on your financial plan for retirement. Step one is to assess your current provision from the state, company schemes and private plans. Step two is to assess the shortfall. Step three is to make good that shortfall through tax efficient investments and savings.

As a very rough guide, if you are over 50 you (and your employer if relevant) should pay in to your pension plan about 13–15 per cent of annual earnings. In the chapters on pensions we give some sensible examples of what constitutes a 'good' pension. Use these as a broad guideline or, to get a more accurate picture, ask an independent financial adviser to assess your situation.

Finally, bear in mind that your plan must be reviewed on a regular basis to take account of changes to your personal circumstances. For example, if you decide you want to contribute to your grandchildren's school fees, or to retire abroad on a larger pension, clearly this will have an impact on your plans to retire early and you will have to adjust your aspirations. We hope the following chapters may help you achieve a happy compromise.

2

YOUR STATE PENSION

This chapter is concerned with the first stage of getting your pension priorities in order and looks at what you can expect from the State schemes.

Pension provision by the state is undergoing considerable change, particularly following recent Labour Government announcements to overhaul the entire welfare system.

The right to a basic retirement pension is one of the planks of the welfare state but as the value of this particular plank continues to erode in relation to earnings, it would be wise not to regard your state benefits as anything more than a relatively minor element of your retirement income.

This chapter looks at state pensions under the following headings:

(1) The state scheme
(2) National insurance contributions
(3) Contributory pension – the basic 'old age' retirement pension
(4) State earnings related pension scheme (SERPS)
(5) Graduated pension
(6) Non-contributory pension
(7) How to find out what you will get
(8) Contracting-out of SERPS
(9) Taking benefits
(10) Welfare and pensions reform.

Your options on the way you may actually take your state pension and the interaction between state pensions and other benefits are covered in Chapter 13.

2.1 THE STATE SCHEME

The state provides two types of basic old age retirement pension through the social security system: a flat rate and an earnings-related benefit.

These pensions may be paid from state pension age. It is not possible to take benefits early though it is possible to take them late (see 2.9.1)

The retirement pension is made up of several components. The basic retirement pension is paid to any man or woman who claims the pension on his or her own contributions record. A widow(er) or a divorced spouse can claim on the contributions record of a former or deceased spouse. A married woman can claim the basic pension (at the lower rate) on her husband's contribution record.

The basic retirement pension is paid at the full rate if enough contributions have been paid. If not, the basic retirement pension is paid at a reduced rate according to the number of contributions you have paid. However, a basic retirement pension at less than 25 per cent of the full rate will not be paid to you. You can increase the basic retirement pension if the claim is deferred and no excluding benefits are paid (see 2.3.2).

In certain cases, a non-contributory retirement pension is available if you are aged 80 or over and not already receiving a basic retirement pension or other benefit at or above the rate of the non-contributory retirement pension (excluding any earnings-related additional pension, guaranteed minimum pension or graduated pension – see 2.6) When you reach age 80, an 'age addition' of 25p is paid.

Additional payments may be made for a dependent adult, so long as the earnings limit is not exceeded. Where the adult dependant is living with you, the limit is £51.40; otherwise the limit is £39.95. Additions for dependent children cannot be paid if your spouse or partner lives with them and earns more than £145 per week for the first child and £19 per week for each extra child. An occupational pension paid to your spouse or partner counts as earnings for this purpose.

If you receive any other contributory benefit at the same time as the basic retirement pension, the benefit is adjusted so that the amount received in total is equal to the highest rate of benefit available.

The earnings-related pension is the state earnings-related pensions scheme (SERPS) or the old graduated pension scheme (or both). Both these additional pensions are calculated according to the contributions you have made. The graduated pension is funded by contributions paid between 6 April 1961 and 5 April 1975. SERPS is funded by certain classes of national insurance contributions made from 6 April 1978. If you paid contributions under both schemes you receive two additional pensions.

2.2 NATIONAL INSURANCE CONTRIBUTIONS

For 1999–2000, national insurance contributions are paid under four 'classes'.

Class 1 contributions are paid by employees as a percentage (10 per cent in most cases) of their 'band earnings'. These are earnings between a lower limit and an upper limit of £66 and £500 per week (£3,432 and £26,000 pa). No contributions are paid on earnings above the upper limit; no contributions at all are paid if an individual earns less than the lower limit.

Class 1 contributions are also paid by employers. These are called 'secondary contributions' (those paid by employees are called 'primary contributions'). Secondary contributions are also a percentage of earnings, but there is no upper limit.

Employers are also liable for Class 1A contributions (at 12.2 per cent) where a company car is available for private use.

Employers are also liable for Class 1B contributions (at 12.2 per cent) on the amount of additional emoluments in a PAYE settlement agreement chargeable under Class 1 or 1A, together with the income tax under the agreement.

Class 2 contributions are payable by self-employed individuals unless their earnings are below £3,770 and they have applied for a certificate of exemption.

Class 3 contributions are a type of voluntary contribution at £6.45 per week paid by people who are neither employed nor self-employed (eg retired but below state retirement age) in order to secure the full benefits under the state retirement pension.

Class 4 contributions are also paid by the self-employed at 6 per cent of a band of their Schedule D earnings from £7,531 to £26,000.

Only Class 1, 2 or 3 counts towards the old age pension (or towards any other social security benefit for that matter).

In addition to actually paying contributions, Class 1 contributions (and sometimes Class 3 contributions) may be 'credited' to you. This means that you are regarded as having paid the contributions, even though you have not in fact done so. Contributions are credited in the following circumstances:

(1) while you are claiming jobseekers' allowance and certain other benefits (see Chapter 13);
(2) while you are undergoing full-time education or training; and
(3) when you reach 60 (if male).

From 6 April 1999, the responsibility for the collection of national insurance contributions has been transferred to the Inland Revenue's National Insurance Contributions Office.

2.3 CONTRIBUTORY PENSION – THE BASIC 'OLD AGE' (RETIREMENT) PENSION

This is normally paid from age 65 for men and 60 for women, although it is possible to defer the pension (see 2.9.1). A state retirement age of 65 for both men and women will be introduced over the period 2010–20. If you are a woman and were born after 6 April 1995, you will not receive your state pension until your 65th birthday. Women born before 6 April 1950 are entitled to their pension from the current age of 60. For women whose dates of birth fall between those dates, a sliding scale applies, so that for each month (or part of a month) that a woman's date of birth is after 6 April 1950, her retirement date will be deferred by one month. Further information on this can be found in Leaflet EQP1a, 'Equality in State Pension Age'.

A man may only claim if he has paid or been credited with sufficient national insurance contributions. A woman may claim either on the record of her own or her husband's contributions. If your contributions are not enough for the full pension, you may get a reduced pension.

The amount of the pension is not affected by any work done, or by how much is earned. However, the extra pension paid for a dependant may be affected by any earnings which he or she may have.

Currently (from 12 April 1999) the rates of retirement pension are:

	£
Basic pension	66.75
Increase for adult dependant	39.95
Increase for eldest/only dependent child	9.90
Increase for subsequent dependent children	11.35
Pension based on spouse's contributions	39.95
Over 80 age addition	0.25

A man who became a widower before age 65 who is not entitled to a full basic pension can have his wife's contributions taken into account to increase his pension. Also, if a man becomes a widower after age 65, and is not entitled to a full basic pension, he can if his wife was aged under 60 when she died have her contributions taken into account. If his wife was over 60, he may be able to receive retirement pension based on her contributions, plus one based on his contributions up to the maximum that a single person could receive. In any event it is only his wife's full rate contributions that are taken into account.

If you are divorced and not entitled to the full basic pension, your ex-spouse's contributions may be taken into account to increase your pension. You do not have to wait until your ex-spouse claims. However, it is only an ex-wife's full rate contributions that are taken into account.

2.3.1 The conditions

The qualifying conditions for a contributory pension are complicated. They combine the number of national insurance contributions you have paid or been credited with, the number of years during which you have built up a minimum record of contributions (referred to as the number of 'qualifying years'), and the number of years that have elapsed since you were age 16 (referred to as your 'working life').

The overall effect is that you qualify for a full pension if you have a record of contributions covering 90 per cent of your working life. If you have less than the required number of qualifying years, you receive a reduced pension – provided that your contribution record contains at least one quarter of the required number of years.

All this makes it extremely difficult to keep track of your pension, but you are written to if for any year your contributions are insufficient. You will be asked if you want to make voluntary Class 3 contributions to preserve your record, and you will be told how much you have to pay. It is normally worthwhile paying these contributions to ensure that you receive the maximum pension.

2.3.2 Deferral

You can earn increments to your pension if you put off receiving your retirement pension. Currently this can be for up to five years, to age 65 for a woman and to age 70 for a man. It is also a requirement that you are not claiming an excluding benefit. When you decide to claim your pension, the weekly rate will be higher. If you are a married woman you can earn increments over the age of 65 on a married woman's pension, if your husband is deferring his pension. As a married woman, you will not earn increments on your married woman's pension if you are receiving an excluding benefit. This includes basic pension on your own contributions or graduated retirement benefit.

2.3.3 Married women

The basic state pension is paid at two rates: one is for a single person (£66.75 from 6 April 1999), the other, higher rate is for a married couple

(£106.10 from 6 April 1999). If you are a married woman, you can qualify for a pension as follows:

(1) If you have paid enough national insurance contributions at the full rate, you can receive a basic pension in the same way as a man or a single woman. This commences from age 60 to 65 (see 2.3) provided that you have paid or been credited with full rate contributions for the required number of qualifying years.
(2) Alternatively, you can receive a lower pension based on your husband's contributions, provided that he is receiving his pension, you are aged over 60 (rising to 65 – see 2.3) and you can be treated as retired. This is worth about 60 per cent of your husband's pension.

The pension that you receive is normally the higher of the two pensions described above (for more details see Chapter 13).

A woman who is widowed before age 60, can, when she reaches age 60, claim retirement pension or continue to receive widow's benefit until she claims retirement pension or reaches age 65.

If a woman is widowed after age 65, she can receive retirement pension based on her own or her late husband's contributions, or she may be able to receive widow's benefit instead.

Reduced rate national insurance claims

Up to 6 April 1977, married women who were employed could pay either a reduced or the full rate of national insurance contributions. If you are still paying contributions at the reduced rate, you do not qualify for SERPS. However, you can usually receive a pension based on your husband's contributions, although this is less than the full single person's pension.

There are certain other benefits that you do not qualify for, so you should consider switching to the full rate. Since October 1989, the rules are such that low earners may pay less in national insurance contributions at the full rate than they would if paying at the reduced rate.

2.3.4 Home responsibilities protection

If you are not working or your earnings are too low, you do not have to pay national insurance contributions. However, you will receive credits if you do not work because you look after dependent children or elderly or disabled relatives. These credits are called 'home responsibilities protection' (HRP) and protect your rights to a basic retirement pension if your working pattern does not enable you to establish qualifying years for pension purposes because of caring responsibilities at home. A married man's HRP can also count towards widow's benefit for his widow if he dies.

The benefit allows you to deduct the number of years during which you meet these conditions from the number of qualifying years required for a pension (down to a minimum of 20).

HRP is available for complete tax years from April 1978 throughout which you have been:

(1) awarded child benefit (see 13.2.3) for a child aged under 16; or
(2) regularly engaged for a least 35 hours per week caring for someone who receives attendance allowance, or the highest or middle rate of disability living allowance or constant attendance allowance (see 14.7.2); or
(3) receiving income support and not having to be available for work, and caring for someone, who for a minimum of 48 weeks in the year receives attendance allowance, or the highest or middle rate of disability living allowance or constant attendance allowance (see 14.2); or
(4) a combination of the above conditions.

HRP is available to both men and women, but a married woman is not eligible for HRP if she normally pays national insurance contributions at the reduced rate.

HRP is awarded automatically if entitlement conditions (1) and/or (3) above apply for a whole tax year and there have been insufficient contributions paid or credited for the year to be a qualifying year. In other cases you must make an application at the end of the tax year concerned. If you are entitled to invalid care allowance for looking after someone who is sick or disabled, you may receive national insurance credits, in which case you do not need to apply for HRP.

2.4 STATE EARNINGS-RELATED PENSION SCHEME (SERPS)

The present state pension scheme began on 6 April 1978. It consists of two pensions – a basic pension with an additional earnings-related pension (SERPS). Employers with an occupational pension scheme providing pensions on a 'defined benefit' basis (see 3.1.1) could 'contract out' of SERPS. Employees who are contracted-out on this basis receive the basic pension from the state and an additional earnings-related pension.

Prior to 6 April 1988, this 'contracting-out' was only possible through an employer-sponsored occupational pension scheme which guaranteed to provide a level of benefits broadly in line with the SERPS benefits being lost. Since 6 April 1998, employers have been able to offer 'contracting-out' on a 'money purchase' basis without having to provide the guarantee previously required. In both cases national insurance contributions are reduced for both the employer and the employee, but with the loss of SERPS benefits.

However, this change still left the decision of whether to offer contracted-out status in the employer's hands. Thus, from 1 July 1988, further changes gave the individual employee the right to contract out of SERPS on an individual basis, without his or her employer's consent. The personal pension plans which enable this to be done are also money-purchase arrangements.

Contracting out through personal pension plans requires the payment of 'protected rights contributions' to the relevant pension contract. The contributions are identified separately from any other contributions paid and create a 'protected rights fund'. The protected rights benefits which are paid out of this fund at retirement replace the SERPS benefit lost as a result of the decision to contract out.

The Pensions Act 1995 introduced a system of contracting-out rebates which applies from 1997–98.

Contracting out via a personal pension plan is an annual decision, and you can 'contract back' into SERPS for the purpose of future benefits. In general, contracting out is of benefit to younger employees, but may not match the likely SERPS entitlement for some older persons and for those on lower earnings.

In recent years the state pension has come under pressure because of increases in life expectancy and larger numbers of retired people in the population. The benefits under SERPS have been reduced so that only those who reach state pension age in 1998 and 1999 will receive the original maximum benefits. If you reach state retirement age in or after 2010 you will receive a pension of only 20 per cent of earnings (within certain limits) instead of 25 per cent as originally intended, and the relevant earnings taken into account will be the average of your lifetime earnings and not the earnings of the best 20 years, as under the original SERPS. There is a sliding scale which operates for those retiring between 2000 and 2009.

SERPS is paid as part of the state pension, and the qualifying conditions are the same as those for the basic pension, ie that you have:

(1) reached the state retirement age; and
(2) have retired from regular employment; and
(3) satisfy the contribution conditions.

2.5 GRADUATED PENSION

This scheme existed between April 1961 and April 1975. People who were employed during this period bought 'units' at the rate of one for every £7.50 of weekly earnings for a man, or £9.00 for a woman, subject to an upper limit. An employer was allowed to 'contract out' employees if they were provided with an equivalent occupational pension; such employees will receive a smaller graduated pension as they will have accumulated fewer units.

Each unit buys an amount of weekly pension. This amount is uplifted each year by the rate of inflation. Currently, the value of a unit is 8.69 pence.

2.6 NON-CONTRIBUTORY PENSION

If you cannot claim a contributory old age pension at all, you can claim a non-contributory pension from the age of 80 (for men and women). The non-contributory pension is sometimes called the 'old person's pension'. This pension is also payable to someone who *does* qualify for a contributory pension but one that is lower than a non-contributory pension. This could apply to anyone who receives a contributory pension of less than 60 per cent of the full contributory pension.

2.6.1 The qualifying conditions

To qualify for a non-contributory pension you must satisfy two conditions:

(1) You must not be receiving either a contributory pension or any other social security benefit of a higher amount. For this purpose you ignore any earnings-related pension, graduated pension or guaranteed minimum pension (see 2.8.3).
(2) You must be 'ordinarily resident' in the United Kingdom (see 12.3.1) and you must have lived in the United Kingdom for at least 10 of the 20 years up to your 80th birthday.

If you already receive other social security benefits when you reach 80, this pension makes little difference to you, as the other benefits are reduced by the amount of pension you receive. However, if you are of independent means, the pension makes a difference as it is not affected by the amount of other income. This could be of benefit, for example, to someone who settled in the United Kingdom in their 60s.

2.7 HOW TO FIND OUT WHAT YOU WILL GET

The results of the various changes over recent years means that your state pension could be a confused amalgam of various payments. You could qualify for one or more of:

(1) The basic state pension.
(2) The graduated pension.
(3) SERPS (and this could be based on a mixture of the old and new rules).

It will be very helpful for you to use the retirement pensions forecast service operated by the Department of Social Security. You should ask for Form BR19 (available from any office of the DSS) and send it to the relevant office in Newcastle upon Tyne. The form asks for some basic information and, in return, you receive a full forecast of the state pensions you qualify for. In addition, there is a small range of useful 'what if?' options. You can, for example, get an idea of the impact on your retirement pension of stopping work before state retirement age or working on beyond it.

Overall, a state pension is unlikely to be adequate to live on. Even with SERPS, it is still likely to fall well short of the benefits provided by a good company or personal pension scheme. In addition, the state scheme does not allow any part of the benefits to be taken as a lump sum, there are no life assurance benefits and there is no provision for early retirement.

However, one advantage of the state scheme is the degree of inflation proofing provided.

There is not a tremendous amount you can do to improve your benefits under the state scheme. What you can do, of course, is to make sure that you qualify for the maximum benefits you are entitled to by making sure that your contribution record is up to date. However, before paying voluntary contributions, ask the DSS what extra benefits you will receive as a result. Also remember that you get no tax relief on national insurance contributions so (provided you are eligible to do so) you might get more value for money if you invest the missed contributions into a personal pension scheme where you do get tax relief.

However, do not forget that it is not just the state pension that is determined by your contributions record. Other benefits (principally widow's benefits) depend on the national insurance contributions you have paid and it could be a false economy to look for alternative methods of saving.

The reverse argument may apply, however, when it comes to SERPS.

2.8 CONTRACTING-OUT OF SERPS

Because of the likely future costs of providing an earnings-related pension, the previous Government took two decisions:

(1) It reduced the ultimate benefits of SERPS. This will start to take effect on those people reaching state retirement age in 1999–2000 and will take full effect on those people retiring in 2009–10.
(2) It introduced incentives to encourage people to leave SERPS and make their own arrangements.

It is only possible to leave SERPS if either you or your employer makes appropriate provision to replace the SERPS benefits with a suitable, Inland Revenue approved private pension. To encourage this, employers who 'contract out' pay a reduced rate of national insurance contributions while employees receive a rebate of contributions which is sent to their pension provider. There are currently three ways in which you can contract out of SERPS:

(1) through an appropriate personal pension (APP);
(2) membership of a contracted-out money purchase pension scheme (COMPS);
(3) membership of an occupational scheme. (Until April 1997 occupational schemes contracted out of SERPS had to guarantee certain benefits but this is no longer the case.)

2.8.1 Appropriate personal pension (APP)

These require no employer involvement at all. In order to contract out, you take out a personal pension plan with a pension provider of your choice (a life assurance company, a unit or investment trust group, a bank, a building society or a friendly society). You and your pension provider must complete a Joint Notice (Form APP1) which is submitted to the DSS. You can use only one APP to contract out at any time and you must contract out for at least one complete tax year.

Once the Joint Notice is accepted by the DSS, payments are made, normally once a year, directly by the DSS to the pension provider. These payments, called 'protected rights' contributions, consist of a national insurance rebate and an element of tax relief on your share of the rebate. From April 1997 the rebate is fully 'age related' and increases with age to compensate for the corresponding increase in the value of SERPS given up. Both you and your employer continue to pay the full rate of national insurance contributions.

The protected rights contributions *must* be used to provide a pension at state retirement age, or a widow(er)'s or dependant's pension or a lump sum on death. The value of these benefits is not guaranteed but depends on how well the fund performs and the price of annuities at retirement (annuities provide a regular income in return for your pension fund; see Chapter 5).

2.8.2 Contracted-out money purchase schemes (COMPS)

These are occupational pension plans where the employer takes the initial decision to contract out on a group basis.

Both you and your employer pay a reduced rate of national insurance contribution but this saving is balanced by the protected rights contributions which your employer must ensure are paid into the pension scheme on a monthly basis. Normally, both you and your employer contribute your respective shares of the protected rights contributions.

The protected rights contributions must be used to provide benefits in the same way as those provided by an APP. As with an APP, the value of benefits is not guaranteed.

2.8.3 Guaranteed minimum pensions (GMP)

Until April 1997 occupational pension schemes had to provide a guaranteed minimum level of pension equivalent to that provided by SERPS. This is no longer the case, although in practice the replacement pension should be broadly equivalent to SERPS.

2.8.4 Contracting-in or contracting-out?

If you contract out using an APP or a COMPS, you must consider whether the benefits provided by the protected rights contributions will exceed the likely benefits from SERPS. A protected rights scheme is a money purchase scheme so the benefits which emerge are dependent almost entirely on the size of the fund built up; there is no guarantee that the benefits will exceed SERPS.

2.8.5 Contracting back into SERPS

Your adviser or pension company should check each year to see whether the value of the rebate is equal to or better than the SERPS benefits given up. Older employees may be advised to go back into SERPS. This is done by sending a completed form APP 2 to the DSS. If you are a member of a COMPS, you have to approach your pension scheme trustees to find out your options, which might include switching into a 'not contracted-out' category of membership whilst remaining in the scheme.

2.9 TAKING BENEFITS

2.9.1 Taking benefits late

Although you cannot take your state pension early, it is possible for you to defer taking your pension if you wish either to continue working or simply put off taking your retirement benefits. Your pension is increased when you finally retire. At present you can only defer drawing your retirement pension for five years after you reach state retirement age (ie to age 65 for a woman and 70 for a man).

The state pension increases at a weekly rate equivalent to an overall increase of about 7.5 per cent for each full year that it is not claimed. If you defer for the full five years, your pension is increased by around 35 per cent (in addition, of course, to any increases introduced automatically through indexation). Under new proposals it may be possible to defer drawing the state pension indefinitely, with an annual increase of 10 per cent.

2.9.2 Contracted-out benefits

If you have contracted-out of SERPS through an occupational scheme providing a guaranteed minimum pension (GMP), the amount of additional pension you would have been entitled to under SERPS is reduced by an amount equal to the GMP. This deduction is called the 'contracted-out deduction'. The GMP ceased from April 1997 but any rights built up before this date must be honoured.

If at state retirement age, the pension derived from a personal pension is *less* than the GMP, the DSS will not make up any shortfall.

2.9.3 Widows, widowers and the divorced

A woman may claim a state retirement pension either on her own records or on her husband's. A widowed or divorced woman may claim on her former husband's records for the longer of:

(1) the period in which she was married to him; or
(2) the period from the start of her working life to the date of her husband's death or of their divorce.

A widower or divorced man may claim on the basis of his wife's standard rate contributions (reduced rate contributions do not qualify) on the same basis as a widow.

Widows' benefits

At state pension age (between 60 and 65, depending on your date of birth), a widow can retire and start to draw the state retirement pension which is based on her own and/or her late husband's contribution record. In the meantime, she receives a widow's pension which is based on her age either at the time of her husband's death or when her youngest child ceases to be dependent upon her. If this age is less than 45, she receives no widow's pension at all and at state retirement age her benefit depends entirely on her own contributions.

It is not essential to make a final decision at state retirement age; it can be put off or changed at any time up to age 65.

Widows' benefits are covered in more detail in Chapter 13.

Widowers' benefits

A widower who is not entitled to a full basic pension may be able to improve it by taking into account his late wife's standard rate contributions. Under the original rules, a widower may claim any SERPS based on his late wife's contributions provided:

(1) both he and his wife had reached pensionable age before she died; and
(2) he had retired from regular employment.

The maximum SERPS a widower may inherit was such that, when added to his own SERPS entitlement, it did not exceed the maximum individual rate.

Since SERPS was modified, the amount of SERPS which a widower may inherit from his late wife is 50 per cent of that calculated on the original basis, if she dies after 5 April 2000.

2.10 WELFARE AND PENSIONS REFORM

In March 1998, the Government published its Green Paper on welfare reform, 'New ambitions for our country: A new contract for welfare', which sets out the framework for the Government's welfare reforms, based on the central principle of work for those who can, and security for those who cannot.

The Pensions Green Paper, 'A new contract for welfare: Partnership in pensions', published in December 1998, proposed a new structure for pensions, including a new state second pension to reduce the extent to which low earners have to rely on means-tested benefits, and encouragement for higher earners to save and provide for themselves.

The Government has introduced these measures in the Welfare Reform and Pensions Bill, the main elements of which are:

(1) The framework for the new 'stakeholder pension schemes' (see 2.10.1).
(2) Provisions for pension rights to be split as part of a divorce settlement, in the same way as other financial assets (see 2.10.2).
(3) A new scheme of bereavement benefits, available to both men and women, to replace the current widows' benefits (see 2.10.3).

2.10.1 Stakeholder pension schemes

The UK pension system is a partnership between the state (providing the basic state pension, SERPS and income-related benefits for pensioners), employers (providing occupational pension schemes) and private pension providers (providing personal pensions). The current pension system is composed of three tiers.

(1) the basic state pension;
(2) a mix of state and mainly private provision which is additional to the basic state pension (this includes SERPS, occupational and personal pensions); and
(3) other voluntary private provision above the compulsory minimum.

All employees and self-employed people, except the very lowest paid, must pay national insurance contributions. These give entitlement to basic state pension. In addition, employees have to pay towards SERPS, unless they opt out and make their own provision (contracting-out). If people are contracted-out of SERPS into a private scheme, their national insurance contributions are reduced or rebated to reflect the value of SERPS foregone.

The minimum that must be paid to a second pension is an average of about 4.6 per cent of earnings – 1.6 per cent from employees and 3 per cent from employers. While employees are required to contribute to a second pension, self-employed people are not. The only second pension choice for them is a personal pension, but many self-employed people make some provision for their retirement through other savings vehicles and investments.

The Welfare and Pensions Reform Bill proposes a new insurance contract with three main elements:

(1) A guaranteed minimum income in retirement, increased year by year as resources allow. Over the longer term the aim is that this should rise in line with earnings.
(2) Improved increased provision for low and middle earners, carers and disabled people through a new state second pension (replacing SERPS).
(3) New, better value, accessible stakeholder pension schemes whereby:
    (i) stakeholder pension schemes are open to everyone but targeted at those earning £9,000–20,000 pa and not in an occupational scheme;
    (ii) there is a simpler tax regime, allowing up to £3,600 to be paid into schemes each year;
    (iii) employers who do not already offer an occupational scheme should identify a stakeholder pension scheme and facilitate access to it for their employees; and
    (iv) stakeholder pension schemes have an approved structure, minimum standards and registration requirements within a legislative framework.

2.10.2 Pension sharing on divorce and nullity

Courts have had to take account of the value of pension rights in divorce and nullity of marriage settlements so that these can be offset against other assets in financial settlements. In addition there are attachment and earmarking provisions in the Pensions Act 1995 that allow courts:

(1) (in England and Wales and Northern Ireland) to require occupational and personal pension schemes to pay maintenance from a member's pension directly to a former spouse; and
(2) (throughout the UK) to order that part or all of a lump sum payable on the death or retirement of a member to be directed to a former spouse.

However, attachment and earmarking have limitations and are little used because of the problems that have arisen, being that:

(1) they do not usually allow a clean break;
(2) title to the pension rights remains with the spouse in whose name the rights have accrued; and
(3) they leave the person receiving the payment at risk of losing the intended retirement income if his or her ex-spouse dies.

The Welfare and Pensions Reform Bill will put in place proposals introducing the option of pension sharing on divorce or nullity of marriage and will:

(1) allow pension rights to be treated like other assets, and the whole or

a proportion of their value to be transferred from one spouse to the other as part of the financial settlement; but
(2) not be compulsory, so that it will still be possible to offset pension rights against other assets or to use the current earmarking and attachment arrangements.

Pension sharing will be available only to those who begin proceedings for divorce or nullity after the legislation has been brought into force.

2.10.3 Bereavement benefits

Under the present widows' benefits scheme, three main benefits are available to women who are widowed. These are based upon the national insurance contributions record of the late husband, rather than the widow herself. The three benefits are:

(1) A widows' payment of a tax-free lump sum payment of £1,000.
(2) A taxable widowed mother's allowance, which is paid to widows with children, and ends when the youngest child ceases to be a dependant. This comprises a basic allowance for the widow herself, plus an allowance for each child and any SERPS.
(3) A taxable widow's pension, which is paid to widows over age 45 who do not have dependent children. This consists of a basic pension plus any SERPS. The amount payable depends on the woman's age when she was widowed or stopped receiving widowed mother's allowance.

Married men currently are not entitled to bereavement benefits.

The proposals under the Welfare and Pensions Reform Bill are that:

(1) All who currently receive widows' benefits will continue to receive them.
(2) Both widows and widowers will be entitled to a tax-free lump sum 'bereavement payment' of £2,000.
(3) Widowed parents with dependent children will receive a weekly, taxable, but non-means tested benefit, the 'widowed parent's allowance', equivalent to and subject to the same entitlement conditions as the current widowed mother's allowance.
(4) Widow(er)s aged 45 and over with no dependent children will receive a weekly, taxable, non-means tested benefit for six months only, the 'bereavement allowance', which will be age-related as for the current widow's pension, but with no SERPS component.
(5) Widow(er)s with children will be guaranteed up to an extra £10 per week through a new disregard of their widowed parent's allowance when calculating entitlement to income-related benefits.
(6) Men and women who are over age 55 at the start of the new

arrangements and who are widowed within the subsequent five years will have access to income-related benefits without any job-seeking requirements. They will also receive a special premium (worth £14.35 a week at April 1998 rates) to help them maintain their income when their transitional bereavement benefit ends after six months.

USEFUL READING MATTER

The following social security booklets contain more details on the state benefits covered in this chapter. They can be obtained from your local DSS office or direct from the Benefits Agency distribution centre (the address is in Appendix 2).

FB 2 – Which benefit? A guide to Social Security and NHS benefits

FB 6 – Retiring? Your pension and other benefits

FB 32 – Benefits after retirement

NP 45 – A guide to Widow's Benefits

NP 46 – A guide to Retirement Pensions

3

IMPROVING YOUR COMPANY PENSION

Once you have assessed the likely value of your state pension it is time to examine and improve your company scheme. Company schemes are the most valuable employee benefit after the pay cheque itself and, following the implementation of the Pensions Act 1995, they are extremely secure.

However, despite recent improvements, some dated concepts are still endemic in company pensions, the principal one perhaps being the need to work for up to 40 years with the same employer in order to obtain the maximum pension permitted under Inland Revenue rules. Given the increasing improbability, in today's world, of such a cosy, long-term relationship, the need to make complementary arrangements is of growing importance. This chapter looks at the following topics:

(1) The structure of company schemes
(2) Finding out what you will get
(3) Maximum benefits
(4) Maximum pensions
(5) Maximum cash lump sums
(6) Special rules for company directors
(7) The framework for improvement
(8) Topping-up company schemes
(9) Additional voluntary contributions (AVCs)
(10) Free-standing additional voluntary contributions (FSAVCs)
(11) Executive pension plans
(12) Unapproved retirement benefit schemes
(13) Leaving your company scheme
(14) Changing your job.

3.1 THE STRUCTURE OF COMPANY SCHEMES

A company pension scheme may be contributory or non-contributory. Contributory means that both you and your employer make contributions to the fund; non-contributory means that only your employer makes contributions.

Typically, you may contribute about 5 per cent of your salary to a contributory scheme. The employer usually contributes a sum between 5 and 10 per cent of your salary, depending on your age and how much the scheme actuary calculates is necessary to enable the pension scheme to pay the promised benefits. Bear in mind, though, that under a final salary scheme you have no right to the *money* in the pension scheme but you do have rights to the *benefits* provided by the scheme.

The type of scheme will either be a final salary scheme or a money purchase scheme and it is important to understand the difference between the two.

3.1.1 Final salary schemes

If you are in a final salary scheme, your pension is calculated as a percentage of your final salary at or around retirement, eg $1/60$ or $1/80$ of your final salary for each year of service to retirement.

This type of scheme (which is sometimes known as a 'defined benefit scheme') saddles your employer with an open-ended liability because the ultimate benefit is based on your future earnings, which makes it difficult to quantify accurately the future cost.

Final salary schemes can either be 'contracted-in' or 'contracted-out' of SERPS (see 2.8).

3.1.2 Money purchase schemes

You may be a member of a money purchase scheme, also known as a 'defined contribution scheme'. This kind of scheme may aim to provide a pension similar to a final salary scheme but there are no guarantees. Your pension depends upon the size of the fund built up when you come to take the benefits. This in turn depends on:

(1) The contributions paid into the scheme by your employer on your behalf.
(2) Any additional contributions which you make yourself.
(3) The investment growth on all the contributions.
(4) The charges deducted by the pension company.
(5) Annuity rates at retirement (that is, how much regular income insurance companies will guarantee to pay in return for your pension fund).

An occupational money purchase scheme gives your employer rather more control over the costs because the commitment is to pay a fixed percentage of your earnings each year into your fund. There is no guarantee what size pension this will generate.

Although money purchase schemes do not guarantee a certain level of pension linked to earnings, the *maximum* benefits that you may receive from either type of scheme *are* restricted by your 'final salary'.

3.1.3 What is 'final salary'?

There is no single definition of 'final salary'. It can be either:

(1) the highest annual salary out of the last five years before retirement age; or
(2) the average of any salary paid over three consecutive years out of the last twelve.

If you are a controlling director (see 3.6.1), only the latter option may be used.

The taxable value of benefits-in-kind (eg company car or free accommodation) may also be included as part of your salary. The value of share option schemes and termination payments is excluded. The Revenue is, however, fairly generous when it comes to determining final salary. For example, it is possible to build in a rate of inflation to previous years' salaries for the purposes of determining your final salary. This is called 'dynamisation' (see 3.4.2).

3.1.4 The main benefits

What you can expect from your pension scheme depends first on the rules laid down by the Inland Revenue, and secondly on the rules of the scheme itself. You may not necessarily get all the benefits that your company pension scheme can provide and the maximum benefits provided by your company scheme may be less than those allowed by the Inland Revenue.

Lifetime income

The principal benefit is a lifetime income payable, on a guaranteed basis, from the moment you retire until the day you die. This is usually expressed as a percentage of your final salary when you retire but your particular pension scheme may have variations. For example, it may be a fixed pension or there may be provision for it to increase at an annual rate which partially or fully compensates you for the effects of inflation. There may be provisions for this lifetime income to continue for your beneficiaries after your death if you die within a very short time of retiring.

Lump sum

Your company pension scheme may also provide you with the facility to take a tax-free cash lump sum when you retire. This is generally expressed as a percentage of your final salary, for example one and a half times final salary, subject to a maximum amount. However, if you take the cash lump sum, then your lifetime income is correspondingly reduced. This is known as 'commutation'.

Widow's/widower's pension

Your scheme may also provide for a pension to be paid to your widow or widower. As with your own pension, the level of income payable is dependent on your salary (but this time at the date of your death).

The maximum widow's/widower's pension is two-thirds of your own maximum pension. Some schemes pay partners' pensions to an unmarried partner, provided financial dependency can be proved.

Life assurance

Many pension schemes also provide life assurance while you are actually employed. This is called 'death in service benefit' and is usually expressed as a multiple of your current salary, up to a maximum of four times salary (see 7.3.3).

3.2 FINDING OUT WHAT YOU WILL GET

The Social Security Act 1985 improved the rights of scheme members. It requires pension scheme trustees to provide information about the scheme and its benefits (including its investment policy and finances) to current members, early leavers and also prospective members.

In addition, you have the right to ask for certain information about the benefits that apply to you. Your company must supply this information within two months, though it has the right to refuse this request if it is less than twelve months since you last received such information. In practice, most companies arrange for some kind of annual statement to be sent out to employees and this will give you a good deal of useful information.

This should set out the pension you can expect to receive at your normal retirement age (your company pension age may well be lower than state pension age) and the value of the cash lump sum you may withdraw at that time. The quoted pension will probably be based on your current salary (ie it will not assume any increase in salary between the date of the statement and your normal retirement date) which in turn will enable you to work out what percentage of your final salary you can expect to draw when you retire. The percentage will not change as it is based on the number of years' service to normal retirement date. The percentage is often lower than expected and prompts many employees to take action to improve their pension.

If your pension is a money purchase scheme, then the rules are different. Every twelve months, your company must tell you how much has been contributed by you, your employer and, where applicable, the DSS. You should find out how much income your fund would buy in the form of an annuity to see if you are on target or need to increase contributions. As a very rough guide, you should pay about 15 per cent of your salary from age 55. Part of this may be paid by your employer.

Many people have a pension arrangement with a previous employer which will pay benefits in the future. If you are not sure what your entitlement will be write to the trustees. If you have lost track of the company, you may be able to find out details of your 'missing' pension through the Pension Schemes Registry. The address is in Appendix 2.

3.3 MAXIMUM BENEFITS

The maximum benefits available to an employee or director from a pension scheme normally depend on your years of service with your employer and your salary at or around retirement. There is, however, a distinction between what the Inland Revenue permits and what a particular pension scheme might provide, which might be well below the maximum permitted. The following sections set out the Inland Revenue limits, and explain how they depend on the date you joined your current scheme. They also describe the overall framework in which improvements to your pension can be planned.

3.3.1 The basic position

Most people are familiar with the underlying Inland Revenue rule on maximum benefits that can be achieved through a company scheme. Provided you have the necessary years of service in your company scheme, you may retire on a pension of up to two-thirds of your final salary. Part of this pension may be commuted into a tax-free cash lump sum that may not exceed one and a half times your final salary.

This, broadly, was the situation up to 1987 and, for people who joined their current employer's occupational scheme before this date, these simple rules still apply.

The first major change came in 1987. The then Conservative Government introduced new rules for high earners which limited the maximum tax-free cash lump sum to £150,000. Somebody with a final salary of, say, £300,000 can still qualify for a pension of £200,000, but the lump sum is restricted to £150,000 and not £450,000.

The next, and rather more substantial, change came in 1989 with the introduction of the 'earnings cap'. This put a limit on the earnings that could be taken into account for contributions and benefits and still enjoy the tax treatment of an approved pension scheme. The limit for 1999–2000 is £90,600 which means a pension (in today's terms) of no more than £60,400 and a maximum tax-free cash lump sum of £135,900, regardless of what your salary is. Once again, this restriction is aimed at high earners but, as increases in the cap are linked to increases in the retail prices index rather than average earnings, it will affect more and more people as time goes by. There are more details about the earnings cap in 3.12.1.

The rules which affect you are determined by the date on which you joined your current employer's scheme.

(1) If your current scheme was established before 17 March 1987, and you joined it before that date (referred to throughout this chapter as a 'pre-1987 member'), you are covered by the old rules with no effective limits to your pension or tax-free lump sum.
(2) If your current scheme was established before 14 March 1989 and you joined it after 17 March 1987 but before 1 June 1989 (referred to as a '1987–1989 member'), your maximum tax-free cash is limited to £150,000.
(3) If you joined your current scheme on or after 1 June 1989, or if you joined a scheme set up on or after 14 March 1989 (referred to as a 'post-1989 member'), you are affected by the earnings cap.

This means that if you change jobs in the future, or join an occupational scheme for the first time, your pension benefits are affected by the earnings cap.

Regardless of what your maximum allowable benefits are, Inland Revenue rules require that you have to belong to your employer's scheme for a minimum period of time before you qualify for the maximum benefits. The rule that most people are familiar with (the 40-year rule) does not always apply and the precise minimum period depends, once again, on the date you first joined your current scheme. The following sections (3.4 and 3.5) set out the details.

3.4 MAXIMUM PENSIONS

3.4.1 The basic position

The Inland Revenue always permits a pension benefit of up to $\frac{1}{60}$ of final salary for each year of service (this is known as the '60ths scale' or 'straight 60ths') so that a maximum pension of two-thirds of final salary is obtained only after completing 40 years' service with the employer – an unlikely event for most people. It is still possible, however, for you to receive the maximum pension of two-thirds of final salary in a shorter timescale (if permitted by the rules of your scheme) depending on when you joined your scheme.

Pre-1987 members

The two-thirds maximum pension is permitted if at least ten years' service has been completed with the employer at normal retirement date. In calculating the maximum pension it is necessary to take account of additional pensions arising from any voluntary contributions (see 3.9 and 3.10) and any 'retained benefits' from previous employment (see 3.4.3).

1987–1989 members and post-1989 members

For people who joined a scheme on or after 17 March 1987, the maximum pension is $\frac{1}{30}$ of final salary for each year of service. The two-thirds maximum is therefore permitted only on completion of at least 20 years' service with an employer at normal retirement date.

There is a further restriction on post-1989 members who are also controlling directors (see 3.6.4).

3.4.2 Dynamised or indexed final remuneration

Final salary may be re-calculated as a notional figure (known as 'dynamised final remuneration' or 'indexed final remuneration') by increasing the actual salary earned in a particular year by the increase in the retail prices index between the end of the year in question and normal retirement date. The result is to produce a pension which is related to the salary which an employee would have received had his previous years' salaries kept pace with the cost of living.

Dynamisation, however, may not be used to increase:

(1) the tax free lump sum (see below) payable to a pre-1987 member unless the pension is increased to the same proportionate extent, ie dynamisation must be justified by an increase to the overall entitlement to benefits;
(2) the final salary of a 1987–1989 member used to calculate the tax-free lump sum beyond £100,000;
(3) the final salary of a post-1989 member beyond the value of the 'earnings cap' as at the date of retirement.

3.4.3 Retained pension benefits

It may well be that you have other pension entitlements in addition to those being provided by your current employer. For example, you may have a deferred pension from a previous employer or you may have built up a personal pension plan through previous self employment. If your current benefits are to be calculated on the 'straight 60ths' scale, then (unless you are a controlling director – see 3.6.4) you need not take any retained benefits into account. However, if your pension is to be improved under any of the methods described above, then any retained benefits are taken into account.

3.5 MAXIMUM CASH LUMP SUMS

In the same way that pensions can be improved up to the maximum level laid down by the Inland Revenue, so can cash lump sums.

3.5.1 The basic position

Most pension schemes allow an employee to give up part of his pension on retirement for a tax-free cash lump sum. This is known as commutation. Inland Revenue rules lay down that the maximum tax-free lump sum that can be provided for any employee is $1\frac{1}{2}$ times his final salary after completing 40 years' service at normal retirement date: this represents $\frac{3}{80}$ of his final salary for each year of service.

Pre-1987 members

Pre-1987 members can obtain the maximum lump sum after 20 years' service with the same employer but *only* if the rules of the pension scheme itself allow lump sum benefits to be built up over 20 years.

1987–1989 members

It is possible to provide the maximum lump sum cash after 20 years (up to a maximum of £150,000) but only if the scheme provides the maximum approvable pension benefits on the accelerated scale for pensions, ie $\frac{1}{30}$ of final salary for each year of service. This means that both benefits must be uplifted in the same way; it is not possible to uplift the lump sum in isolation. If the rules of your scheme are such that the pension provided is between $\frac{1}{60}$ and $\frac{1}{30}$ of final salary for each year of service, an enhanced cash lump sum may be payable according to a laid down formula.

Post-1989 members

The maximum lump sum is the greater of:

(1) $\frac{3}{80}$ of final salary (capped at £90,600 in 1999–2000 – see 3.12.1) for each year of service, and
(2) the pension multiplied by 2.25. 'Pension' is the amount before commutation or any reduction in favour of widows/dependants and is calculated on the basis on which it will actually be paid, eg in monthly instalments, increasing in payment at 5 per cent per annum compound (see 5.3 for details on the various ways in which pensions may be taken).

3.6 SPECIAL RULES FOR COMPANY DIRECTORS

The Inland Revenue regards company directors, particularly controlling directors, as a special category for whom membership of a company pension scheme involves certain restrictions. Directors of investment companies are in a particularly difficult position. The company itself may not be able to set up an exempt approved pension scheme if the membership includes controlling directors and such directors are prohibited from contributing to personal pension schemes.

3.6.1 The definition of controlling director

There are two definitions depending on the date that you joined your company scheme.

(1) If you joined your scheme on or after 1 December 1987, you are treated as a controlling director if, at any time after 16 March 1987 and within ten years of retirement or leaving pensionable service, you were a director of the company and able to control, either

directly or indirectly, 20 per cent or more of the company's ordinary share capital. To assess the degree of control you exercise, the shareholdings of your 'associates' is taken into account; 'associates' in this context includes relations and partners, trustees of settlements where you are the settlor etc. All the shareholdings are added together and, if they exceed 20 per cent, you are a controlling director even if you do not own or control any share capital yourself.

(2) If you joined your scheme before 1 December 1987, then you are regarded as a controlling director if, at that date, you were a director who either alone or along with your wife and minor children controlled 20 per cent or more of the voting rights of the company. This 20 per cent also includes any rights held by the trustees of a settlement of which you or any relative is or were a settlor.

The definition in (1) applies to all controlling directors who want to transfer benefits to a personal pension plan (see 3.14.3).

3.6.2 Restrictions on all controlling directors

Final salary

The definition of final salary (see 3.1.3) and dynamised final remuneration (see 3.4.2) must be averaged over a period of three or more consecutive years within the last ten years before retirement.

Maximum contributions

For schemes set up before August 1993, the maximum contributions payable by a controlling director have been reduced as a percentage of earnings. The old, higher levels remain in place for existing schemes but, if contributions are increased, the new, lower basis must be used from then on.

3.6.3 Restrictions on pre-1987 and 1987–1989 members

Normal retirement date

The earliest normal retirement date is 60 for both men and women. However, there are a number of occupations where a reasonable case can be put to the Inland Revenue for a lower retirement age. Acceptance is never automatic: each case has to be argued on its merits. Also, if accepted, you may have to take the benefits at the agreed date; it is not possible to defer them.

Benefits on late retirement

If you delay taking your pension benefits beyond your normal retirement date, you get no additional credit up to age 70 though you get an increase if you defer your retirement date beyond age 70 (see 5.7.6).

3.6.4 Retained benefits

With the exception of post-1989 members, all benefits from retirement annuity contracts or personal pension plans must be taken into account when calculating the maximum benefits from a company scheme or executive pension plan.

For post-1989 members, there is no need to take account of any benefits from such schemes set up during earlier periods of self employment or with a previous employer *unless* your benefits under your current scheme are being provided in a shorter timescale (see 3.4.1). Benefits from any personal pension schemes relating to your current employment must always be taken into account and are treated as if they were benefits from your occupational scheme.

3.7 THE FRAMEWORK FOR IMPROVEMENT

Once you have found out what pension you are likely to receive from your employer's occupational scheme, you can see to what extent you can improve it. However, there is an important distinction to be drawn between the limits laid down by the Inland Revenue and the rules of your own company scheme. The Inland Revenue lays down the maximum benefits that may be taken from any approved company scheme and the timescale over which these benefits may accrue. The rules of your own scheme cannot exceed these limits, but they can fall short.

Consequently, there are three principal reasons why you may not qualify for the maximum pension to which you are entitled:

(1) You may not have achieved sufficient years of service with your employer when the time comes for you to retire. This means that you do not qualify for the maximum pension allowed by the rules of your company scheme.
(2) The maximum benefits allowed by the rules of your company scheme may be less than the maximum benefits allowed by the Inland Revenue.
(3) If you change jobs, for various reasons the number of 'years' built up in the old scheme may buy less 'years' in your new employer's scheme.

For example, you may belong to a company scheme that is based on the 60ths rule so you have to complete 40 years' service to achieve a maximum pension. The Inland Revenue rules, however, permit you to take a maximum two-thirds pension after only 20 years. There is nothing to prevent you from retiring at any time to suit yourself but the trustees of your company scheme are not obliged to start paying you a pension until you reach the normal retirement age of your company scheme.

Even if they do agree to pay you a pension early, it may not be the maximum because you have not worked the required number of years. The rules of your scheme may also include an early retirement penalty which reduces your pension still further.

Clearly it is important to see how the Revenue's rules and those of your own scheme apply. If you wish to retire at a certain age on full pension, what are the maximum benefits the Inland Revenue will allow you to take, what are the maximum benefits provided by your company scheme, and how do you plug the gap?

There are other benefits permitted by the Inland Revenue rules which may not be offered by your company scheme. Your company scheme may provide you with a fixed pension whereas Inland Revenue rules allow you to take one which is index-linked. Your company scheme may not have the benefit of a dependant's pension. Finally, your company benefits may be related to your basic salary and take no account of other forms of remuneration such as bonuses, company car, private medical insurance contributions and other fringe benefits, all of which can be included in the definition of 'salary' (or, more correctly, your 'total remuneration') for the calculation of contributions and benefits.

Consequently, in drawing up plans to improve your company pension, you can consider the exercise, not just from the point of view of increasing the amount of your pension, but also increasing the overall level of benefits and perhaps taking benefit at an earlier age. As the next sections show, there are a number of options for you to improve the situation either in conjunction with your employer or through private arrangements.

3.8 TOPPING-UP COMPANY SCHEMES

There are essentially four ways in which you can improve your company benefits:

(1) Additional voluntary contributions (AVCs)
(2) Free-standing additional voluntary contributions (FSAVCs)
(3) Executive pension plans
(4) Funded unapproved retirement benefit schemes (FURBS).

3.9 ADDITIONAL VOLUNTARY CONTRIBUTIONS (AVCS)

The Inland Revenue allows you to contribute up to 15 per cent of your total remuneration into a pension scheme. If you are already paying, say, 5 per cent to your company scheme, then you may pay the balance (10 per cent) into a supplementary scheme. However, the earlier point about basic salary versus total remuneration (see 3.1.3) may be valid here. If your employer pays a percentage of your *basic salary* into the pension scheme, you are free to pay the balance of 15 per cent of your *total remuneration* into an AVC scheme, that is you can also include the 'shortfall' on your employer's contributions.

You have a choice of investing AVCs through either your employer's scheme ('in-house' AVCs) or through a free-standing scheme (see 3.10).

The general rule for an in-house AVC scheme is that it runs parallel to a company scheme. The whole of your contributions are deducted from your pay before tax which means that you get tax relief at the highest rate you pay. The purpose of AVCs is to improve on the benefits provided by your company scheme up to the level of benefits allowable by the Inland Revenue rules (although AVCs started after 8 April 1987 may only provide a pension; no part of the benefits may be taken as a lump sum).

As a general rule, your employer's AVC scheme is likely to offer better value for money than FSAVCs because the employer usually bears the charges, whereas with FSAVCs you pay these yourself. However, for younger employees, the investment choice of FSAVCs may outweigh the disadvantages of higher charges.

3.10 FREE-STANDING ADDITIONAL VOLUNTARY CONTRIBUTIONS (FSAVCS)

FSAVCs were introduced on 26 October 1987. An FSAVC is an individual retirement plan and does not normally require any involvement on the part of your employer. It may be arranged through insurance companies, banks, building societies and unit and investment trust groups. You have total freedom of choice when selecting your pension provider.

An FSAVC scheme has the following characteristics:

(1) It can be used to provide income in retirement only, not tax-free lump sums.
(2) Contributions are subject to the normal limits. The maximum contributions you may pay must not exceed 15 per cent of your

salary (including any personal contributions which your employer may require you to pay under an occupational scheme or under a separate executive pension plan). Contributions paid by post-1989 members are also subject to the earnings cap (see 3.12.1).

(3) Benefits are also subject to the normal limits applying under occupational schemes.

(4) The scheme is completely separate from your employer's occupational scheme. When benefits become payable, eg on retirement, the trustees of your employer's scheme inform your pension provider of the maximum benefits permitted under Inland Revenue rules, and the amount being provided under the employer's scheme. The balance may be provided by the free-standing scheme. If there is a surplus when benefits become payable, it is returned to you minus a tax charge (see below).

(5) You pay contributions net of basic rate tax (similar to the basis on which you would obtain tax relief on mortgage interest payments). Any higher rate tax relief is obtained through your tax return.

3.10.1 Over provision

If the combination of benefits under the main occupational scheme and your free-standing scheme provides excessive benefits, the surplus arises under the free-standing scheme, ie the main scheme benefits are not reduced. Your pension provider can return to you this surplus but is obliged by law to deduct tax at 35 per cent from the surplus fund and this tax cannot be recovered even if you are a non-taxpayer at the time. If you are a higher rate taxpayer, further tax at 15 per cent is payable on the grossed up equivalent to the amount retained.

3.10.2 Contribution levels

If you plan to take early retirement but are not keen to let your employer know about your plans, there is nothing to prevent you from setting up a free-standing scheme to provide the funds.

However, you will probably want to know how much you can contribute to the free-standing scheme to top up the benefits to the Inland Revenue maximum. This information can only be provided by the main scheme trustees. The pension provider who runs the free-standing AVC may request this information on your behalf.

If you want to contribute £2,400 per annum or more, you have to give your pension provider information about the main scheme and any retained benefits. Your pension provider then checks if this level of contribution will lead to over provision. If this is likely, your pension provider will tell you what your maximum contributions can be to ensure that overall benefits do not exceed Inland Revenue limits.

If you intend contributing less than £2,400 per annum, the pension provider does not have to carry out an initial check (but will do so should your contributions exceed £2,400 per annum at any time in the future).

3.10.3 Benefits at retirement

As an investment, one disadvantage of a free-standing AVC scheme is that you cannot take part of the fund as tax-free cash. It must be used to buy an annuity. In practice, though, this problem may be overcome by looking at the combined benefits emerging from the free-standing scheme and your other pension arrangements.

Your first step should be to enquire about the rules of your company scheme. The rules of occupational schemes often contain powers of augmentation allowing the trustees to increase the tax-free lump sum (and other benefits) up to the maximum permitted by the Inland Revenue. You could, therefore, take increased cash from your occupational scheme, leaving a lower income from that scheme which would be topped-up by the pension from your free-standing scheme. Post-1989 members may also be able to benefit from the '2.25 times pension' rule (see 3.5.1).

There are more details on the options open to you when taking your pension in Chapter 5 (see particularly 5.2).

If you are keen to retain maximum flexibility consider investing in individual savings accounts (ISAs), which replaced personal equity plans (PEPs) on 6 April 1999, either instead of or as well as AVCs/FSAVCs. The tax treatment is different from pension schemes but is very attractive and you can take the fund as tax-free cash at any time (see 6.5.6).

3.11 EXECUTIVE PENSION PLANS

Another way of supplementing your pension benefits is to ask for your employer's co-operation in setting up an executive pension plan (EPP) for you. This is a separate plan; it is not part of the group scheme. EPPs are particularly tax efficient if your employer pays the contributions to the plan on your behalf and subtracts the amount from your gross salary.

However, if your benefits are to be topped up by means of a separate EPP, your employer *must* contribute at least 10 per cent of the total costs. If your employer is unwilling to bear any additional expenditure, his contribution can be offset by an equivalent deduction in your salary (known as a 'salary sacrifice').

There is no need for the EPP to mirror the group scheme. This flexibility offers certain benefits. The Inland Revenue permits categories of employees to have (effectively) two normal retirement dates. A director or executive can, for example, be a member of a group pension scheme with a normal retirement age of 65 (when the majority of employees will retire), and also be a member of an EPP arranged specially for him with a retirement age of 60. To calculate the maximum approvable benefits under the EPP, the benefits payable under the main scheme at the earlier retirement age have to be taken into account.

The precise way in which the EPP can be used to top up your group scheme depends, of course, on the date you joined the main scheme.

3.11.1 The range of additional benefits

By combining an EPP with a group pension scheme, you can achieve one or more of the following benefits:

(1) A full two-thirds pension at an earlier age.
(2) Increases in dependants' benefits.
(3) A pension which increases in line with RPI.
(4) Increases in the tax-free lump sum up to the maximum permitted.
(5) More flexibility when you change jobs. If you leave your company, your benefits (often in the form of an individual policy) can be transferred to your new employer. Even if it is not transferred, it continues to benefit from future investment growth. However, watch out for penalties if you stop contributions.
(6) Improved death in service protection (life assurance).
(7) The use of dynamised final remuneration.
(8) Improved benefits on early retirement.
(9) Greater control over the investment medium in which your contributions are invested and greater privacy over your retirement provisions.
(10) Pay which is not normally pensioned, eg bonus, commission, is more easily accommodated under an EPP.

3.12 UNAPPROVED RETIREMENT BENEFIT SCHEMES

3.12.1 The earnings cap

The 1989 Finance Act introduced the earnings cap. This imposes a ceiling (£90,600 for 1999–2000) on the salary that can be taken into account for pensions and applies to all post-1989 members.

The then Conservative Government's intention was to limit the amount of pension that could be built up with the full benefits of tax relief. The level was originally set at £60,000 and was index-linked to rises in the cost of living. However, indexation is not guaranteed and may be suspended by the Government (as it was in 1993–94 when the cap stood at £75,000).

In practice the number of people currently caught out by the cap is not high and it only applies to people who joined their company scheme since 1989. However, by linking annual rises to prices rather than annual earnings, and by reserving the right to suspend even this limited index-linking, the cap is steadily being reduced in real value compared to average earnings. Higher paid people moving jobs and developing their careers could well expect their salary to grow in excess of the rate of increase in average earnings and, for them, the earnings cap could soon become a bar to adequate pension provision.

For example, if we assume that inflation really is beaten and stays at about 2 per cent per annum, the cap could rise to just under £94,000 in ten years' time (assuming the Government does not freeze the cap in the meantime). Somebody earning £30,000 today would need an annual salary increase of around 12 per cent per annum to hit problems in ten years' time. If that rate of salary increase seems over-optimistic, salary increases of just over 8.5 per cent per annum would take the employee to the cap threshold in 15 years' time.

3.12.2 The introduction of FURBS

Fortunately, for high earners, the Government introduced unapproved schemes at the same time as the earnings cap. These allow the employer to:

(1) provide additional lump sums on retirement;
(2) offer a pension greater than the normal maximum of two-thirds of capped final salary;
(3) provide a full two-thirds pension where the normal rules would not allow it;
(4) provide lump sums or pensions on earnings above the earnings cap.

3.12.3 Funded or unfunded?

If your employer wishes to provide additional benefits for you under an unapproved scheme, he has a choice in the way these benefits are provided. The benefits are either paid at retirement out of company funds and shown on the balance sheets (the unfunded method) or out of money set aside in advance to meet the future benefits (the funded method).

Most people will probably prefer the far greater security of the funded method where money is set aside each year by the employer and ear-marked specifically for the individual member. The arrangements can be incorporated into a contract of employment and, if held in trust for the employee, the money cannot normally be reclaimed even if the employer is taken over or goes into liquidation.

3.12.4 The tax position of the funded route

The following is an overall summary of the tax implications of funded unapproved retirement benefit schemes (FURBS):

(1) The contributions paid by your employer are treated as an expense against profits and normally qualify for tax relief, as for approved schemes. However, from April 1999 employers will pay national insurance contributions on these payments.
(2) Contributions paid by your employer are regarded as income in your hands and are treated as a benefit in kind; the full amount of contributions paid is reported on your annual P11D. Alternatively, provided you are not a director, your employer may pay this tax for you as part of your total remuneration package in which case the contributions do not appear on your P11D.
(3) You should not pay any contributions yourself as this could have adverse consequences on your tax position.
(4) At retirement, the fund is paid to the trustees who in turn pay it to you as a lump sum. You may then reinvest the lump sum to provide a regular income if you prefer. As the funds usually already have been taxed on their income and capital gains, the lump sum is entirely tax-free but the annuity is taxable – hence the popularity of the lump sum. However, if your FURBS was established after 30 November 1993 and the income and capital gains have not been subject to UK tax (eg an offshore scheme), the lump sum is taxed at your top rate.
(5) In the event of your death before retirement, a lump sum can be paid to your dependants. As with approved schemes, this is free of inheritance tax.

In exchange for a tax regime that is less advantageous than under an approved scheme, there is no limit to the benefits that can be provided by a FURBS.

3.13 LEAVING YOUR COMPANY SCHEME

From 6 April 1988, it has been possible for you to leave your employer's scheme if you wish and it is no longer possible for employers to make membership of the pension scheme a condition of employment. Generally speaking, however, if you have the option to join the scheme, this will provide better value and guaranteed benefits which cannot be matched by a personal pension.

If you leave your company scheme, you have two options:

(1) to make no private provisions at all and rely on state pension benefits; or
(2) to take out a personal pension plan.

It is possible that your employer might be prepared to contribute to your personal pension plan as he will not be contributing on your behalf to the occupational pension scheme that you have left. However, your employer is under no obligation to do this and could refuse to allow you back into the company pension scheme at a later stage.

3.13.1 Should you leave?

The factors that you should consider vary according to your personal circumstances and the benefits provided by the company scheme, but, in general, you should take care to note the following points:

(1) If you take out a personal pension plan, will your employer contribute to it?
(2) What benefits will you be giving up if you leave? Scheme benefits can vary enormously (for example, they could include life assurance and long-term sickness benefits) and it is expensive to replace these by taking out a personal pension plan and private insurances.
(3) Is your company pension scheme contributory or non-contributory?
(4) Does the company scheme provide benefits on a final salary basis (which guarantees the level of your pension) or on a money purchase basis? Even if it is a money purchase scheme the employer will probably pay the charges and make a contribution on your behalf.
(5) Are the transfer values offered attractive?
(6) If you leave, can you rejoin?

3.14 CHANGING YOUR JOB

Most people change jobs around five times during their career. There are a number of options open to you to make sure that your future pension is not jeopardised.

Until 1975, many pension schemes provided nothing for the job mover whether he was dismissed for misconduct, was made redundant, or left of his own accord. Since then, the position has changed dramatically. The Social Security Act 1973 significantly altered the benefits of early leavers with effect from 6 April 1975, and the subsequent Acts of 1985, 1986, 1990 and 1998 have made further improvements. The position now for people who leave their company scheme is that company schemes have to provide benefits at or after normal retirement date and (in the case of final salary schemes) must revalue preserved pensions in line with increases in the retail price index up to a maximum of 5 per cent per annum.

The options normally available to employees are set out below, although some may not be available, either as a result of the preservation requirements under the Act or because the employer's pension scheme does not provide them. Essentially, you have the choice between leaving your pension where it is or taking the transfer value and investing it in an alternative pension arrangement.

If you have been a scheme member for less than two years you can claim a cash refund, less a deduction for cash and for back payments to SERPS if the scheme was contracted out.

If you were a member for more than two years you cannot obtain a cash refund of your contributions (subject to a tax charge) and your options are as follows:

(1) A deferred pension (sometimes known as preserved, paid up or frozen pensions) may be provided by your current scheme, payable when you reach normal retirement age, although early and late retirement options may be permitted.
(2) A cash transfer from your current scheme may be used to purchase a deferred annuity from an insurance company – so-called 'Section 32 annuities' (sometimes called 'buy-out plans').
(3) A cash transfer from your current scheme may be paid into a personal pension plan.
(4) A cash transfer from your current scheme may be paid to your new employer's pension scheme.
(5) You may be assigned an executive pension plan by the trustees of the original scheme.

3.14.1 Deferred pension

A deferred pension is generally limited to a proportion of your total final remuneration at the date of leaving your employment. The deferred pension must be revalued in line with the cost of living between the date of leaving and normal retirement age, subject to a maximum of 5 per cent per annum. Part of the pension may be exchanged for a lump sum on reaching normal retirement age. The maximum lump sum is calculated on the same basis as for early retirement (see 5.7.5).

In most cases a deferred pension or a transfer to your new employer's scheme would be the best options.

3.14.2 Section 32 annuity

Rather than providing deferred benefits under the scheme as above, the trustees may effectively transfer the benefits by purchasing (from an insurance company chosen by you) a deferred annuity in your name. A series of such annuities may be purchased (not necessarily from the same insurers) allowing benefits to be taken in stages.

The maximum pension and the maximum tax-free cash lump sum permitted by the Inland Revenue is endorsed on the policy issued by the insurer. These benefits may be increased between the date on which the transfer is made and the date of retirement in line with increases in the retail prices index subject to a maximum of 5 per cent per annum. One of the specific benefits of a Section 32 annuity until April 1997 was that if part of your current scheme consisted of a guaranteed minimum pension (see 2.8.3) then the GMP element was transferred into the annuity.

The Section 32 annuity itself may include an open market option (see 5.4) and power to surrender the policy and transfer it to a new scheme, including a personal pension scheme.

Benefits (pension and tax-free cash lump sum) may be taken from age 50 onwards (but not later than age 75), regardless of whether you have retired or are continuing to work. Also, the cash lump sum entitlement may be increased each year in line with movements in the retail prices index between the date of leaving and the date of drawing benefits.

3.14.3 Personal pension plans

An individual leaving his employer's scheme also has the option of transferring his benefits into a personal pension plan. In most cases this would not be advisable because you would give up guaranteed benefits for a higher risk, non-guaranteed pension.

In the rare cases where a transfer makes sense, a personal pension may be more flexible than the Section 32 annuity described above because the transferred benefits are subject to the personal pension legislation which allows you to pay future contributions if you have 'net relevant earnings' (see 4.7.2).

However, before benefits may be transferred to a personal pension plan, the trustees of your original company scheme must provide certificates as required in Inland Revenue regulations, as follows:

(1) *A controlling director's/high earner's certificate* This certificate is required for anybody who is a controlling director (see 3.6.1) or was a high earner (defined, in 1999–2000, as anybody earning £90,600 or more – the same level as the earnings cap), at any time during the ten years prior to the date in which the transfer value is applied for. The certificate must confirm that the transfer value does not exceed the cash equivalent of the maximum benefit that could have been paid under the rules of the transferring scheme.

(2) *A cash sum certificate* This certificate is required for anybody who is a controlling director or high earner (as defined in (1) above) or who is over age 45 at the date that a right to a transfer value is applied for. This certificate must state the maximum cash lump sum payable under the transferring scheme at normal retirement date based on salary and service at the date of leaving.

3.14.4 Transfer values into your new scheme

When you leave one employment to take up another, your benefits under the original pension scheme may be transferred to the new pension scheme provided it is willing and able to accept a transfer value.

If your new employer's scheme is a money purchase scheme, the transfer value is simply the value of your fund, although there might be penalties if you stop contributions early. If it is a final salary scheme, the position is more complicated as the transfer value is credited to you in the form of 'added years' service' with your new employer's scheme. There is no hard and fast rule on how many added years you should get; it could be a matter for negotiation with your new employer.

Right to a transfer value

If you leave your company scheme, you have a right to a transfer value if you had been in the scheme long enough to qualify for benefits – normally two years. There is no right to a transfer value if you are already receiving a pension from your current scheme or if you have less than one year to go before reaching the previous scheme's normal retirement age.

3.14.5 Assignment of an executive pension plan

If you had set up an executive pension plan as part of your retirement arrangements with your previous employer, it is possible for the policy to be assigned to a new employer. However, this is be regarded by the Inland Revenue as a new scheme set up by the new employer in order to bring the maximum benefits into line with your new company scheme, which means that it is restricted by the earnings cap.

There are two further options:

(1) the trustees of the original scheme could assign the executive pension plan to you personally; or
(2) the policy may continue to be held by the trustees and will participate in any future growth.

Both of these options keep the plan under the existing rules which means that benefits may not be affected by the earnings cap.

3.14.6 What about your AVCs?

If you leave your company, the in-house AVCs are regarded as part of your contributions. They may be included as part of the transfer value or as part of the deferred pension.

In contrast, free-standing AVCs are completely portable and can be taken with you, regardless of what happens to the rest of your pension contributions. However, beware of penalties if you reduce or stop contributions.

3.14.7 To defer or transfer?

There is no simple answer to this question. Your first step must be to find out what deferred pension you can expect and then to find out what benefits your transfer value might provide through the other options. Part of the problem is getting a fix on the underlying value of any transfer value you are offered. There is no standard method of calculating transfer values and, although the trustees are supposed to offer you a transfer value that is fair and reasonable, opinions may vary as to exactly what *is* fair and reasonable.

It is a decision that needs careful thought and competent independent advice; your future pension is a vital part of your long-term financial security and it is an area which should be covered in any negotiations with a potential employer as part of your overall remuneration package. If you decide to move to a new scheme, you are then affected by the earnings cap (even if you were previously unaffected by it) and this needs to be taken into account in any discussions with a future employer, for example you may wish to discuss a FURBS.

4

IMPROVING YOUR PERSONAL PENSION AND RETIREMENT ANNUITY

This chapter looks at personal pensions and retirement annuites under the following headings:

(1) Personal pension plans and retirement annuities
(2) What type of plan?
(3) Finding out what you will get
(4) The framework for improvement
(5) Limits on benefits
(6) Maximising contributions
(7) Earnings
(8) Maximum contributions
(9) Carry forward/ carry back facilities
(10) Investment strategy.

4.1 PERSONAL PENSION PLANS AND RETIREMENT ANNUITIES

Background

Retirement annuities were, until recently, the main pension arrangement for the self-employed. The term 'self-employed retirement annuity' is, however, misleading as it suggests that eligibility was confined to one group: in fact, employed people who do not have access to a company scheme have also taken out these contracts in the past.

On 1 July 1988, personal pension plans were launched and no new retirement annuities were available from that date. However, retirement annuities taken out before 1 July 1988 may still be maintained and may even accept increases in contributions. Some people may well have one or more of each type of plan.

The basic rules of eligibility remain unchanged; if you are self-employed or employed by a company that does not have an occupational pension scheme, you may build up your own pension through a personal pension plan.

The benefits

Three types of benefit may be provided by both types of pension scheme:

(1) A pension at retirement with provision for taking part of the benefits as a tax-free cash lump sum.
(2) A pension for the wife (or husband) or for any one or more dependants of the planholder.
(3) A lump sum on the death of the planholder before age 75. The lump sum can be paid in instalments to provide income for dependants.

The principal differences between the two types of scheme are the limits on benefits (see 4.5) and on contributions (see 4.8).

4.2 WHAT TYPE OF PLAN?

Personal pension schemes are sold by life offices, unit and investment trust groups, banks, building societies and friendly societies. There are a number of different basic structures of plan but the most common are with-profits plans and unit-linked plans, although a small but growing number of unit trust and investment trust plans are available.

4.2.1 With-profits policies

Many pension plans on the market fall into this category and are issued by traditional life offices. The policy is either:

(1) a 'pure endowment' where a guaranteed capital sum is payable on retirement, converted into an annuity at an annuity rate that may be guaranteed in the policy; or
(2) a deferred annuity with a guaranteed annuity payable on retirement, possibly with a guaranteed cash option.

If you are investing in a conventional with-profits policy, you may well have been offered a 'projected capital fund per £1,000 of annual contribution' made up of three elements:

(1) A minimum guaranteed amount payable at retirement age.
(2) An annual bonus, which is not guaranteed, and which depends on the actual results achieved over the year, although returns are 'smoothed' to hold back some profit in good years in order to maintain decent bonuses in poor investment years. This additional sum

(known as a 'reversionary bonus') is normally expressed as a percentage of the minimum guaranteed amount in (1) and usually benefits from a compounding effect.

(3) A final additional amount (known as a 'terminal bonus') which depends on economic and financial conditions prevailing at the time of retirement.

Once a reversionary bonus has been declared by the insurance company, it cannot subsequently be removed even if future investment results fail to match expectations.

In recent years, there has been a general reduction in reversionary bonuses and more emphasis on terminal bonuses. There is no guarantee with terminal bonuses, however, as these are discretionary payments depending upon investment conditions when the policy matures.

4.2.2 Unit-linked policies

The 1970s saw an upsurge of insurance companies offering policies on unit-linked principles. The unit-linked route has become so popular that companies which traditionally marketed only with-profits policies now also offer unit-linked policies.

Under a unit-linked policy, you can choose the asset class in which you would like your contributions to be invested and you may switch between sectors from time to time. The contributions paid are used to buy units in one or more of the chosen funds and the value of the units rises and falls in line with the underlying investments in the funds.

On retirement, the units are encashed and the proceeds are used to purchase an annuity. No bonuses are declared and the value of units is not guaranteed.

4.2.3 Unit trust plans

These are similar to unit-linked plans in that the value of your units fluctuates in line with the value of the underlying investments.

4.2.4 Investment trust plans

An investment trust is a British company listed on the UK Stock Exchange, which invests in the shares of other companies in the United Kingdom and overseas. The share price is affected by the value of the underlying assets and by supply and demand. This makes the shares potentially more volatile than units in unit trust and unit-linked plans (see above).

4.3 FINDING OUT WHAT YOU WILL GET

Personal pension plans are money purchase schemes. The final benefits you can expect depend on the size of the fund built up and this, in turn, depends on the amount of money you have paid in, investment performance over the period and the charges deducted. In this way, they are no different in structure from occupational money purchase schemes except that, unlike company schemes, the benefits you can take out are not restricted by final salary. However, there are restrictions on the amount of money you can pay into these schemes (see 4.8).

At retirement, the fund built up is used to buy an annuity which, in return for your pension fund, guarantees an income for life. The 'rate' or income depends on your age and sex and on long-term interest rates generally available at the time (see below). You may also take a proportion of the fund in tax-free cash (see 4.5) with a corresponding reduction in pension.

4.3.1 Getting a quotation

Your pension provider should give you an illustrative quotation of what the benefits are likely to be. Bear in mind these are based on certain assumptions – for example investment returns – and are by no means guaranteed. There are, moreover, two points to bear in mind if you intend to compare these quotations with the quotation received when you first started contributing to your pension (especially so if it was before 1988).

(1) The basis on which projections of benefits are now made is more rigorously controlled.
(2) The annuity rate you were originally quoted may no longer be relevant.

4.3.2 The projection of benefits

The quotation system before 1995 produced unrealistic projections. Companies were free to use more or less any basis of future investment return which they considered reasonable and this frequently led to some quite remarkable projections of future fund values (the so-called 'telephone number' projections). It was also difficult to compare quotations from different companies because each used its own specific charging structure to arrive at the final estimates.

In 1988 standard growth rates were introduced. In January 1995 the current system was completed. Companies today must use set rates of annual return (9 per cent in the case of pension plans) and must allow for the deduction of their own charges. All pension providers and advisers are regulated under the Financial Services Act and/or the Financial Services and Markets Act 1998.

4.3.3 Annuity rates

In addition, the annuity income the funds will generate changes frequently. In providing you with a pension for life, the company actuary has to invest those funds where he can be sure of obtaining a known rate of income for a substantial number of years and where he knows the capital will be safe. The only forms of investment that meet these requirements are long-dated Government gilt-edged securities (see 6.3.4) and some of the safer corporate bonds. When quoting future annuity rates to you, your insurance company will have based its quotation on the yields on long-dated gilts.

4.4 THE FRAMEWORK FOR IMPROVEMENT

Contribution limits for personal pensions are very generous, starting at 17.5 per cent of net relevant earnings up to age 35, rising to 40 per cent for those over age 61 (see Table 4.1). Contributions are restricted by the earnings cap – as is shown in the table. The contributions to retirement annuities are lower in percentage terms but the cap does not apply (see 4.8.1).

4.5 LIMITS ON BENEFITS

There are limits on when benefits may be taken and also in the way the tax-free cash lump sum is calculated. The limits differ between retirement annuities and personal pension plans.

4.5.1 Retirement annuities

The limits are as follows:

(1) Benefits must be taken between ages 60 and 75 (or earlier, if you work in a specialised occupation (see 4.5.3)).
(2) The tax-free cash lump sum is limited to three times the annuity remaining after the cash lump sum has been taken. This calculation can be carried out by your adviser or your pension provider. The Inland Revenue rules allow the lump sum to be calculated on the

most favourable terms, ie on the basis of the highest possible annuity even if you do not actually choose that form of annuity (there are more details in 5.3 on the various ways in which annuities may be taken).

(3) If, at retirement, the plan is converted into a personal pension plan under the open market option (see 5.4), the limits below apply.

4.5.2 Personal pension plans

The limits are as follows:

(1) Benefits may be taken between ages 50 and 75 (or earlier, if you work in a specialised occupation – see below).
(2) Up to 25 per cent of the fund may be taken in cash.
(3) If any part of the fund relates to protected rights contributions (see 2.8.1), this cannot be used to generate tax-free cash.

4.5.3 Lower retirement ages for specialised occupations

The Inland Revenue permits a pension age lower than age 50 (under personal pension plans) and lower than age 60 (under retirement annuity contracts) for certain specialised occupations where early retirement is customary. Anybody in one of these occupations has the option of paying contributions into a personal pension scheme which provides benefits to commence at the earlier pension age allowable. If the individual's job changes to one which does not fall into the definition of a specialised occupation, he has to stop paying contributions to the original contract and divert future contributions to a new contract which specifies the normal range of pension ages from 50 to 75.

4.6 MAXIMISING CONTRIBUTIONS

Maximum contributions are governed by two factors. There is an overall limit in place which applies to your 'net relevant earnings' (see below). These earnings are carefully defined and it may be possible for you to increase the amount you may contribute to a personal pension scheme by calculating your net relevant earnings more accurately.

The second factor relates both to your age (which stipulates the maximum percentage of your 'net relevant earnings' that you may contribute) and also to an upper monetary limit which may apply to personal pension plans (but not retirement annuities).

The following sections look in more detail at the following topics:

(1) Earnings
(2) Maximum contributions
(3) Carry forward/carry back facilities
(4) Investment strategy.

4.7 EARNINGS

4.7.1 Relevant earnings

It is necessary to have 'relevant earnings' to be eligible to pay contributions to a personal pension plan or retirement annuity. The relevant earnings for an employee or director taxed under Schedule E are his actual earnings during the fiscal year beginning on 6 April and ending on 5 April.

4.7.2 Net relevant earnings

'Net relevant earnings' means the amount of relevant earnings less business expenses including any deductions for losses or capital allowances. Personal charges such as maintenance payments, charitable covenants and non-business interest do not reduce net relevant earnings.

Contributions to both types of personal pension, although deducted from earnings in order to arrive at total income for tax purposes, are not deductible for the calculation of net relevant earnings.

4.7.3 Schedule E taxpayers

If you are in non-pensionable employment taxed under Schedule E, you normally have no deductions to make from your relevant earnings: your gross earnings from your employment are your net relevant earnings and all deductions (such as tax, national insurance contributions, maintenance payments, covenants and interest), whether or not allowable for tax, are ignored.

If you are a member of an approved personal pension plan, you do not pay income tax on your employer's contributions.

4.7.4 Schedule D taxpayers

If you are self-employed and taxed under Schedule D, you must make the following deductions from your gross profits in order to arrive at your net relevant earnings:

(1) all expenses incurred in earning the profits, such as rent, rates, business interest, employees' salaries, etc;
(2) losses, whether:
    (a) incurred in the current tax year; or
    (b) incurred in a previous tax year and carried forward to set against profits in the current tax year; or
    (c) incurred in a previous tax year, relieved against other income, and not yet deducted from net relevant earnings;
(3) capital allowances.

Personal mortgage interest and covenants to charity can be ignored.

4.8 MAXIMUM CONTRIBUTIONS

As mentioned, the maximum contributions differ for retirement annuities and personal pension plans.

4.8.1 Retirement annuities

Contributions (as a percentage of net relevant earnings) which may be made to retirement annuity contracts for the tax year 1999–2000 and onwards are:

Age on 6 April	*Maximum contributions (%)*
Up to 50	17.5
51 to 55	20.0
56 to 60	22.5
61 to 74	27.5

All the above figures are inclusive of any contributions for life assurance (see 7.3.3) and waiver of contribution benefit (see 7.5.3). Part of any lump sum life assurance benefit can instead be taken as a pension for dependants.

4.8.2 Personal pension plans

The maximum contributions which may be made to a personal pension plan are the lower of a percentage of net relevant earnings and a monetary limit, as shown in Table 4.1 below. Up to 5 per cent of net relevant earnings for life assurance are included in the maximum contributions in Table 4.1, as is the cost of waiver of contribution benefit. Part of any lump sum life assurance benefit may be taken instead as a pension for dependants.

Where a personal pension plan is used for contracting-out of SERPS (see 2.8.1), the contributions paid by the DSS are in addition to the maximum contributions,

The monetary limits shown in Table 4.1 are the relevant percentage of the earnings cap (personal pension plans carry the same restrictions as occupational schemes).

Table 4.1 Maximum contributions to personal pension plans

Age on 6 April	*Maximum contribution*	*Monetary Limit* 1994–95 £	1995–96 £	1996–97 £	1997–98 £	1998–99 £	1999–2000 £
up to 35	17.5%	13,440	13,755	14,385	14,700	15,330	15,855
36 to 45	20.0%	15,360	15,720	16,440	16,800	17,520	18,120
46 to 50	25.0%	19,200	19,650	20,550	21,000	21,900	22,650
51 to 55	30.0%	23,040	23,580	24,660	25,200	26,280	27,180
56 to 60	35.0%	26,880	27,510	28,770	29,400	30,660	31,710
61 to 74	40.0%	30,720	31,440	32,880	33,660	35,040	36,240
Maximum contributions for life assurance		3,840	3,930	4,110	4,200	4,380	4,530
Earnings cap		76,800	78,600	82,200	84,000	87,600	90,600

4.8.3 Personal pension plans versus retirement annuities

Many people who contribute to existing retirement annuities also wish to take advantage of the higher contribution limits available under personal pension plans. However, special conditions apply in these circumstances. If you want to pay contributions to both a personal pension and a retirement annuity in the same year, then the personal pension limits apply, including the earnings cap. If you are careful you can pay on an alternative year basis and maintain both sets of contribution limits.

4.9 CARRY FORWARD/CARRY BACK FACILITIES

It is possible to take advantage of these two facilities to maximise your pension contributions and obtain the best possible tax advantages on those contributions.

4.9.1 Carry forward of unused relief

This allows you to pay a higher contribution than you would normally be able to in the *current* year in order to catch up for missed contributions in *previous* years. If you do pay higher than normal contributions then, if you are contributing to a retirement annuity, the Inspector of Taxes automatically refers back over the previous six years to discover any unused reliefs which can be carried forward to soak up the excess contributions. If you are contributing to a personal pension plan, you must make an election.

Tax relief, however, is always against the *current* year; there is no impact on tax paid in previous years. Also, tax relief is only available up to the level of tax payable on earned income for the current year, ie there is no tax relief on contributions in excess of the level of taxable earnings. For Schedule E employees, the position is slightly better. Their contributions are paid net of basic rate tax and must not exceed their net relevant earnings for the current year (which are generally higher than their taxable earned income because of personal allowances, mortgage interest relief, etc).

4.9.2 Carry back provisions

A contribution (or part of a contribution) may be carried back to the tax year preceding the year of payment regardless of whether there are relevant earnings in the year of payment. If there were no net relevant earnings in the preceding year, the contribution may be carried back one further year.

The contribution is taxed as if it had been paid in the year to which it is carried back. The contributions allowed for that year are the normal maximum for that year plus any unused reliefs for the previous six years as described in 4.9.1.

Consequently, a contribution paid in 1999–2000, and carried back to 1998–99, is allowed against your income tax bill for 1998–99. It can also include an amount relating to missed contributions carried forward from a previous year.

If you are a Schedule E employee, only your own personal contributions may be carried back; there is no facility to carry back contributions made by your employer.

4.10 INVESTMENT STRATEGY

Your eventual retirement income depends to no small extent on investment growth over the period. As most personal pension plans give you a choice of investments, you are in a position to influence the risk/reward profile of your fund.

However, the guidelines in Chapter 6 are relevant here. Although you may regard your retirement fund as a long-term investment, it ceases to be such as you get to within, say, five years of your retirement date, unless you plan to keep your fund fully invested in early retirement (see 5.9.2).

The important point to bear in mind is that your pension fund is a source of guaranteed income for the rest of your life. Although you may be able to take some risks with your choice of investments over the long term, as you get closer to retirement your pension plan becomes more a source of guaranteed long-term income than a short-term investment opportunity. There may come a time when you have to regard it as a short-term investment and move to a fixed interest fund.

If you are tempted to maintain your exposure to equities until the last minute, remember October 1987. And if you think that it cannot happen again, remember the 1974 oil crisis.

5

TAKING YOUR PENSION

When the time comes for you to take the benefits of your pension plans (which may not necessarily coincide with full retirement), the complexity of choice does not diminish.

This chapter covers the following topics:

(1) What is an annuity?
(2) Pension versus cash lump sum
(3) Types of annuity
(4) The open market option
(5) Dealing with low annuity rates
(6) Impaired lives
(7) Company pensions
(8) Personal pension schemes
(9) Working into retirement.

5.1 WHAT IS AN ANNUITY?

An annuity is the purchase of a lifetime income in exchange for a lump sum payment. In many ways, it can be looked at as the reverse of a life assurance policy where, in return for the payment of a regular series of premiums (which depend on the policyholder's age and sex), a lump sum is paid on death. An annuity reverses that by agreeing to pay, in exchange for a lump sum, a regular series of payments (which are determined by the annuitant's age and sex) until the annuitant's death.

Annuities for older lives are higher than for younger people (because the insurance company assumes that fewer payments will be made) and are usually lower for females (as women have a life expectancy of between four and five years longer than a man of the same age). There are two principal types of annuity:

(1) Compulsory purchase annuities
(2) Purchased life annuities.

A compulsory purchase annuity is, as its name suggests, an annuity you are required to buy with the proceeds of certain pension plans. The funds built up under an approved money purchase pension plan, after the cash lump sum has been deducted, *must* be invested in a compulsory purchase annuity. If the cash lump sum is not taken, the whole fund must be invested in a compulsory purchase annuity.

Unapproved plans (see 3.12) do not have this restriction; the whole fund may usually be taken as tax-free cash.

A purchased life annuity, on the other hand, is an annuity which you can purchase at any time with your spare capital. If you have a sum of money available (the tax-free cash lump sum from your pension, for example) and you decide to invest it in an annuity, then you would buy a purchased life annuity.

The difference between the two types of annuity lies in the way they are taxed. With the compulsory purchase annuity, the *whole* of the income is taxed. With the purchased life annuity, part of each payment is regarded as a return of capital and this is not taxed. The *balance* is regarded as income or interest and is therefore taxable.

As you get older the element which is classed as a return of capital increases, so the taxable interest element reduces correspondingly. As a rough guide, a 65-year-old man is taxed on 50 per cent of the income whereas for an 80-year-old the taxable element is about 38 per cent.

Given the tax treatment, if you decide to use your *entire* pension fund to provide you with an annuity, then the best approach is to take the largest amount of cash you can out of your fund and use this to buy a separate purchased life annuity rather than use the whole fund to provide you with a compulsory purchase annuity.

5.2 PENSION VERSUS CASH LUMP SUM

Most people at retirement take the cash lump sum because this gives them greater flexibility in the way they use their retirement benefits. As mentioned, even if you need the maximum possible income from your pension, it may still make sense to take the cash lump sum and re-invest the proceeds in a more tax-efficient purchased life annuity.

This is certainly true of money purchase schemes but you should consider your overall options more carefully if your occupational pension is a final salary scheme. Under these circumstances, your pension is guaranteed (in that it is a fixed percentage of your final salary), it probably guarantees a pension for your spouse if you die first and may well benefit from increases in the future (see 5.7.7). If you take the cash lump sum, you reduce this guaranteed pension in return for the option of perhaps buying a purchased life annuity on the open market. At a time of low annuity rates, you need to make quite sure that your replacement income is not inferior to the pension you are giving up out of your final salary scheme. The position is eased if you have a supplementary pension plan (see 5.7.4).

5.3 TYPES OF ANNUITY

If you are in an occupational scheme that provides you with a pension based on your final salary, you will probably find that you have very little choice in the type of pension you may draw owing to the inflexibility of the scheme rules. With money purchase company schemes, for example FSAVCs and personal pensions, you may have considerable flexibility in the way you take your pension. The following are the various types of annuity that are available.

Single life versus joint life

The annuity can either be chosen for the life of one person or can be a lower annuity which lasts for the lifetime of two people, ending on the second death.

Frequency of payment

The amount depends on the frequency of payment. Payments can be made monthly, quarterly, half yearly or annually.

In advance versus in arrear

Annuities can either be paid at the start of the period of frequency or at the end (monthly in advance, annually in arrear and so on).

For example, if you choose a quarterly annuity payable in advance, you receive your first payment immediately and your second payment in three months' time. If the annuity were payable in arrear, you receive your first payment in three months' time.

Level versus escalating

You may choose a level pension or one which increases each year at a predetermined rate of compound interest. Typical examples are annuities which escalate at 3 per cent, 5 per cent or are linked to rises in the retail prices index.

Term of annuity

You may choose between an annuity which is paid for life or one that is paid for a guaranteed number of years, even if death occurs in the meantime. With a purchased life annuity, you have the further choice of a temporary annuity (one that is paid for a fixed term of years) or a deferred annuity (one that does not start to be paid until the end of a fixed term of years).

5.3.1 The impact of choice

For a given age and a given purchase price, the highest type of annuity is a level, single life annuity, paid for life with no guarantees on early death and paid annually in arrear. For a man aged 65, with a fund of £100,000 invested in a compulsory purchase annuity, he could draw an income of £10,468 before tax.

The following list gives an idea of the impact of the various options on the level of annual net income.

Table 5.1 How options affect gross annuity rate for £100,000 purchase

	Male 65	*Joint – male 65, female 63**
Level	10,468	9,461
3% increases	8,314	7,311
RPI increases	7,350	6,366
5 year Guarantee	10,320	n/a

*Spouse's pension is worth 50 per cent of main pension. These rates are for a compulsory purchase annuity with Prudential for a purchase of £100,000. Income is paid monthly in arrear. Figures shown are gross.

Source: *The Annuity Bureau, June 1997*

The level of annuity can vary enormously depending on which options you select. The above figures merely give an indication of options; the impact of several options working together can be even more dramatic. For example, a joint life annuity, escalating at RPI payable monthly in arrear, would be £6,366 compared to the £10,468 achieved on a level, single life basis.

The range of choice is clearly very wide and there are further options which are not immediately apparent. For example, it may seem automatic for a married man to choose a joint life annuity. This means that, in return for a lower overall annuity, there is at least the guarantee of an annuity for his wife if he dies before her. However, his wife might die first in which case he has given up the higher single person's annuity for nothing. A better result might be obtained by taking a single life annuity (on the husband) and using part of the income to pay for a life assurance policy (on the husband's life) so that, in the event of the husband's death, his wife can use the proceeds to buy a single life annuity for herself.

The message is to use this flexibility in the best way you can. You have to do some very careful analysis of the type of income you want from your pension and then to make your decision. The important point is that, once you have made your decision and started to draw your pension, you cannot change your mind at a later date. Consequently, it is absolutely vital that you consider exactly what type of pension you want and get a range of quotations from different companies.

The most important step to achieve the best annuity is to shop around, preferably through an independent adviser. This facility is known as the open market option.

5.4 THE OPEN MARKET OPTION

Pension plans usually permit an 'open market option' where the accumulated fund can be transferred, at retirement, to another insurance company. You will normally wish to do this if another insurance company offers better annuity rates than those of your original pension provider. You may occasionally incur a penalty if the monies are transferred to another insurance company and, if you use the services of a specialised service, you will have to pay a fee or commission for the pensions 'search'. Generally speaking, the advantages of getting a higher pension usually outweigh these costs.

Personal pension schemes arranged through banks, building societies, unit trusts and investment trusts are not allowed to provide pension benefits on retirement directly. The underlying funds (after the tax-free cash has been paid) have to be transferred to an insurance company which then provides the annuity.

5.5 DEALING WITH LOW ANNUITY RATES

Chapter 4 covers the impact of low interest rates on the yields on long-dated Government securities. When rates are low, there are some who would argue that conventional annuities are poor value for money. However, as a rule, when annuity rates are low, equity prices are high so your fund size should compensate. Unfortunately this does not always follow. Clearly, timing is everything and some people may be tempted to delay taking their pension in the hope that things may improve. However, this argument has two major flaws. In the first place, you are not getting any income at all in the meantime and, in the second place, there is no guarantee that interest rates are going to move up significantly in the short term.

One way out of this dilemma is to recognise that long-term yields may not recover substantially in the immediate future and to consider alternative forms of annuity. There are some more specialised forms of annuities where the income is not related to the yield on long-dated gilts but is instead linked to the future performance of an underlying investment. These include with-profits annuities and unit-linked annuities.

5.5.1 With-profits annuities

Due to the 'smoothing' of returns and guaranteed reversionary bonuses (see 4.2.1) with-profits funds are considered less volatile than unit-linked funds. Here the annual pension is based on the performance of the underlying fund. The percentage chosen initially is based on anticipated bonuses (eg 8 per cent per annum) but the future income depends on the value of the underlying fund. If this were to grow steadily over the years, the bonuses would also grow and hence the annual income.

Some companies will offer you a guaranteed minimum level of annual bonus; others will not and you will have to take whatever level of bonus is declared.

The risks are those of any long-term asset-backed investment; there is no guarantee that the value of funds will continue to rise (by their very nature, there will be some years when values will fall) and the value of bonuses will also fluctuate. The basic argument in favour of such annuities is that they are unlikely initially to be much poorer than conventional annuities when yields are low (but they do not look initially so attractive when conventional yields are high).

It is also important to remember that the investment management and administration are packaged together so, if the performance is poor, you cannot switch to a different manager.

5.5.2 Unit-linked annuities

Here the value of units is linked directly to the value of assets, so the income fluctuations will be more volatile. The annual income is taken by encashing a fixed percentage of units. The number of units that are encashed each year is calculated by dividing the total number of units by the expected number of payments according to the annuitant's life expectancy. Once again, provided that unit growth is consistent over the longer term, this type of annuity may provide a secure and rising income. Nevertheless, the investment risks are very real and you cannot change the manager if performance is poor.

The most important point to stress about these alternative annuities is that they are not for the faint hearted. They do involve some risk (principally that of falling values over the shorter term) and, if you need a guaranteed income, then you should stick with a conventional annuity. If, however, you have other sources of income in retirement that could make up any shortfall in the lean years, and if you are in reasonably good health, then the alternative forms of annuity could prove to be a suitable long-term choice, particularly at a time when the yields from conventional annuities are low.

5.5.3 Index-linked annuities

Conventional indexation is typically RPI or 5 per cent, whichever is the lower. A fully indexed annuity is adjusted in line with movements in RPI regardless of what inflation will be in the future. When inflation was high, such annuities provided a very low level of income in the early years but, with inflation at an historically low level, the RPI annuity rates are similar to a fixed 5 per cent escalation. Typically, the loss in the early years will be about 30 per cent but you have the assurance that the income you start with will retain its real value for the rest of your life.

5.6 IMPAIRED LIVES

Just as there are specialised forms of annuity for those people who can take a long-term view of their retirement, there are also specialised annuities for those people who have a medical condition that is sufficiently serious as to affect their normal life expectancy. Such annuities increase the level of income as the annuitant's life span is shorter. There are no clear guidelines; each case is treated on its own merits though it is perhaps worth emphasising that the annuity is based strictly on life expectancy and not quality of life.

This clearly is a very specialised area and advice should be sought from one of the specialist annuity offices.

5.7 COMPANY PENSIONS

In this section, the options open to you are covered as follows:

(1) The overall position
(2) Options on retirement
(3) The impact of other plans
(4) Benefits from supplementary schemes
(5) Early retirement
(6) Late retirement
(7) Pension increases in retirement.

5.7.1 The overall position

When the time comes for you to retire from your company, you could have several sources of pension:

(1) There is the pension from your current occupational scheme, which is either a final salary scheme or a money purchase scheme.
(2) You may have augmented your company scheme with additional voluntary contributions.
(3) You may have the benefits of a separate executive pension plan.
(4) You may have set up a separate free-standing additional voluntary contributions scheme.
(5) You may have deferred pensions from previous periods of employment.
(6) You may have a personal pension as a result of previous self-employment or employment with a company that did not provide you with a company pension.
(7) As a controlling director, you may have a personal pension relating to your current employment or to previous employment.
(8) You may have been contracted out of SERPS at some time through an appropriate pension and have a protected rights fund.

On top of all that, you may be retiring earlier or later than the normal retirement date laid down by your current scheme.

5.7.2 Options on retirement

The maximum pension benefits you may take are laid down by the Inland Revenue rules and the way these may be taken depends in part on when you joined your company scheme (see 3.3) and its rules.

You have to decide whether to take the cash lump sum (and, if so, what to do with it) and, in the case of money purchase schemes, you also have to decide whether to take the pension being offered to you by your company scheme or to use the open market option.

On reaching normal retirement date, it is normally possible (depending on the rules of your company scheme) to:

(1) take all the benefits, ie tax-free cash lump sum and pension;
(2) defer all the benefits;
(3) take the tax-free cash lump sum and defer the pension (or vice versa).

For post-1989 members, the benefits may only be taken at actual retirement date (ie it is not possible to take the benefits if you intend working on beyond normal retirement date). Also, option (2) is of limited value because the maximum approvable pension is not increased beyond normal retirement date (see 5.7.6) and option (3) is not permitted.

There may be circumstances where it would be better for a pre-1987 member to receive the benefits applicable to a post-1989 member. If you are in this position, then you should ask the trustees of the scheme to see if they are prepared to allow your benefits to be augmented.

If you are a 1987–1989 member, you can opt to be classed as a post-1989 member if the results are beneficial to you. There is no requirement to ask the trustees for permission; you have the right to make that decision by law.

5.7.3 The impact of other plans

Protected rights plans

Your company pension is not affected by any protected rights benefits (which, in any event, cannot be taken until you reach state retirement age).

Personal pension schemes and retained benefits

Your pension is not normally affected by any personal pension plan you may have taken out in the past. Also, if your pension is based on the 'straight 60ths' scale (see 3.4.1), you do not have to take into account any retained benefits (ie deferred pensions) from earlier employments. However, if you have been building up your company pension under one of the enhancement methods, then your total pension from your company scheme plus any retained benefits must not exceed two-thirds of your final salary.

Similar rules apply to controlling directors (see 3.6.4).

5.7.4 Benefits from supplementary schemes

If you are contributing to an additional voluntary contribution scheme to augment your company scheme, the benefits will probably follow the normal maximum limit of your company scheme, ie there may be an overall limit to the benefits you can draw. It is also usually the case that the benefits of both schemes have to be taken at the same time.

If you are contributing to a supplementary money purchase scheme, the problem of whether people in a final salary scheme should take the tax-free cash (see 5.2) is largely solved. Under these circumstances, you can draw the full pension from your final salary scheme and use the fund built up from the supplementary plan to provide the tax-free cash.

Free-standing AVC schemes

If you are contributing to a free-standing scheme, it will be completely separate from your employer's scheme. However, when benefits become payable, the trustees of both schemes liaise to ensure that you do not receive more than the maximum allowable benefits under Inland Revenue rules. The benefits from your company scheme is always topped up by the benefits from your FSAVC fund; if there is a surplus on your FSAVC fund, the excess is returned to you, less a tax charge (see 3.10.1).

Although FSAVCs may not be commuted to a cash lump sum, the pension provided may (for post-1989 members) be used in the '2.25 × pension before commutation' calculation to increase the tax-free lump sum provided by your employer's scheme (see 3.5.1). However, if your employer's scheme is a final salary scheme, it may not necessarily be in your best interests to take any cash from it because it will reduce your guaranteed pension.

As your supplementary scheme is a money purchase scheme, you can take advantage of the open market option.

5.7.5 Early retirement

You can take an immediate pension and cash lump sum from age 50 if your employment is terminated or if you retire early.

You will not, of course, get the benefit of any state pension until you reach state retirement age. Some occupational schemes make good this shortfall by paying a 'bridging pension' which is paid until state retirement age.

Pre-1987 members and 1987–1989 members

Maximum benefits on early retirement can be calculated in accordance with the following formulae:

$$\frac{N}{NS} \times P \quad \text{or} \quad \frac{N}{NS} \times LS$$

'N' is the number of years of service which have been completed to the point of early retirement (maximum 40).

'NS' is the number of years which could have been completed from the date of joining service to normal retirement date.

'P' and 'LS' are the maximum pension and tax-free lump sum you would have been entitled to had you retired at your normal retirement date but based on your final remuneration at the date of your early retirement. These are the overall limits and include the value of any retained benefits which must be deducted from the value of P and LS before doing the calculation.

Post-1989 members

The maximum benefit is $\frac{1}{30}$ of final remuneration for each year of service completed up to the date of early retirement. For example, if you have completed 20 years' service, a maximum pension of two-thirds of final remuneration may be provided from age 50 onwards (this is one set of circumstances where it could be advisable for a pre-1987 member to request the benefits of post-1989 membership).

Early retirement through ill health

If for reasons of physical or mental incapacity you are unable to follow your normal employment or have your earning capacity impaired, you can take early retirement. The maximum benefits are those based on your years of service had you reached your normal retirement date, but are based on your final salary at the date you are required to take early retirement.

If your incapacity is such that your expectation of life is very much shorter than normal (ie measured in months rather than years), you may be able to exchange the whole of your early retirement pension for an immediate cash lump sum. However, this lump sum will not be totally tax-free.

Money purchase schemes

In general terms, the early retirement pension limits as described above do not apply. The permitted maximum is the same as that on early retirement through ill health, that is it is based on potential service to normal retirement age and final salary at the date of early retirement.

Transfers to a personal pension plan

If you leave your employer's scheme as a result of early retirement, you also have the option of transferring the benefits into a personal pension plan. However, in most cases this would be very unwise, owing to the excellent guarantees offered by company schemes. In exceptional cases you may wish to take advantage of 'phased retirement' or 'income drawdown'.

This allows you to take part in the process known as 'staggered vesting' (see 5.9).

If you have contracted out of SERPS (see 2.8), then any part of your pension that results from protected rights must be taken at state retirement age and so is not available to you before then.

5.7.6 Late retirement

Except for post-1989 members (who receive no additional benefits at all from working on after normal retirement age), you can be provided with additional benefits up to the maximum which would apply if your actual retirement date were your normal retirement date.

1987–1989 members also receive a credit for extra years worked. If you have achieved 40 years' service or more at normal retirement date, you can increase the pension to a maximum of $^{45}/_{60}$ of final salary (and the cash lump sum to $^{135}/_{80}$). If you have worked less than 40 years' service at your normal retirement date, the increased pension that you receive at your actual retirement date is calculated on an actuarial basis.

Controlling directors

If you defer drawing benefits beyond your normal retirement date, the limits on your pension and tax-free cash up to age 70 are exactly the same as those that would have applied had you retired at your normal retirement date, that is, you receive no increments.

If you defer your retirement beyond age 70, there are two ways you can increase your benefits:

(1) Your benefits, based on your years of service and final remuneration at age 70, can be increased by the greater of an actuarial increase (ie one that takes into account your age) or an increase in the retail prices index.
(2) Your benefits can be based on your years of service and final remuneration at your normal retirement date. Provided you have at least 40 years' service at age 70, you can receive an extra $^1/_{60}$ of final remuneration for each year you work beyond age 70 up to a maximum of $^{45}/_{60}$.

If you are a pre-1987 or 1987–1989 member, and you have the option to take the tax-free cash and defer your pension, the position is slightly different. If you take the cash before age 70, the maximum residual pension may only be increased by reference to RPI up to age 70. After age 70, it may be increased by the greater of an actuarial increase or an increase related to RPI.

5.7.7 Pension increases in retirement

Many schemes allow the escalation of pensions in payment. These are normally limited to a fixed percentage, say 3 per cent or 5 per cent per annum compound, while other schemes provide increases on a discretionary basis from time to time. Following the Social Security Act 1990, the trend is to provide escalation of pensions in payment at 5 per cent per annum, or the rate of increase in the retail prices index, whichever is less. This is known as Limited Price Indexation (LPI).

It is also possible for your employer to increase a pension in payment up to the level of the maximum approvable pension which would have been payable at retirement, subsequently increased in line with RPI. If you retired before 31 August 1991, this maximum approvable pension need not take into account any pension commuted for a cash lump sum.

5.8 PERSONAL PENSION SCHEMES

5.8.1 Income in retirement

The purpose of a personal pension scheme is to provide an income in retirement commencing (in the case of a retirement annuity) at any time between the ages of 60 and 75 or (in the case of a personal pension plan) between the ages of 50 and 75. An annuity can be drawn regardless of whether you are working and it is possible to stagger the benefits over that period by one of two methods (see 5.9).

The facility to take benefits under a personal pension plan from age 50 compared with age 60 under a retirement annuity is attractive, but not a sufficient reason for stopping contributions to a retirement annuity in favour of a personal pension scheme. Most people do not have sufficient funds to provide a worthwhile income at age 50 while annuity rates for this age group are very low.

5.8.2 Lump sums

Up to 25 per cent of the personal pension fund may be taken as tax-free cash (except where the money was transferred from an occupational scheme).

Retirement annuities have different rules. The tax-free lump sum is restricted to three times the remaining annual pension after the cash has been taken. The Inland Revenue allows this calculation to be done on the most favourable basis (ie to base the calculation on the highest possible annuity) whilst at the same time allowing the annuity *after* the lump sum has been taken to be calculated on a different basis.

Although more complicated, this method usually provides more tax-free cash. However, that is not a hard and fast rule and, at a time of low annuity rates, it could be that the 25 per cent rule under the personal pension plan legislation gives a more favourable result.

5.8.3 The open market option

Both personal pension plans and retirement annuities are able to take advantage of the open market option. If this is done with a retirement annuity, then the fund is transferred to a personal pension plan under which the tax-free cash is limited to 25 per cent of the fund. However, the most important point is to get the best annuity rate.

5.9 WORKING INTO RETIREMENT

Working part time before you retire, whether as an employee or freelance consultant, has a significant effect on your financial plans. Understandably your chief concern is to achieve the right level of immediate income from your earnings and pensions but it is important not to focus solely on current cashflow at the expense of future income.

As part of your overall financial planning it is essential to maintain a lifelong cashflow projection. If this identifies a future shortfall you may decide to continue part-time consultancy for longer than you initially intended.

If your semi-retirement income includes your pensions, remember that although you may be able to draw on your company scheme and private plans early, you cannot claim your state pension until age 65 for men and, currently, age 60 for women.

Some company schemes pay what are known as 'bridging' pensions to make good the shortfall between the date you retire and the date you qualify for the state benefit. But many do not, and in this case you need to cater for the shortfall. Moreover, most occupational schemes reduce your pension substantially if you retire early – typically by 5 per cent for each year. Where the normal company pension age is 65, this could mean a staggering reduction of 50 per cent in your pension if you go at 55.

5.9.1 Deferring your pension and making further contributions

Provided your freelance earnings are sufficient you may be able to defer your pension until you retire fully. In theory this should raise your eventual pension income – whether it is derived from a company scheme or private plans – because by deferring you increase the period your money is invested and reduce the number of years you actually draw the benefit. But in practice things are never quite so simple so do not rely on this theory – check with your pension company or the trustees of your occupational scheme.

Where your consultancy earnings are substantial you could make further pension contributions, although this depends on the nature of your pension arrangements and whether you were also making any withdrawals.

Investing in a pension plan in your 50s and 60s can be very tax efficient. For example, you could contribute 30 to 40 per cent (depending on age) of your annual earnings to a personal pension and qualify for full tax relief. This is particularly tax efficient if you are a higher rate taxpayer now and receive 40 per cent relief on your investment, yet in retirement expect to pay basic rate tax at 23 per cent on your pension income. And do not forget, you can take up to 25 per cent of your pension fund completely tax free.

Despite its manifest attractions, eleventh hour pension planning requires considerable skill. In particular, finding the right type of pension plan can be difficult if you intend to invest for a relatively short time. For most people the best option is to invest lump sums rather than lock in to a regular contribution plan – particularly when you do not know for sure how long your work will continue. Lump sum investments help to maximise flexibility and minimise charges. Moreover, under Inland Revenue rules you can invest substantial single premiums to your pension plan and mop up unused tax relief from previous years, provided you first make the maximum contributions for the current year.

5.9.2 Flexible pension options

The pension and annuity options previously discussed have required a once and for all decision at retirement. However, when it comes to phasing your pension income to combine it with other sources during semi-retirement, personal pensions can be very flexible. Flexibility is also important even if you plan to retire fully. Given the trends towards early retirement and increased longevity, your retirement could last 20 years or more.

As a result, an increasing number of investors are taking advantage of more flexible alternatives to standard pension, known as 'phased retirement' and 'income drawdown'. Both are available as packages but a better arrangement is to separate the investment management from the administration so if performance is unsatisfactory you can change the manager responsible.

These complicated annuity substitutes are only suitable in certain circumstances. You must have a substantial pension fund (many advisers recommend a minimum of £250,000), you must be able to tolerate a fair degree of investment risk, and, ideally, you should have other sources of retirement income. The object of the exercise is to keep the bulk of your pension fund fully invested so you continue to benefit from equity returns while you draw an income. By age 75 at the latest you must convert your remaining fund to a conventional annuity, so you cannot avoid the annuity issue – you can only defer it.

With phased retirement your pension fund is segmented. Each year you take one or more segments in the form of a small annuity and a small amount of tax-free cash to provide your income. In this way, instead of buying one big annuity at retirement, you convert your fund to annuities in stages so you can tailor your income to meet your requirements. This is useful if, for example, you want to work part time in retirement and draw very little from your pension fund in the early years but then boost the income level later on.

One disadvantage with phased retirement is that you have to use your tax-free cash allocation to generate part of your income, so if you have set your heart on a capital project – a second home or dream holiday, for example – this is not for you. On the plus side are good inheritance planning opportunities. If your fund is held within a trust it can pass on tax free to your beneficiaries.

Under income drawdown you can take all of your tax-free cash at retirement. The rest of your fund remains invested and you draw an income which must be between a minimum and maximum set by the Inland Revenue. Should you die your fund goes to your beneficiaries. However, if your beneficiaries take this as cash rather than as continued income, there is a 35 per cent deduction for tax.

It is possible to combine phased retirement and income drawdown for maximum tax efficiency and flexibility but do watch out for the high costs associated with the more complicated arrangements.

Finally, remember that with phased retirement and income drawdown it is unwise to leave the annuity purchase until the last moment. The timing is critical and depends partly on your personal circumstances. It also depends on a combination of equity returns – which determine your fund size – and gilt yields – which determine annuity rates. The chances of you spotting the right conjunction are slim, hence the need for expert independent tax and investment advice.

6

INVESTMENTS

There are many books on investment, some of which are dedicated to a single topic. A chapter in a book of this nature cannot set out anything other than to provide an overview in the context of your overall retirement planning.

Before looking at alternative investments it is essential to analyse your current pension arrangements and do what is necessary to maximise your future pension (which is probably going to be the most important investment of all).

This chapter looks at the range of investments suitable to compensate for a shortfall in your pension income or for long-term low to medium risk capital growth. Further details on all of the investments in this chapter can be found in the *Allied Dunbar Investment and Savings Handbook*.

The chapter covers the following topics:

(1) Introduction
(2) Short-term investment
(3) Tax efficient short-term investments
(4) Long-term investment
(5) Collective or pooled investments
(6) The home as an investment.

6.1 INTRODUCTION

Before looking at specific investments, this section covers some basic criteria for success:

(1) The overall approach
(2) Investment criteria
(3) The four aims of investment
(4) Asset-backed investment versus inflation
(5) The comfort factor
(6) Investor protection.

6.1.1 The overall approach

For the purpose of this chapter 'investment' refers to genuinely spare capital. It is impossible to say how much should go into any one particular type of investment as each portfolio will be arranged to suit individual circumstances. However, it is important to get the right balance between immediate access funds and short, medium and long-term investments.

The overall objective is directed towards your medium to long-term capital (defined here as capital you do not need for five years or more). Before you get to that point, you need to set aside a sum of money that can be used in an emergency. You may also feel more comfortable if some of your money is available in no more than five years' time.

As a general point, short-term investment should be concerned with capital protection. The longer the term, the more your concern should be protection from inflation and therefore the focus should be on capital growth.

6.1.2 Investment criteria

The *Allied Dunbar Investment and Savings Handbook* suggests that there are a few simple criteria to be borne in mind when considering investments.

Diversification

The first maxim for practically every investor should be diversification through a spread of investments to reduce the risk of over-concentration. Diversification can be achieved by investing in various asset classes directly or through 'pooled' investments such as unit trusts.

Balance

Every investor should, as far as possible, have a balanced portfolio. Part of your capital should be earmarked for security and invested in, for example, building society or bank deposits. However, investors should also look for a measure of capital appreciation as a hedge against inflation so a part of your capital should be invested in equity type investments which tend to give higher returns over the long term. The precise balance depends on the individual circumstances and attitude to risk of the particular investor.

Getting advice

Be prepared to seek expert advice and to shop around for the best value in terms of performance, charges and flexibility.

Taxation

Your investment policy should not be dictated by tax considerations alone. Clearly, you should take advantage of all the tax benefits you can, but the investment decision should come first, not the tax benefit. There is no guarantee that an investment with tax benefits will produce a better return than an investment which has no tax benefits at all. Learn to distinguish between the assets themselves – equities and bonds, for example – and the tax efficient wrappers in which you can place these assets – pensions and ISAs, for example.

6.1.3 The four aims of investment

Capital and income

Two basic aims of an investment are capital growth and income. At one end of the scale, the capital remains constant while the income produced may vary (for example, bank and building society deposits); at the other end, there are non-income-producing assets (such as the capital shares of split capital investment trusts) where no income is produced but the capital value should appreciate.

Inflation

An essential third element in evaluating investments is inflation. Beware the current popular view that inflation is 'dead'. The double digit inflationary days of the 1970s and 1980s are not so long ago and who is to say that they will not return during the course of a 20-year retirement?

Investment period

The fourth dimension is the investment period and knowing when to buy and sell. These decisions are taken out of your hands with pooled investments, but you still need to judge when it is best to buy and sell your units.

6.1.4 Asset-backed investment versus inflation

One of the longest running investment surveys in the United Kingdom is the BZW Equity Gilt Study which monitors the performance of various asset classes back as far as 1918. Despite the major events of the last 80 years (including the Second World War and the catastrophic impact of the oil price rise in the early 1970s), investment in equities with the income reinvested has produced the best overall return and one that has provided the best hedge against inflation. However, there are always periods when interest rates are high and gilts provide a better short-term bet.

6.1.5 The comfort factor

Comfort has a great deal to do with investment choice. There are literally thousands of different investments, but the ones that are likely to be the best for you are those that you understand and feel comfortable with. However, that is not a reason for excessive caution or for sitting back once you have made your investment decisions. There is an important relationship between risk and reward and some of your long-term capital should be placed where it has a higher risk of short-term falls but long-term growth prospects.

Comfort also has a lot to do with the balance of a portfolio. If you have only £5,000 spare capital, almost certainly you should stick to 'safe' investments such as deposits and National Savings. By the same token, anybody with £50,000 to invest would be excessively cautious to take the same approach but nor should they necessarily plunge the whole lot into equities. A sensible balance is the aim.

6.1.6 Investor protection

Outside the range of deposits offered by banks and building societies, other types of investment will generally fall under the regulations of the Financial Services Authority (FSA). Widespread concern following the collapse of several investment institutions in the early 1980s led to the Financial Services Act 1986. Today, with very few exceptions (such as the Bank of England and members of Lloyd's), any person or organisation giving investment advice or carrying on investment business in the United Kingdom must be authorised to do so under the terms of the Financial Services Act; to do otherwise is a criminal offence. The FSA maintains a central register of all such authorised people and organisations.

Investor protection is now provided through a series of Self-Regulating Organisations (SROs), Recognised Professional Bodies (RPBs), Recognised Investment Exchanges (RIEs) and Recognised Clearing Houses (RCHs), each of which is responsible to the FSA for ensuring that the firms authorised by them to conduct investment business do so in a tightly controlled way.

All SROs, RPBs, RIEs and RCHs are required to ensure that their member organisations follow the basic principles laid down by the FSA. There are compliance and monitoring procedures in place backed up by disciplinary powers, including powers of expulsion against those who fail to meet the required standards. These requirements include the responsibility to obtain information about customers before giving advice on specific investments. Consequently, when seeking advice from any source, you must be prepared to give your adviser a good deal of information about your financial circumstances so he can help you make an informed judgement about the suitability of specific investments.

The one area of investment which is not covered by the Financial Services Act is residential housing and mortgages. All forms of borrowing are covered by the Consumer Credit Act and the monitoring of firms offering credit is handled by local trading standards officers under the overall guidance of the Office of Fair Trading.

The duties and responsibilities of these various regulatory bodies are brought together under a single organisation, the Financial Services Authority (see the Financial Services and Markets Act 1998).

6.2 SHORT-TERM INVESTMENT

For the purposes of this book, short-term investment covers anything invested for up to five years. Within the market for short-term capital investment, there is a whole range of types of investment. Some offer fixed rates of interest, some have variable rates. In most cases, the interest is taxed at source; occasionally it is paid gross.

For the majority of people, the most obvious home for their short-term capital is a bank or building society deposit. However, there are alternatives which could be worth keeping an eye on.

The following are covered in this section:

(1) Bank and building society accounts
(2) National Savings
(3) Other forms of deposit
(4) Guaranteed income bonds.

Although the security of these sorts of investments is generally taken for granted, there is some statutory protection in that most providers are either an approved institution under the Banking Act 1987 (under the terms of which 75 per cent of individual deposits up to £20,000 are safeguarded) or are covered by the Building Societies Act 1988 (under the terms of which 80 per cent of deposits up to £20,000 are safeguarded).

Safeguards for life assurance-based guaranteed income bonds are provided by the Policyholders Protection Act 1975 which protects up to 90 per cent of the value of your investment.

Throughout these early sections, the distinction is drawn between those interest-bearing investments which pay interest net of tax and those which pay interest gross. With most of them, interest is paid net of tax but, in the majority of cases, non-taxpayers can apply to have it paid gross. Form R85 (available from banks and building societies) should be completed for each account earning interest; interest is then paid gross. As soon as the individual's total income rises over the tax threshold, the accounts must be de-certified.

Parents or guardians can make similar application for children under 16. The certification automatically expires at age 16; the account-holder must then re-apply on his own behalf.

6.2.1 Bank and building society accounts

For your emergency fund probably the best home is a bank or building society deposit account. With building societies, there is a growing number of postal accounts which tend to offer slightly higher rates of interest. It really does pay to keep on top of these rates because they do change and some institutions are not in any hurry to tell you that your particular type of account is no longer paying the best rate.

There are various publications (of which *Moneyfacts* is probably the most comprehensive) which keep you up to date on rate changes.

Interest is generally paid net of tax (but see 6.2.3) although a number of banks and building societies have offshore branches (eg the Dublin International Financial Centre, the Isle of Man and the Channel Islands). Interest on these accounts is paid gross.

A few building societies offer special accounts to people over 55 (some reduce this to 50; others raise it to 60). The rates of interest are not necessarily better, but there are occasional perks such as shopping discounts.

6.2.2 National Savings

National Savings accounts

National Savings provide two types of account – the ordinary account and the investment account. Interest on both of these is paid gross.

The interest on ordinary accounts is low, but the first £70 of interest is tax free, which makes a limited investment in this account of interest to higher rate taxpayers. Interest is taxable to the extent that it exceeds £70, and must be declared on the tax return. The maximum deposit is £10,000. There is instant access to the extent of £100 per day (but regular customers can withdraw up to £250).

The interest on the investment account is fully taxable and must be declared on the tax return. The maximum holding is £100,000, including capitalised interest. One month's notice is required for withdrawals, but immediate withdrawal can be made with the loss of 30 days' interest.

Interest on both accounts is credited annually on 31 December.

National Savings income bonds

Interest is paid gross on a monthly basis. There is a loss of part of the interest if any withdrawals are made in year one. Subsequent withdrawals are allowed (subject to three months' notice), but at least £2,000 must be left deposited.

The minimum initial purchase is £2,000. The minimum subsequent purchase is £1,000. The maximum holding is £250,000. The bonds can be held for up to ten years.

The interest on the investment account is fully taxable and must be declared on the tax return. A bonus is earned on holdings of £25,000 or more. Three months' notice is required for withdrawals, but immediate withdrawal can be made with the loss of 90 days' interest.

These bonds are generally of interest to those non-taxpayers who can tie up £2,000 for at least 12 months.

First option bonds

These are a lump sum savings vehicle where the interest rate is guaranteed for one year at a time. On the anniversary, the net interest is capitalised and the whole amount can be withdrawn or reinvested for a further year.

No interest is paid on any money withdrawn in the first year; withdrawals during the second and subsequent years accrue interest at half the stated rate, unless the withdrawal is made on the anniversary date.

The minimum purchase is £1,000. The maximum holding is £250,000. The bonds can be held for up to ten years.

The interest on the investment account is paid net of basic rate tax, and is fully taxable and must be declared on the tax return. A bonus is earned on holdings of £20,000 or more.

Premium bonds

These can be bought and sold at any time and qualify for a prize after they have been held for one clear calendar month (so the best time to buy them is towards the end of the month). The minimum holding is £100, and the maximum is £20,000. Prizes are free of income tax and capital gains tax.

6.2.3 Other forms of deposits

Fixed rate accounts

A number of organisations offer fixed rate accounts where the rate of interest is determined by the size of the deposit and the time period (which usually ranges from one to seven years, although some banks and building societies offer accounts for one, three and six months).

Interest usually is paid net. The frequency of interest varies with individual accounts. Some pay monthly but the majority pay annually or at maturity.

Some banks and building societies offer offshore fixed rate accounts. They also offer what are called 'money market term deposits' though the minimum level of deposit is usually very high, eg in excess of £50,000. Interest on both these types of account is paid gross.

Escalator bonds

A limited number of building societies offer escalator bonds (also known as 'rising bonds'). These are fixed term investments where the initial rate of interest is fixed and guaranteed to increase each year of the term. The interest is always paid net of tax.

6.2.4 Guaranteed income bonds

These are issued from time to time by various insurance companies. In return for a lump sum investment, the insurance company guarantees a monthly or yearly income with a full return of capital at the end of the term. The income is paid net of basic rate tax but is not reclaimable by non-taxpayers. Higher rate taxpayers may have an additional liability to tax when the bond matures.

Beware of guarantees that depend on a certain percentage rise in one or more stock market indexes. If the anticipated rises do not take place, your 'income' is paid partly out of your capital.

6.2.5 Summary

Most of these investments can play a part in your financial planning. Your choice will depend on personal preference. Do remember it always pays to shop around for the best rates.

6.3 TAX EFFICIENT SHORT-TERM INVESTMENTS

For investments where you are prepared to put your capital on one side for up to five years, the range of options increases. All the investments mentioned in 6.2 are valid here but committing funds for longer periods of time should only be done where you can obtain some additional benefits, eg capital or income guarantees or tax incentives (you can also get the benefit of regular savings which are covered in more detail in 6.9).

However, these guarantees and tax benefits do require some level of commitment and so, with the exception of gilt-edged securities, all the investments in this section only provide the full benefits if they are held for the full term. Also, only gilts and guaranteed equity bonds offer any scope for capital growth.

The following investments are covered:

(1) National Savings
(2) TESSAs and ISAs
(3) Guaranteed equity bonds
(4) Gilt-edged securities.

6.3.1 National Savings

National Savings certificates

These are guaranteed by the Government. A number of issues have been made. An issue can be withdrawn at any time. The maximum holding varies from issue to issue. No interest is payable but the certificates are redeemed for a higher value than the original purchase price. The full benefit is gained only if the certificates are held for five years.

The gain is totally tax free which makes them attractive for higher rate taxpayers. Holdings should be reviewed from time to time, particularly if interest rates are rising. Certificates can be held in addition to PEPs, TESSAs and ISAs.

Index-linked certificates

These are designed to provide inflation proofing. A typical issue guarantees a rate of return equal to rises in the retail prices index over a five-year term plus an additional rate of interest which equates to 3 per cent per annum over the five-year term. All gains are free of income tax and capital gains tax which make them attractive to higher rate taxpayers.

Index-linked certificates can also be held in addition to PEPs, TESSAs and ISAs. The minimum investment is £100; the maximum is £10,000 per issue.

Capital bonds

These accrue interest which is capitalised on each anniversary of the purchase. The interest is taxable and must be declared. The capitalised interest accrues at an increasing rate – the full benefit requires a bond to be held for five years. The capital can, however, be withdrawn in whole or in part at any time.

Capital bonds could be suitable for people who pay little or no income tax and who can tie up funds for five years. However, their overall attraction depends on the level of interest rates generally available; as with any fixed interest investment they could become unattractive if interest rates start to move up.

The minimum purchase is £100 and the maximum is £250,000 in all series except Series A.

Pensioners' guaranteed income bonds

These were introduced in 1994. They are available to people aged 65 or over. The minimum purchase is £500 and the maximum is £50,000 per series. They provide a regular monthly income guaranteed for five years. The income is taxable but is paid gross.

The money invested may be withdrawn without penalty at the fifth anniversary; earlier withdrawals require 60 days' notice and no interest is payable during the period of notice.

6.3.2 TESSAs

Tax Exempt Special Savings Accounts offered by banks and building societies may be absorbed into the new Individual Savings Account in 1999. Currently you may invest up to £9,000 through an initial deposit of up to £3,000, followed by three annual deposits of up to £1,800 with a final payment of up to £600.

Interest accrues during the five-year period net of basic rate tax. After five years, a bonus equal to the amount of basic rate tax deducted is added back into the TESSA, ie it effectively becomes a tax-free investment.

Interest added to a TESSA does not count towards 'total income' for the purposes of the higher age-related personal allowance (see 8.4.2).

During the five-year period, the net interest can be withdrawn without affecting the tax exempt status of the account but, if any *capital* is withdrawn, the right to the tax bonus is lost. If you run a TESSA for, say, four years and then close it, any remaining accrued interest is taxed in the year of closure even if it actually arose in earlier years.

TESSAs are therefore best seen as a five-year investment with tax-free interest. The rates of interest are variable (though a small number of building societies offer fixed rate TESSAs). You may only own one TESSA at a time but you may switch it to another bank or building society to get a better rate (though this may involve you in a transfer fee).

When your TESSA matures you can reinvest your original £9,000 in a new account and enjoy a further five years of tax-free growth.

A saver may continue to invest in an existing TESSA until the end of its original five-year term. When a TESSA matures, the capital (but not the interest) can be reinvested in a special extra TESSA which does not affect the ISA limits for that year. Alternatively, investment can be made into the cash element of an ISA (ie £3,000 for 1999–2000, or £1,000 thereafter).

6.3.3 Individual Savings Accounts (ISAs)

ISAs were introduced from 6 April 1999. They are free of both income tax and capital gains tax, and withdrawals can be made without losing the tax benefits. They can comprise up to three components:

- Cash
- Life insurance
- Stocks and shares.

A cash ISA can be invested in a bank or building society, a National Savings account, money market deposits or cash unit trusts.

In the first year, up to £7,000 may be invested in an ISA. Of this, a maximum of £3,000 may be invested in the cash component and £1,000 in the insurance component. After the first year, the limits reduce to £5,000 with a maximum of £1,000 in both the cash and insurance components.

If any money is invested in either the insurance or the cash component of a 'maxi' ISA, the amount that can be invested in stocks and shares is reduced by the amount invested in that component. For example, investing £500 in the cash component reduces the maximum that can be invested in the stocks and shares component (in the first year) from £7,000 to £6,500.

There is no upper limit on the cumulative amount that can be held within ISAs.

A maxi ISA is managed by one provider. It must include a stocks and shares component, and may include a cash component and/or insurance components as well. Offering only the stocks and shares component allows up to £7,000 (£5,000 after the first year) to be invested in this component in a tax year.

A 'mini' ISA can only consist of one ISA component. It is permissible to invest in up to three mini ISAs, each from different providers, in any one tax year. Each mini ISA has to be invested in different ISA components. It is not permitted to have, for example, two mini cash ISAs.

Thus, a maxi ISA can hold all three types of investment, while a mini ISA can only hold one type of investment.

6.3.4 Guaranteed equity bonds

There is a huge range of 'guaranteed' equity bonds available, particularly from the insurance companies, but also from an increasing number of unit trust groups and personal equity plan managers. These products are complicated and it is difficult to compare the different types of guarantee, so do seek expert independent advice before taking the plunge. Remember, the main attraction of these funds is their potential for capital growth so it is important to check what your exposure is to the upside of a market movement, as well as to check your level of protection from the downside. Maximum growth is essential because these funds generally do not benefit from investment yields, yet over a 10-year period reinvested dividends on the FTSE-100 index account for roughly half of the return.

Most funds, particularly in the insurance sector, effectively lock you in for five years. If easier access is important, consider one of the unit trusts where the guarantee has no specific term or for a quarterly lock-in.

To back their guarantees companies buy a type of derivative known as an option. At the risk of over-simplification, this can be regarded as an insurance contract which gives the fund manager the right to buy or sell assets on a future date at a price agreed at the outset. If the fund's value falls below a certain level, the company backing the option pays up. The cost of this option can be high – typically an extra 1 per cent or 1.5 per cent on top of the annual charge. The returns must be substantial to cover these costs.

A five-year guaranteed equity bond provides a return of your original equity at the end of five years if markets go down. If they go up the bond provides something between 120–140 per cent of the growth in the relevant index – but not the dividends.

Many of these bonds operate as a term deposit where the relevant gain in the FTSE-100 Index is credited to the bond as interest. This interest is paid net of tax. Basic rate taxpayers pay no further tax, but higher rate taxpayers face an additional liability in the year of maturity if the maturity value exceeds the original investment.

6.3.5 Gilt-edged securities

Gilt-edged securities represent borrowings by the British Government and are guaranteed to be repaid in full (at 'par') at maturity (the redemption date). The period to run to redemption is used to classify gilts as follows:

(1) 'Shorts' – less than 5 years to redemption
(2) 'Mediums' – 5 to 15 years
(3) 'Longs' – over 15 years
(4) 'Undated' – stocks with no fixed redemption date.

Shorts and mediums are the gilts of most interest to people planning for retirement.

The year of redemption may be precisely defined (eg Treasury 6% 1999) or lie within a range (eg 11½% Treasury Stock 2001–2004). The precise date of redemption varies from stock to stock, but is the anniversary of its date of original issue. That is also the reference point for the half yearly payments of interest. The amount of interest paid is determined by the 'coupon': for example, £100 of Treasury 6% 1999 will pay £6 per annum each year until redemption.

Interest used to be paid net of tax except in the case of any stock bought through the National Savings Stock Register (NSSR). However, since the July 1997 Budget it has been possible to get gilt interest gross if you buy direct or through a stockbroker. Gilts are exempt from capital gains tax.

People living abroad are exempt from all UK taxes on a range of gilts (see 12.7) known as the FOTRA stocks (Free of Tax to Residents Abroad).

Gilts are guaranteed to be redeemed at par at the redemption date, ie £100 of nominal stock will be bought back by the Government for £100. In the meantime, the price will vary according to the coupon and the general level of interest rates. Prices decrease as interest rates rise and increase as interest rates fall but always converge eventually towards the par value at redemption.

The return from gilts is, therefore, a combination of two factors: the rate of interest paid and the rise (or fall) in value between the date of purchase and the date of redemption. This total return is called the redemption yield and, in very broad terms, the redemption yield tends to follow prevailing interest rates.

At a time when interest rates are high, locking in to a high coupon gilt (ie one with a coupon more or less equal to outside interest rates) can:

(1) guarantee a high level of income until redemption (should interest rates fall in the meantime); and
(2) hold out the prospect of a tax-free capital gain should interest rates fall between the date of purchase and the date of redemption.

Index-linked gilts

These have been available since 1981. The redemption value and annual income are linked to changes in the retail price index. The income from index-linked stocks is relatively low as the main advantage is through the inflation proofing given to the capital (provided it is held to maturity). The income payments increase every six months to reflect changes in the retail price index.

6.3.6 Summary

These medium-term investments certainly have a part to play in planning for retirement. National Savings, TESSAs and ISAs have the attraction of tax-free income, guaranteed equity bonds offer the opportunity to participate in stockmarket growth and gilts offer a known level of income with the guarantee of repayment of capital, often with a tax-free gain thrown in.

The downside is that they require a committed term of investment to get the *full* benefits and, if you are close to retirement, you need to assess what your tax position might be at the end of the term to make sure they are still attractive.

You also need to remember their appeal varies according to movements in interest rates. If rates rise National Savings certificates could start to look unattractive, TESSAs and ISAs will benefit, gilts will fall and, although guaranteed equity bonds in themselves will not be affected, they could lose their attraction if the interest rate increase is sufficient to rattle the Stock Market.

In conclusion, even investments with guarantees and tax benefits have to be watched and managed.

6.4 LONG-TERM INVESTMENT

6.4.1 Introduction

'Long-term' in the context of this chapter means over five years, but not more than ten. Investing for the long term incorporates the riskier forms of investment which carry far greater potential for protecting the real value of our money. Most of this money should usually be invested in real assets such as equities, and in some cases property. Gilt-edged securities can play a part in this type of portfolio, but bear in mind that the guarantees inherent in gilts (the guaranteed income and repayment value) do mean sacrificing much of the potential for growth.

You can either invest directly in the asset itself (eg by buying ordinary shares in a specific company through a stockbroker) or through one of the 'pooled' investments which reduce the risks by diversification and economies of scale.

Direct investment is clearly more risky because you are concentrating risk in one or more individual companies. There can also be much administration involved. For most investors direct investment is not appropriate.

6.4.2 Individual investments

Securities is the general name for all stocks and shares. Broadly speaking stocks are fixed interest securities and shares are the rest. The four main types of securities listed and traded on the UK Stock Exchange are:

(1) UK ('domestic') equities – ordinary shares issued by UK companies
(2) Overseas equities – ordinary shares issued by non-UK companies
(3) UK gilts – bonds issued by the UK Government to raise money to fund any shortfall in public expenditure
(4) Bonds or fixed interest stocks – issued by companies and local authorities, among others.

The following guide may help the uninitiated.

UK equities

UK equities are the quoted shares of companies in the United Kingdom and tend to dominate most private investors' portfolios, whether the investments are held directly or are pooled. Companies 'go public' by being quoted on The Stock Exchange or Alternative Investment Market in order to raise finance by issuing shares. A share literally entitles the owner to a specified share in the company's profits and, if the company is wound up, to a specified share of its assets.

The owner of shares is entitled to the dividends – the annual or six-monthly distribution to shareholders of part of the company's profits. The 'dividend yield' on equities is the dividend paid by a company divided by that company's share price. This is an important feature for income seekers.

There is no set redemption date for an equity: if the holder wishes to realise its value he must sell it through a broker. The price varies from day to day so the timing of the purchase and selling of shares is critical.

There are different classes of shares. 'Ordinary' shares give the holder a right to vote on the constitution of the board of directors. 'Preference' shares carry no voting rights but have a fixed dividend payment and have preference over ordinary shareholders if the company is wound up.

There are several sub-classes of equities or equity-related investments. For example, convertibles confer a right to convert to an ordinary share or preference share at a future date. You might also come across warrants, which confer a right, but not an obligation, on the holder to convert to a specific share at a predetermined price and date. The value of the warrant, which itself is traded on the stock market, is determined by the difference or premium of the share price over the conversion price of the warrant.

'Derivatives', as the name suggests, derive their value from the price of an underlying security. This is the generic term given to futures contracts and options both of which can be used to hedge risk in a fund or even in a large private portfolio.

Overseas equities

Overseas equities are similar in principle to UK equities but there are differences in shareholder rights. Investment overseas offers the opportunity to gain exposure to foreign currency and younger, fast growing economies but there can be tax penalties on the investments because some or all of the withholding tax on dividends deducted by the foreign country may not be recoverable. Moreover, in the case of developing markets there may be a risk of sequestration.

Bonds

Bonds behave like sophisticated IOUs. UK bonds are issued by borrowers, for example the Government (these bonds are known as gilt edged or gilts) and companies (corporate bonds). Bonds are also issued by local authorities, overseas governments and overseas companies.

In return for the loan of your money the borrower agrees to pay a fixed rate of interest for the agreed period and to repay your original capital sum on a specified date, known as the maturity date.

The point to remember about fixed interest securities is that the investment return is determined more by the level of interest rate than the issuing company's profitability. Provided the issuer remains sufficiently secure to honour the future coupon payments (the regular interest) and redemption payment (the return of the original capital) you know exactly what your return will be if you hold the bond to maturity. Gilts offer the highest degree of security because they are issued by the UK Government.

If the fund manager sells a bond before its maturity date, then the value of the future coupon and redemption payments depend on the prevailing interest rates at the time of sale. If interest rates are high then the value of the fixed interest security is lower because you could get a similar return for less money elsewhere. Conversely if interest rates are low, then the value of the fixed interest security is higher because it provides a greater stream of income than you could get from alternative sources. This volatile pattern of behaviour is more apparent with fixed interest securities which have a long period to run to maturity since they are more likely to be traded before redemption date.

Index-linked gilts are issued by the UK Government and are guaranteed to provide interest payments and redemption proceeds which increase in line with inflation. For this reason they are one of the lowest risk assets for income seekers. The return on index-linked gilts in excess of the retail price index varies but usually it is possible to buy these securities in the marketplace at a price which guarantees a real rate of return to the holder, assuming that the stock is held to maturity.

Property

In investment terms, 'property' usually refers to the ownership of land and buildings that are used by a business or other organisation. The owner receives income from rent charged to the tenant and, over time, this rent is expected broadly to keep pace with inflation. The dominant factor in the value of a property is the desirability or otherwise of its position.

There are two problems in particular with property. First, it is often sold in large blocks which cannot be easily split for investment purposes. As a result only the larger institutional funds can afford (or are wise) to own property directly. Secondly, property is a very illiquid asset and it can take several years for the right selling conditions to arise.

6.5 COLLECTIVE OR POOLED INVESTMENTS

6.5.1 Unit trusts

A unit trust can invest in a range of assets which are suitable for its overall aim; for example, it can aim to produce an income through investment in high yielding UK equities, or to generate capital growth through investment in new or expanding industries or, more riskily, in emerging markets.

Unit trusts sold to the public are authorised by the chief financial services regulator, the Securities and Investments Board. The trusts are 'open ended', which means they may create or cancel units on a daily basis depending on demand.

Investors purchase units in the fund, the value of which fluctuate in line with the value of the underlying assets. Most funds invest mainly or wholly in equities, although the number of corporate bond funds, which invest in corporate bonds, preference shares and convertibles, among other assets, is growing rapidly.

6.5.2 Investment trusts

An investment trust is a British company, listed on the UK stock exchange, which invests in the shares of other quoted and unquoted companies in the UK and overseas. As public companies, investment trusts are subject to company law and Stock Exchange regulation. The prices of most investment trusts are published daily in the *Financial Times*.

Investment trust companies have a fixed number of shares so unlike unit trusts, 'units' cannot be created and cancelled to meet increased and reduced demand. As with any quoted company, the shares are only available when other investors are trying to sell. This means there are two factors that affect investment trust share prices. The first is the performance of the underlying assets in which the company invests. This factor also affects the price of units in a unit trust.

However, where unit trust prices directly reflect the fund's net asset value, investment trust share prices may not. This means that the market forces (supply and demand) to which investment trust shares are subject may make the shares worth more or less than the underlying value of the company's assets.

If the share price is lower than the value of the underlying assets the difference is known as the discount. If it is higher the difference is known as the premium. This is explained in more detail below.

Investment trusts can borrow money to invest, an activity known as gearing. This adds extra flexibility and if the shares purchased with the borrowed money do well, the trust and its shares will benefit. A poor return on the shares reduces the profitability of the company.

'Split capital' investment trusts can have two types of shares – one that has a right to all the income and one that has a right to the capital growth.

6.5.3 Life assurance investments

Life assurance investment policies offer an alternative form of collective investment which in some ways is very different from unit trusts, investment trusts and open ended investment companies.

Despite the confusing array of investments offered by insurance companies to the public, most fall into one of three main categories:

(1) Maximum investment plans (MIPs) are regular monthly or annual premium investments and usually run for ten years. Once this term is complete you can either take the proceeds or leave the fund to continue to benefit from investment growth. You can also make tax efficient annual withdrawals.
(2) Insurance company investment bonds are similar to MIPs but here you invest a single premium or lump sum.
(3) Endowments combine investment with a substantial element of life assurance.

With maximum investment plans and insurance company investment bonds your premiums are invested in a choice of funds, most of which are unit linked, similar in concept to unit trusts in that your premiums buy units in a collective fund and the value of those units rises and falls in line with the value of the underlying assets.

Although sold by life assurance companies, most of these regular and single premium plans offer minimal life cover, as their main purpose is investment. If you die the company might pay out 101% of your original investment or the value of the fund, whichever is greater.

The third category – the traditional endowment – is most commonly used as a repayment vehicle for a mortgage. The distinguishing feature of an endowment is that it combines a significant element of life assurance with your savings plan so that if you die during the term of the policy, the combination of the value of your fund plus the life assurance is sufficient to repay the debt.

There are three investment options. With-profits and unitised with-profits endowments invest in a mixture of equities, bonds and property and have a rather idiosyncratic method of distributing profits. You can also invest in unit-linked endowments, which share the same investment characteristics as other unit-linked funds.

Taxation of life assurance policies

The whole area of the taxation of life assurance policyholders is under review but at the time of writing the Inland Revenue is seeking consultation on its proposals and has not issued a date for any changes to come into effect. To avoid confusion, this chapter explains current practice.

At the end of the investment period, the proceeds of a life assurance policy are treated as though the fund had already paid the equivalent of basic rate tax. For lower and basic rate taxpayers that is the end of the story. But what happens next for higher rate taxpayers depends on whether the policy is classed by the Inland Revenue as 'qualifying' or 'non-qualifying'.

With a qualifying policy there is no further tax liability. However, to attract this special tax status the policy must abide by various conditions. First, it must be a regular premium plan where you pay a predetermined amount each month or each year. Secondly, it has to be a long-term plan – usually a minimum of ten years. Thirdly, it has to provide a substantial amount of life cover.

This means that single premium investment policies are non-qualifying but the regular premium MIPs may be classed as qualifying depending on the level of life cover provided. Mortgage endowments, which tend to be long-term regular premium plans, usually are qualifying due to the substantial element of life cover.

The important point to note about life assurance policies is that the income tax cannot be reclaimed so, generally, these policies are not considered suitable for non-taxpayers. Moreover, the capital gains tax paid by the fund cannot be offset against an individual's exemption – as is the case with unit and investment trusts. Financial advisers tend to regard this feature as a serious drawback.

However, there are circumstances in which the unique features of investment bonds can be attractive to certain investors. With bonds there is no annual yield as such since income and growth are rolled up within the fund. But up to 5 per cent of the original capital can be withdrawn each year for up to 20 years. The Inland Revenue treats these withdrawals as a return of capital and therefore at the time of payment they are free of tax, so the higher rate tax liability is deferred until you cash in your policy. (Withdrawals above 5 per cent are treated by the Inland Revenue as though they are net of basic rate tax – so the higher rate liability must be paid, not deferred.) You can make withdrawals from your MIP in the same way, although usually this feature does not apply until you have completed the ten-year initial investment period.

Even if you invest in a non-qualifying life policy you may be able to reduce or avoid the deferred higher rate tax bill due to the effect of top-slicing relief. Top-slicing relief averages the profit over the number of years the bond has been held and adds this profit slice to an investor's income in the year the bond matures. If part or all of this falls into the higher rate bracket, it is taxed. However, with careful tax planning investors can avoid this liability by encashing the bond when they become lower rate taxpayers – in retirement, for example.

Higher rate taxpayers who have used their full capital gains tax allowance may also find bonds attractive because the 5 per cent withdrawals do not have to be declared for income tax purposes in the year of withdrawal.

6.5.4 Offshore funds

In certain cases for more wealthy, risk tolerant investors it may be appropriate to consider offshore funds. Whether an offshore fund is suitable depends on the tax jurisdiction of the fund, the way the fund itself is taxed and your own tax position as an investor.

Points to consider with offshore funds include the charges – which often can be very high compared with UK funds – and the regulation; for example if it is outside of the United Kingdom, what protection do you have if the company collapses or the fund manager runs off with your money?

As a general rule for a UK investor investing in UK securities, unit and investment trusts are likely to prove more cost effective and simpler than offshore funds. Investors who may gain by going offshore include UK and foreign expatriates who are non-resident for UK tax and who can benefit from gross roll up if they do not pay tax in the country where they live. Higher rate taxpayers may also benefit from the gross roll up but they do have to pay tax when they bring the money back into the United Kingdom, although of course they may have switched to the lower tax bracket if they have retired by the time the bond matures.

Finally, offshore bolt holes always appeal to investors who, for whatever reason, require total confidentiality – or, to put it bluntly, those who want to hide their investments from the tax and legal authorities.

6.5.5 Open ended investment companies (OEICs)

These investments were introduced in 1997. OEICs, as the name implies, have a corporate structure rather than one based on trust law. Like unit trusts, they can invest in any securities which can be bought and sold on the open market. The fund's profits and income are pooled. Also like unit trusts, OEICs are 'open ended' which means the management company can increase or reduce share capital on a daily basis – in the same way that a unit trust manager can create or reduce the number of units in line with supply and demand.

This means that investors in OEICs buy and sell at net asset value, so there is not the added complexity of a differential between the net asset value and the share price, as is the case with investment trusts.

One of the main differences between OEICs and unit trusts is that the former can have different classes of share, with different aims. OEICs do not have a different selling and buying price, known as the bid/offer spread. Instead they have just one mid-market price – literally the mid-point between the bid/offer spread – at which investors both buy and sell. As with qualifying unit trusts, qualifying OEICs are PEPable.

6.5.6 Personal equity plans (PEPs)

From 6 April 1999, no further investment can be made in PEPs. Existing holdings remain unaltered and thus remain a very attractive tax-efficient investment. The changes to the rules do not affect your existing PEP holdings.

A PEP is not an investment in its own right but is simply a tax-efficient basket in which you hold your portfolio to shield it from income and capital gains tax. Up to £6,000 a year could be invested in a general plan and a further £3,000 a year in a single company plan where the shares of just one company were bought.

The list of 'qualifying' investments that you can hold in a PEP is extensive.

Direct investment

(1) The ordinary shares of companies registered in the United Kingdom or in other EU countries.
(2) The corporate bonds and convertibles (fixed interest securities which may be converted to equities at some future date) of UK companies. The companies must not be authorised credit institutions so, for example, this would exclude banks. Corporate bonds must have a minimum lifespan of five years at the time of purchase.

(3) The preference shares (shares that pay dividends at a fixed rate) of UK and other EU companies.

All the investments must be in quoted companies.

Collective funds (unit trusts, investment trusts and OEICs)

(1) The full £6,000 allowance could be invested in 'qualifying' collective funds which hold at least half their assets in the above categories for direct investment. The investments could be in both quoted and unquoted companies.
(2) Up to one-quarter of the allowance (£1,500) could be invested in 'non-qualifying' collective funds, which hold at least half of their assets in ordinary shares listed on EU stock exchanges and in shares on international exchanges recognised by the Inland Revenue. It is the PEP manager's responsibility – not the private investor's – to ensure compliance with these rules.

If a fund does not fall into one of these two categories it is classed as ineligible for PEP investors.

For the general plan, you could invest directly in equities and bonds or through unit trusts, investment trusts and the new OEICs. You could only invest in one general PEP a year but if you opted for a 'self-select' plan you could use this to hold a range of qualifying investments, so you were not restricted to the funds of just one management group. Self-select plans are for experienced investors.

PEP tax benefits

The tax benefits of PEPs are considerable. If you hold bonds outside a PEP then the interest payments are taxed at your top rate of income tax. In the case of equities, dividends paid to shareholders also are taxed at your top rate of income tax.

Within a PEP, both interest and dividends are tax free. For a lower rate taxpayer PEPs provide relief at the rate of 20 per cent – in other words your interest and dividends are worth 20 per cent more than if you held the shares outside of a PEP and did not qualify for relief. If you are a basic rate taxpayer, the relief is 23 per cent for 1999–2000, while for higher rate taxpayers the relief is at 40 per cent.

This is very useful for investors looking for a regular income, who can use the dividends from equities or the interest from bonds without eating into their original capital. Investors seeking capital growth can benefit considerably from the compound effect of reinvesting dividends on their equity holdings.

Normally when you sell shares you incur a tax penalty on any 'capital gains'. The gain is simply the difference between the price at which you bought the shares and the price at which you sell, after taking account of inflation to 5 April 1998 and taper relief. In other words, the Revenue only charges capital gains tax on the gains an investment has made over and above inflation. For shares held within a PEP the capital gains are tax free. However, if you make any losses within your PEP these cannot be offset against gains made outside the plan.

In practice very few investors pay capital gains tax because gains can be offset against the annual exemption of £7,100 in 1999–2000 tax year. Investors holding less than around £100,000 of equities usually can manage their investments in such a way that they would not expect to pay capital gains tax. For this reason it makes sense to use your PEP allowance to shelter from income tax the interest on corporate bonds and the dividends on high yielding equities.

The bulk of the PEP market is in collective funds – largely in unit trusts. Here you automatically hand over responsibility for managing the fund – and your money – to the company. For obvious reasons this type of fund is sometimes called a managed fund.

The alternative is to invest through a 'self-select' plan. In this case in effect you are buying the PEP wrapper separately from the assets. Provided you stick to the rules on investment choice you can run your own portfolio or ask a stockbroker to do this for you.

Notwithstanding the prohibition, from 6 April 1999, on further investments in PEPs, an investor can keep all existing PEPs.

6.5.7 Individual savings accounts

ISAs were introduced from 6 April 1999 and can comprise up to three components.

Cash

A cash ISA can be invested in a bank or building society, a National Savings account, money market deposits or cash unit trusts.

Life insurance

An insurance ISA comprises a life insurance policy insuring the life of the ISA holder. However, the following contracts are not eligible:

- Annuities
- Personal portfolio bonds
- Pensions

Stocks and shares

A stocks and shares ISA can comprise investments in shares listed on a recognised stock exchange, unit trusts, investment trusts, open-ended investment companies (OEICs), corporate bonds, gilt-edged securities, shares bought through savings-related share option schemes (SAYE), or cash held for buying stock market investments. ISAs cannot hold unlisted shares or shares quoted on the alternative investment market (AIM). Shares arising on privatisation or demutualising building societies or insurers cannot be transferred into an ISA.

For investment limits, conditions, the tax position and details on 'maxi' and 'mini' ISAs, see 6.3.3.

6.6 THE HOME AS AN INVESTMENT

No chapter on investment would be complete without a section on houses. For most people, their home represents their biggest single financial commitment and, as we prepare for retirement, it may well represent our biggest single debt. This section of the chapter looks at topics related to residential property and financial planning:

(1) Paying off the mortgage
(2) Home income plans
(3) Furnished holiday accommodation
(4) Rent-a-room relief.

6.6.1 Paying off the mortgage

The majority of people buy their home with the help of a mortgage and the idea of continuing with a mortgage is almost second nature. However, at or near retirement such a large debt is not attractive and paying off the mortgage might make sense financially.

Tax relief on loan interest is limited to the first £30,000 of the loan. This was fixed in 1983 and has not been adjusted since. In addition, the rate of tax relief has come down over the years. In 1991, it was changed so that higher rate tax relief was no longer available; a further change in April 1994 limited the tax relief to 20 per cent, with a further reduction to 15 per cent from April 1995. The July 1997 Budget reduced this further to 10 per cent from April 1998. It will be withdrawn entirely from 6 April 2000. As a result of these factors, many of the arguments for keeping a mortgage need re-examining.

The question, of course, is – if you have the funds available, do you pay the mortgage off, or reinvest the money elsewhere in the hope of doing better with it? The interest you pay on money you have borrowed is almost certainly more than the interest you are likely to get from any guaranteed investment. Add to that the fact that, from April 1998 to April 2000, you will only be getting 10 per cent relief, and thereafter nothing, on the first £30,000 you have borrowed compared to the 40 per cent you may pay on the interest that you earn and you can see that there is probably no way that you will ever be able to match your mortgage interest payments unless you go for high-risk investments.

The big drawback, of course, is having to write out a cheque for such a large amount. The decision inevitably comes down to one of peace of mind. If you are happy to sign the cheque, then pay it off (or at least pay enough of it off to bring you down to the £30,000 level). If you prefer to leave your options open and retain flexibility for the future, then invest the funds elsewhere.

6.6.2 Home income plans

Home income plans allow you to gain access to the equity in your home and use this to generate an extra income without having to sell up and move. You can take the money as a regular income or as a lump sum, depending on the scheme rules. All you have to do in return is pay interest on the loan, where applicable, and agree that the debt will be repaid out of the proceeds of your house sale when you die.

Back in the 1980s, early versions of the home income plan proved to be a financial disaster for many elderly people because these schemes relied on the flawed assumption that bond investment returns would always outstrip mortgage interest rates. They did not, and as a result many elderly homeowners were left with a mortgage debt larger than the combined value of their house and the insurance bond. In 1990 these investment schemes were banned.

Today there is a second generation of respectable equity release plans. In particular four companies – Allchurches Life, Carlyle Life, Home & Capital Trust and Stalwart Assurance – joined together in 1991 to form SHIP, the Safe Home Income Plans company. SHIP secretary is based at the independent advisers and home income plan specialists Hinton & Wild. The code of practice offered by members of the organisation is as follows:

(1) You have complete security of tenure and are guaranteed the right to live in the property for life, no matter what happens to interest rates and the stock market.
(2) You have freedom to move house without jeopardising your financial situation.

(3) You are guaranteed a cash sum or regular income; your money is not sunk into uncertain investments.

There are two basic types of safe home income plans: where a mortgage on the property is used to produce an income, and those which involve the sale of part or all of your property to produce an income or cash lump sum. In each case the loan is paid off when you die.

Mortgage annuities

This type of plan allows you to remortgage part of the value of your house, usually up to £30,000. The lump sum is used to buy a 'purchased life annuity' from the lender which in return guarantees an income for life. This pays the fixed rate of interest on the mortgage and whatever is left is yours to spend how you wish.

The income generated by the annuity remains static or, at an extra cost, rises at a fixed rate or in line with inflation. SHIP states that the minimum age for a mortgage annuity plan is 69 for a single person; for couples their combined ages must total at least 145, with the youngest aged 70 or over. Below these ages the annuities are unlikely to offer attractive rates. The loan usually is repaid on the death of the individual, or on second death in the case of a couple.

The normal minimum loan is £15,000 and the maximum is £30,000, although the over-80s may be able to raise slightly more. Depending on the size of the loan and interest and mortgage rates, this might buy a gross flat rate annual income guaranteed for life of £1,200 for a woman age 75 rising as high as £4,000 for a man age 85. This is the surplus income after the mortgage interest net of MIRAS (mortgage interest relief at source) is deducted.

Purchased life annuities are regarded as tax efficient because only part of the income is taxed. The rest is treated as a return of capital.

Reversion plans

This is where you sell, rather than mortgage, part or all of your house. Reversion plans fall into two categories. With a *reversion annuity* the purchase price is used to buy an annuity which operates in the same way as the mortgage annuity described above, although there is no mortgage interest to pay so your income is higher. However, because you have sold rather than mortgaged, you do not gain from any rise in house prices on that portion of your property.

Under the *cash option* you sell part or all of your home in return for a lump sum which is tax free provided the house is your main residence. You continue to live there, rent free, until you die. You can, if you wish, use the money to buy an annuity, but this is not obligatory.

According to SHIP the minimum age for reversion plans is 65 to 70. The minimum sale is usually between 40 per cent and 50 per cent of the value of the property and with most companies you can sell up to 100 per cent. SHIP says that for homes priced over £70,000 the benefits under a reversion plan often are appreciably higher than the mortgage plans.

6.6.3 Furnished holiday accommodation

Property can be used as an investment, providing you with an income and some useful tax benefits. The first option is holiday letting where property in the United Kingdom is used for the specific purpose of furnished holiday accommodation (the benefits do not apply to overseas property).

There are certain requirements that must be fulfilled:

(1) The property must be let on a commercial basis (ie it must be let at a realistic rent).
(2) It must be furnished.
(3) During any 12-month period:
  (a) the property must be available for letting as holiday accommodation for at least 140 days;
  (b) it must be let for 70 such days;
  (c) it must not normally be occupied by the same person for more than 31 days during a period of seven months in the 12-month period.

Tax benefits

Provided these conditions are fulfilled, the following tax benefits apply:

(1) Interest on loans used to buy the property should qualify as an expense.
(2) You may get capital allowances for equipment, furniture and furnishings.
(3) Expenditure incurred before you actually start letting your property may be allowed as a loss.
(4) Any overall loss (after taking into account items (1), (2) and (3)) may be offset against your other income.
(5) Your profits could be regarded as 'relevant earnings' (see 4.7.1) for the purposes of personal pension plan and retirement annuity contributions.
(6) On a sale, your capital gains may be rolled over if further business property is purchased.
(7) On a sale, capital gains tax retirement relief is available (for disposals prior to 6 April 2003).

(8) Furnished holiday accommodation is a business asset for capital gains taper relief.
(9) A chargeable gain on furnished holiday accommodation can be re-invested in 'eligible shares' in a 'qualifying company'.

The term 'holiday accommodation' should not be taken to imply that it must be a cottage in the country or by the sea. Provided it is used for the purposes of holidays, it could be in the centre of a town and it could just as easily be a mobile home.

Overall, there are some attractive features to the purchase of property for use as holiday accommodation, though it is clearly an area where an accountant's advice is needed.

6.6.4 Rent-a-room relief

Under this relief, you can get total exemption from tax for income of up to £4,250 per annum for letting part of your only or main residence for use as a separate residence. Not only can this be a useful source of income, it is also a source of income which does not form part of your 'total income' for the purposes of your eligibility to the higher age-related personal allowances (see 8.4.1).

7

FINANCIAL PROTECTION

Any prudent arrangements for a smooth transition from earning a salary to living on a retirement income must take account of the unpredictable events that can suddenly threaten our welfare and that of our family. There is nothing new in this; the practice of insuring life can be traced back to Roman times.

This chapter looks at the most common forms of financial protection and covers the following topics:

(1) Introduction
(2) Life assurance
(3) Personal life assurance
(4) Business assurance
(5) Illness protection
(6) Medical insurance
(7) Redundancy and unemployment.

7.1 INTRODUCTION

This chapter looks at a number of ways in which we can insure ourselves against death, disability and sickness. However, there has to be a balance. To take no action is both foolish and irresponsible. But if we paid all the necessary premiums on every form of insurance, to protect ourselves up to the hilt from every one of life's potential problems, then we would certainly be well protected. We might also be destitute.

It may not even be you who is the one to suffer. Your business could be affected by the absence of a key individual.

There are no magic formulae. The only thing you can do is to ask yourself the question of what the financial implications would be, for you or your family, following the death, ill health or accident either of yourself or somebody close to you. Then you have to find out the cost of covering yourself or your family against these implications. The decision you face is whether you are prepared to accept a modest fall in your current living standards today in order to maximise the chances of maintaining that slightly lower standard of living in the future if the worst happens.

7.2 LIFE ASSURANCE

Life assurance is the most important form of personal protection. It has a long history but, although a simple form of life assurance was available in England in the sixteenth century, the birth of the modern life assurance industry took place in 1762. It was then that policies were first issued where the premiums related to age and type of policy.

Life assurance is also one of the few permanent forms of insurance. Once you have been accepted, and provided you continue to pay the premiums, you are covered regardless of what happens to you in the future.

7.2.1 The types of life assurance

There are three broad categories of life assurance.

Term assurance

This is the simplest form of life cover and provides a guaranteed amount if death occurs within a certain fixed period (the term). The term can be set for any number of years to suit the purpose. At the end of the term, the cover lapses and there is no residual cash value.

Endowment assurance

Endowment assurance has a term but it also has a growing investment value as well. Throughout the term, the policy provides life cover. At the end of the term (the maturity date) the plan provides a sum of money, often used to repay a mortgage.

Whole of life assurance

These policies provide a guaranteed level of cover for as long as premiums continue to be paid. They may also build up a cash value.

7.2.2 The forms of life assurance

The principal aim of a life policy is to provide the funds to cover any financial difficulties likely to arise on the death of a named individual (the life assured). The amount of cover is agreed at the start of the plan and, provided premiums are maintained, this life cover can never be taken away.

With whole of life modern life policies, the initial premiums are set at the best rates the life company can offer, based on assumptions of future mortality and investment conditions. At the end of a period of time (usually ten years), the position is reviewed. If the overall environment is better than the assumptions, the level of cover is increased; if worse, then premiums are increased to maintain the same level of cover. This then remains the position until the next 'policy review'.

There are two main types of policy: with-profits and unit-linked.

With-profits policies

The policy's underlying value is related to the value of assets in which the life company invests the premiums. Any growth which can be passed on to the policyholder is awarded as periodic bonuses throughout the term of the policy (called 'reversionary bonuses') with a final bonus (the 'terminal bonus') payable at maturity. Once declared, a bonus is guaranteed but, in the case of endowment policies, companies reserve the right to re-calculate the figures if the policy is surrendered before its maturity date.

Unit-linked policies

The policy's underlying value is expressed in the number and value of units that the policy holds in the relevant funds. The funds themselves reflect the value of the underlying assets and so, as the value of the assets fluctuates, so does the value of the policy.

The policy's value can therefore be continuously assessed; there are no periodic or final bonuses as for with-profit policies.

7.2.3 The variations in life policies

The simplest form of policy is an 'own-life, own-benefit' arrangement. The policy is arranged by the policyholder on his own life and, when he dies, the policy proceeds form part of his estate for inheritance tax purposes (see 9.2).

Other forms are joint-life policies, written jointly on married couples. Here, the life cover can be paid out either when the first person dies (joint-life, first-death) or when the second person dies (joint-life, second death).

It is also quite common to take out life assurance on somebody else's life if you would suffer financially if that person died (referred to as having an 'insurable interest'). Such policies are called 'life of another' policies. The insurable interest (and hence the maximum amount of life cover) is the potential financial loss to you if the life assured died.

Husbands and wives have unlimited insurable interest in each other. A policy taken out by one spouse on the life of the other can come under the provisions of the Married Women's Property Act 1882, which gives the policy a certain element of protection (eg a policy taken out by a wife on her husband would be protected in the event of the husband's bankruptcy).

Policies may also be taken out under the terms of a simple trust. This is usually done to ensure that the policy proceeds do not fall into the life assured's estate on death but, instead, become payable to nominated beneficiaries. This is frequently used in conjunction with joint-life, second death plans for the mitigation of inheritance tax (see 9.5) and also in certain types of business assurance (see 7.4).

There is also the straightforward practical point that policies written in trust means that cash is available without having to wait for grant of probate. Consequently, there is a case for saying that every life policy taken out for family protection should be written in trust.

7.3 PERSONAL LIFE ASSURANCE

7.3.1 The need for personal life cover

It is rare for anybody with any level of family or financial responsibility to have no life assurance. Anybody taking out a loan or a mortgage, for example, usually has life cover equal to the loan whether they want it or not because the lender usually wishes to ensure that the loan is protected in the event of the borrower's death.

If you have family responsibilities, where others are dependent on your income, then you have to consider what they would do without that income. The life cover you need is the sum of money which, when invested (and taking into account the level of interest rates generally available), produces the income they need and which also covers any outstanding debts or future financial commitments.

Tax relief

There is no general relief for life assurance premiums but certain policies taken out before 13 March 1984 continue to benefit from life assurance premium relief (LAPR). This relief is currently equal to 12.5 per cent of premiums paid and represents a good reason for continuing to pay the premiums on such policies for as long as the policy remains eligible.

7.3.2 The uses of personal life cover

The type of life cover generally follows the requirement it is needed to fulfil.

(1) A short-term debt (eg a bank loan) could be covered by term assurance with the life cover equal to the amount borrowed.
(2) A mortgage on a house is frequently covered by endowment assurance. The basic intention is for the maturity value to pay off the loan at the end of the term but the life cover ensures that the mortgage is protected during the term of the loan.
(3) Where the need for cover is effectively limitless (eg family protection), whole of life plans are used to provide the required level of cover. Such plans are also written in trust where family protection or inheritance tax mitigation is the objective (see 9.5).

7.3.3 Pensions related life cover

Occupational pension schemes

Company schemes usually provide a level of life cover while you remain employed and a member of your company scheme. Inland Revenue rules allow life cover of up to four times your final remuneration to be incorporated in your pension plan and, in this context, final remuneration means your remuneration at death. This definition means that your life cover keeps pace with your earnings, a form of in-built indexation.

For post-1989 members (see 3.3.1), the earnings cap affects this which means that for 1999–2000, the maximum level of life cover is £362,400 (ie 4 × £90,600).

The recipients of the lump sum payment are at the trustees' discretion and the payment is normally free of inheritance tax. However, the scheme rules usually allow you to nominate your preferred beneficiaries although, strictly speaking, the trustees are not bound by your nomination.

Additional voluntary contributions

Generally, any additional voluntary contributions (see 3.9) paid to a company scheme are returned in full, although the scheme rules determine whether they are returned with interest. Usually, the full investment value is repayable.

With free-standing additional voluntary contributions (see 3.10), the full investment value is payable to the beneficiaries.

Funded unapproved retirement benefit schemes (FURBS)

With FURBS (see 3.12), any employer looking to increase the life cover of an employee caught by the earnings cap has to set up an ordinary life assurance policy written in trust (and the premiums paid are regarded as a benefit in kind and so taxable).

On death, the benefits are distributed by the trustees and it is unlikely that any inheritance tax would be due.

Personal pension schemes

In the event of death before retirement, the retirement fund is payable as a death benefit. The total death benefit under personal pension schemes can be written in trust and with generally favourable inheritance tax consequences. The form of trust can either be interest in possession or discretionary (see 11.3). Putting existing schemes into trust may have some inheritance tax implications.

However, it is possible to arrange a totally separate life policy within a personal pension scheme. The main benefit here is that the contributions are fully allowable against tax. The maximum amount that may be paid into a life policy set up separately from the personal pension scheme is 5 per cent of net relevant earnings (see 4.7.2). However, the percentage does not vary with age, unlike the proportion that may be invested to provide retirement benefits. The 5 per cent also counts towards the overall maximum percentage that may be contributed to a personal pension scheme (see 4.8).

Life assurance policies set up together with a personal pension scheme may be assigned, which can make them useful as collateral security in certain business assurance situations (see 7.4.3).

7.4 BUSINESS ASSURANCE

Just as there is a need to protect the family against sudden death, there is an equal need within the business. Covering the financial consequences of the loss of a key person (eg the repayment of guaranteed loans, arrangements to prevent the breakup of shareholdings and partnerships and so on) are all areas where the smaller business should make use of a suitable life policy. This is a complex area and one where competent advice should be sought. The following sections provide only an outline of the types of areas where life assurance can play a part in business protection.

7.4.1 Key person assurance

Area of risk

A key person is an employee or working director whose existence is crucial to the company's continued activities. His or her loss could lead to a drop in sales, in profits or in confidence. In an extreme case, it could mean the winding-up of the company. The individual could have given personal guarantees for loans and may even have made personal loans to the company.

Regardless of the specific circumstances, cash could be required, for example, to repay loans, hire and train replacements, and spend time on reassuring nervous customers.

Level of risk

The potential loss in each case will vary. Where a loan is guaranteed, the position is clear. Where a sales director's value to the company is being considered, the potential loss is less easy to ascertain. It could be a multiple of salary (ie a replacement cost), the loss in net profits or the potential fall in share value.

Type of policy

The most appropriate form is often a term policy but whole of life plans may give further options. It is generally taken out on a 'life of another' basis as the proceeds belong to the company.

From the tax point of view, if the proceeds are likely to be treated as a trading receipt (and therefore taxable), the premiums are allowable as an expense for corporation tax purposes. This tends to be the case when life cover is arranged on a short-term basis to meet the expense of replacing a key person. Where, however, the proceeds are unlikely to be seen as a trading receipt (eg if the policy is taken out to protect a loan), then the premiums are not allowable as an expense against corporation tax.

In all cases, you should get confirmation of the tax position from your local Inspector of Taxes.

7.4.2 Share purchase assurance

Area of risk

There are many thousands of companies with just two or three shareholders. The death of any one of them could have problems for the company's future direction as the remaining shareholders may not welcome the involvement of the deceased shareholder's family. When a shareholder dies, his shares fall into his estate and pass to his beneficiaries under the terms of his will. If there is no will, the rules of intestacy apply (see 10.2), leading to a potentially even more unwelcome situation.

The most likely position is that the existing shareholders will wish to buy the shares so that they can retain full control of the overall shareholding. However, that may not always be easy; the new shareholders may be unwilling to sell or may put too high a price on the shares.

Level of risk

The most popular solution is an arrangement with options to buy and sell the shares. This is usually referred to as a 'cross-option' agreement.

The agreement gives the holders of the shares (ie the deceased's executors) the option to sell the shares at the market price and gives the other shareholders the option to buy them.

The agreements provide for adequate life cover to be taken out to cover the costs of purchase of the shares. Determining the precise level of life cover is not easy because it is related to the market value of shares, so you need a flexible policy which allows for future increases in the level of life cover to be arranged.

Type of policy

The most common arrangement is for each shareholder to take out a policy on his own life, written in trust for the other shareholders. On death, the proceeds are paid to the other shareholders who then have the money to buy the shares from the executors. Either a term policy or a whole of life policy may be used; a whole of life plan may provide greater flexibility.

7.4.3 Partnership protection

Area of risk

The death of a partner is legally the end of the old partnership and the start of a new one. The partner's widow is in a difficult position; the main source of her income may have disappeared and, while she may have inherited her husband's share in the partnership, she may have little interest in it. Her need is for cash but a share in a partnership is a difficult thing to sell except to the remaining partners and they may not have the money. She may be able to have the partnership dissolved in order to realise her interest in it, but this could be a lengthy and unsatisfactory process which could be a major problem for the remaining partners as well.

Level of risk

Once again, a suitable life policy can provide the answer. The most common arrangement is for each partner to take out a policy written in trust for the benefit of the other partners for a sum assured appropriate to his share in the partnership. A suitable form of option agreement is set up including the necessary cross-option arrangements to make sure that a willing seller is bound to find willing buyers.

Type of policy

From the point of view of a traditional life policy, a whole of life arrangement may provide greater flexibility. However, it might also be taken out as a separate plan alongside a personal pension scheme. This may also have the added advantage of full tax relief on the premiums.

7.4.4 Tax implications

The tax implications of share purchase and partnership arrangements can be quite complex. The major impact is on inheritance tax and business property relief (see 9.8).

Clearly, no inheritance tax applies if property is left to the spouse, but, in all other cases, inheritance tax may be payable. This is a case where business property relief comes into its own as up to 100 per cent relief can be given on the transfer of shares and interests in partnerships. However, this relief could be lost if, at the time of death, there is a binding contract for sale. This could be a problem where there is a long-standing 'buy and sell' agreement which may well constitute a binding contract for sale.

However, the Inland Revenue view is that a cross-option agreement is not regarded as a contract for sale for these purposes and so the relief is not lost. Clearly a correctly drawn up cross-option agreement is an essential part of all shareholder and partnership protection. Most life companies can advise you on a suitable form of agreement.

In general, there are no inheritance tax implications on the payment of premiums or of proceeds, particularly where there is an arrangement within a group of people to 'cross insure' each other for commercial purposes; under these arrangements the premiums are not regarded as gifts.

There may be tax implications if a new shareholder or partner joins an existing arrangement.

7.5 ILLNESS PROTECTION

Most people will, if pushed, reluctantly concede that they are not immortal and that their life will at some point come to an end ('but not for some years yet'). Serious illness, however, for its survival, is often regarded as an even more unlikely occurrence, a view which flies in the face of all the evidence.

The chances are that one in four men reading this book have either had, or will have, a critical illness before they reach state retirement age. Each year, hundreds of thousands of people are diagnosed as having cancer, or suffer from a heart attack or stroke.

Over and above these critical illness figures, many hundreds of thousands of people are unable to work as a result of sickness, accident or disability. For all manner of reasons, over half a million people are unable to work at any moment in time for medical reasons and have been unable to work for at least three years.

This section looks at three areas of financial protection against illness and covers the following:

(1) Critical illness cover
(2) Income protection
(3) Waiver of premium.

7.5.1 Critical illness cover

Not so very long ago, a critical illness, such as a heart attack, was frequently fatal; very few people expected to survive. Today, medical science has made dramatic improvements in the treatment of a whole range of such illnesses and an increasing number of people survive them. Each year, half a million people suffer heart attacks or strokes, or are diagnosed as having cancer, but after 12 months over half of them are getting on with their lives.

However, while they may survive, their finances often do not. A heart attack may not lead to a permanent disability but it may lead to a permanent change of lifestyle. It could mean a less stressful (and less well-rewarded) job; it could mean no job at all.

Critical illness cover is a relatively new type of insurance which is designed to meet the financial problems of survival. It provides a cash lump sum on the survival of a range of critical conditions or certain types of major surgery. The cash can be used for any purpose such as necessary home alterations or paying off the mortgage.

The range of plans available is growing all the time. They are also growing in terms of the options they can provide; some plans now provide additional life cover and some can be written on a 'joint-life, first claim' basis.

They may also be incorporated into cross-option agreements for shareholder and partnership protection (see 7.4.2 and 7.4.3) to cover the purchase of business interests in the event of serious illness, as well as death.

7.5.2 Income protection

An illness does not have to be classified as 'critical' illness in order to prevent you from working. Some of the less severe illnesses can lead to long periods of absence, as could an accident or other forms of disability.

A regular income at times like this can arise from three sources: the state, a company scheme or a personally arranged income protection plan.

State benefits

Sickness benefit and invalidity benefit were replaced from April 1995 with a new incapacity benefit (see 13.6.3). The overall effect has been a reduction in the amount of state help after an initial 28-week period.

In addition to the cut in long-term sickness benefits the Government also changed the definition of qualifying disability from 'cannot do *own* job' to 'cannot do *any* job'. If you can sweep the streets you are classed as fit for work and receive no benefit. The long-term incapacity benefit is taxable and if your claim started after 13 April 1995 you will not get an earnings-related top up.

Company benefits

The principal benefit is incapacity benefit which employers pay for up to the first 28 weeks of illness. There are a number of requirements to be fulfilled by the employee. Once this ends, then you may have to rely on state benefits.

Some occupational pension schemes also provide a disability pension but this is only usually paid if you are so disabled that you are in no position to continue with your job and have to leave the company.

For many people, therefore, the possibility of a long illness could leave them protected by a sick pay scheme of some sort or other for just over six months with the prospect of having to live on state benefits after that.

Income protection plans

These are contributory insurance plans which usually provide you with up to about 75 per cent of your gross annual salary, less any entitlement to incapacity benefit. These plans are designed to replace your earned income and so usually commence paying benefit when your regular source of income stops as a result of your illness or disability. The income then continues until you are fit to resume work or until the cover ceases (which is usually your date of intended retirement). The income is tax free if derived from a personal policy, but is taxable if drawn from an employer's scheme.

There is usually a range of options. One is to choose that the income does not start for a defined period of time after you have to give up work. This allows the plans to mesh in with other sick pay arrangements. These 'deferred periods' are typically one, three, six or twelve months and the longer the deferred period, the lower the premiums.

Other options include the facility to index-link your benefits in line with your rising income.

7.5.3 Waiver of premium

Many forms of financial protection (life assurance policies, critical illness plans and pension schemes) require that you pay regular contributions, often monthly. Although many of them have the facility to catch up on any missed payments, there are usually limits to the extent you can do this, some imposed by the Inland Revenue.

Most of these plans therefore incorporate a 'waiver of premium' where, in return for a small increase in your regular contributions, you have the reassurance that your contributions will continue to be credited for if you are off work due to illness or disability. There is usually a built-in 'deferred period' of three months before this starts.

With personal pension schemes, it may seem odd that contributions can continue to be paid during a period of incapacity, ie at a time when, by implication, net relevant earnings are not arising. However, in practice what happens is that contributions are not paid on behalf of the planholder, the life company credits them.

Overall, this benefit can be very important in maintaining plans that are being used for inheritance tax mitigation or as the repayment vehicle for a mortgage and extremely important if it maintains your personal pension scheme during a period of incapacity.

7.6 MEDICAL INSURANCE

Regardless of political persuasion, most people accept the view that the NHS offers an unbeatable level of care in emergencies but that for more routine, non-life threatening conditions, we either join the queue at the NHS hospital or pay extra and go to a private hospital.

The growth of private medical insurance has mushroomed in recent years, particularly in corporate schemes, usually presented as a 'staff benefit' but equally to the employer's benefit if it gets expensive staff back to work as fast as possible. Nevertheless, prompt medical treatment can remove a source of stress and, for the self-employed and those who run their own business, fast, timely treatment is a key ingredient in preserving their income and their business.

Medical insurance companies offer a range of options which allow you to select the type of treatment that you want and can afford (for example, where you only resort to private treatment if NHS treatment is unavailable to you within a certain timescale). PMI is a complex product and independent advice is essential to obtain the right type of policy for your needs at the best price.

If you need treatment, you should always check with your insurers first to ensure that your condition qualifies and that the bills will be paid in full. If you take on treatment which is outside their limits, you will have to pay the difference yourself.

Finally, remember that PMI does not cover chronic conditions – only acute, curable conditions. Chronic illness is covered by permanent health insurance, which provides a replacement income (see 7.5.2). Medical insurance does not cover residential or nursing home care. This can be provided for to some extent by long-term care insurance (see 15.6).

Tax relief

There is no general relief for medical insurance premiums except for people aged 60 or older. However, this relief was limited from 5 April 1994 to the basic rate of income tax – 23 per cent (see 8.4.2). In the case of a joint policy, tax relief is given if either the husband or wife is over 60.

For policies taken out before 2 July 1997, income tax relief is given at basic rate (at source) until 6 April 1999. No relief is given for post-2 July 1997 policies unless the proposal for the contract was received by the insurer prior to that date, provided that the contract is in place and the first premium was before 1 August 1997.

7.7 REDUNDANCY AND UNEMPLOYMENT

As if illness and disability are not enough, there is always the chance you may lose your income through other factors beyond your control. It is an unpalatable fact that older people are often first in the queue when it comes to 'rationalisation/slimming down' exercises when ability and experience often carry little weight with companies looking for youth and vitality which, coincidentally, often comes with a lower salary.

If you do face the 'five o'clock walk', it is vital to know your rights and to do everything possible to protect your position.

7.7.1 Your statutory rights

You are entitled to a statutory redundancy payment if you have worked continuously for your employer for at least two years (five years if you are in part-time work) and you had to leave your job because it ceased to exist and there was no suitable alternative. The amount of payment is a multiple of your normal weekly gross earnings at the time you were made redundant (up to a maximum of £6,300).

The overall maximum level of statutory redundancy pay for an older person being made redundant after 20 years of work is therefore £205 × 20 × 1½ = £6,150. The calculation is different (ie less attractive) if, at the time of your redundancy, you are less than 12 months from state retirement age.

These are your statutory rights; there is nothing to stop your employer making a more generous payment. The taxation of these payments is covered in 8.2.1.

What is important, of course, is that you take all the steps you can to protect your pension. You should make quite sure that your pension arrangements are an integral part of your negotiations with your employer, particularly if you are taking voluntary redundancy. There are full details on your options when leaving your employment in 3.14.

7.7.2 Redundancy insurance

Redundancy insurance is very limited. It tends mainly to apply to loans and mortgages and, specifically, to new loans and mortgages. There are also a number of conditions on most forms of redundancy insurance which tend to limit eligibility.

The premiums can be quite high. The borrower decides the level of cover he needs and the insurance cost could be in the region of £7 per

£100 (eg to protect a monthly payment of £500, the additional monthly payment would be £35).

The definition of redundancy is usually fairly strict:

(1) For employed people, the redundancy must be through no fault of their own and must not be voluntary.
(2) Self-employed people may only be able to claim on being made bankrupt.
(3) Company directors may only be able to claim if their company is in compulsory liquidation.

One frequent problem with many types of redundancy insurance is that the test for eligibility is done at the time of claim, not at the time of taking out the insurance. It is often the case that a policyholder, having paid the premiums for some time, only finds when he comes to claim that, for example, a subsequent change of job has rendered him ineligible.

7.7.3 Unemployment

If you lose your job, then you are eligible for jobseekers' allowance. This is described in more detail in Chapter 13.

Jobseekers' allowance can, of course, only be claimed by people who have been employed; the self-employed are not covered. More specifically, it is only paid to those people who have actually paid (rather than been credited with) Class 1 national insurance contributions (see 2.2) in one of the last two complete tax years before the year benefit is claimed.

Once you become eligible for benefit, and for as long as you qualify for benefit, you are credited with national insurance contributions in order to preserve the full value of your state pension and other benefits.

8

INCOME TAX AND CAPITAL GAINS TAX

The emergency Budget of the first Labour Government for 18 years did very little to alter tax planning. However, FA 1998 made major changes to capital gains tax.

Against this background, it is essential that in planning for your future retirement, you take every step you can to reduce your tax burden to the absolute minimum. As Lord Clyde remarked in a famous judgment, nobody is obliged to arrange his affairs 'to enable the Inland Revenue to put the largest possible shovel into his stores'. The Inland Revenue takes every opportunity it can to reduce our income and our wealth and we have the right to take every legal step we can to prevent this.

This chapter looks at taxation specifically from the point of view of people approaching or in retirement and covers the following topics:

(1) Introduction
(2) Employees about to retire
(3) Self-employed people about to retire
(4) Taxation in retirement
(5) Independent taxation
(6) Capital gains tax
(7) Tax saving areas.

8.1 INTRODUCTION

The UK system works on the basis that all your income and capital gains for a tax year, after deducting certain reliefs and allowances, and allowing for certain exemptions, are effectively aggregated together and taxed at varying rates according to the total amount. Within this system, you have some control over the total amount of tax you pay by following three simple guidelines:

(1) Claim your entitlements
(2) Check Inland Revenue documents
(3) Keep your tax affairs in order.

8.1.1 Claiming your entitlements

Although the range of reliefs, allowances and exemptions has diminished over recent years, there are still a valuable number to be claimed. However, it is up to you to see if you are entitled to a particular allowance. This chapter does not detail all the allowances and reliefs that are available because that would be beyond the scope of the book. The most important ones from the point of view of retirement planning are covered; details of others can be found in the *Allied Dunbar Tax Handbook*.

8.1.2 Checking Inland Revenue figures

Given the money it has invested in computer technology, it might seem odd for the Inland Revenue to make mistakes in its calculations. Unfortunately, it does, for example, make incorrect notices of coding, incorrect assessments and incorrect payment claims.

Once again, it is up to you to make sure that you are not being over-taxed (or under-taxed), and to notify the Inland Revenue accordingly. Any errors should immediately be brought to the attention of your Inspector of Taxes, including any that are in your favour (if you 'benefit' from a mistake by the Inland Revenue and fail to declare it, you could face stiff penalties).

8.1.3 Self-assessment

Legislation introduced over recent years, in particular on self-assessment, has transferred a great deal of responsibility to the taxpayer and has given the Inland Revenue much greater powers in dealing with tax offenders. Failing to declare sources of income, making late returns and even making mistakes in returns all carry quite serious penalties in contrast to the redress you have against the Inland Revenue for mistakes made against you.

Under self-assessment, the onus is on you. If you have been sent a tax return covering your personal tax affairs for 1998–99, you must have that return, fully completed, in the hands of your Inspector, by 30 September 1999 if you want the Inland Revenue to calculate your tax liability or if you want liabilities coded out through pay as you earn (PAYE). If you calculate your own liability you have until 31 January 2000 to file. For further information telephone the Revenue's leaflet line on 0645 000444.

Under self-assessment the Revenue requires interim payments of tax on 31 January during the tax year and 31 July following the tax year; these are both 50 per cent of the previous year's tax bill. Any under or overpayment is then picked up when the tax return is finally submitted to the Inland Revenue.

The new system applies mainly to the self-employed and those with investment income. Employees continue to be taxed under PAYE, as is pension income.

8.2 EMPLOYEES ABOUT TO RETIRE

The most valuable exercise you can undertake is a general 'clean-up' of your tax affairs in the year immediately before the year in which you intend to retire. The last thing you want to do is carry forward unpaid tax bills into your retirement.

You should check your notice of coding carefully. This usually comes out in advance of your final tax year of employment. Make sure that it accurately reflects the deductions that should be made due to your allowances and any additions made due to the benefits in kind to which you are entitled.

Benefits in kind

The impact of the taxation of benefits in kind (eg a company car) are spread over the 12 months of the tax year. Consequently, if you retire part way through a tax year, you should apply, shortly before you retire, to your Inspector of Taxes for your notice of coding to be amended with effect from your date of retirement. This then ensures that the correct amount of tax is deducted from your pension payments (if you start these straight away) and that your net pension payment is more or less correct. Clearly, you cannot avoid some tidying up after the end of the tax year (your form P11D, for example, is not generally sent out by your employer until a couple of months after the end of the tax year) but keeping the Revenue informed helps to ensure that the position is as well organised as possible.

Car fuel benefit

If all your petrol, including your petrol for private use, is paid for by your employer, you are taxed on the full benefit regardless of the amount of fuel provided. If you only fill the tank once during the tax year, you have to pay tax on the full amount of car fuel benefit (though if you give up your company car part way through the tax year, you only have to pay tax on a proportion of the car fuel benefit).

Depending on your anticipated private mileage in the tax year during which you intend to retire, it could pay you to forgo this benefit and to reimburse your employer for the full cost of fuel used for private purposes. If you intend to take this decision, you should make quite sure that it is clearly recorded in writing between you and your employer before the end of the preceding tax year.

8.2.1 Termination payments

It could be that you are retiring early from your job because your employment has been terminated. Under these circumstances, it can make a difference whether your employment is terminated at the beginning or end of the tax year. Part of any payment that you receive may be treated as taxable income in the year in which your employment is terminated; if this takes place at the beginning of the tax year, it could benefit from a lower rate of tax if your other income for the remainder of the year is low. In this case it might be tax efficient to defer taking your pension for a few months.

Redundancy payments

If you are taking early retirement as a result of redundancy, any statutory redundancy payment (see 7.7.1) is exempt from tax although it may need to be taken into account in computing the tax payable on a termination payment (see below). Payment from a non-statutory redundancy scheme is exempt if it meets certain Inland Revenue requirements.

Golden handshakes

If your contract of service is terminated, it may be possible for a compensation or *ex gratia* payment to be made either wholly or partially tax free provided you are not entitled to it under the terms of your contract, and it is not regarded as benefit under a retirement benefit scheme.

The various types of termination payments that are wholly exempt from tax are as follows:

(1) Any made where you have to give up your job because of illness or disability.
(2) Any special contributions made by your employer into an approved retirement benefit scheme.
(3) Any payment made where you have worked abroad for your employer (subject to certain, fairly lengthy, minimum periods of service abroad).

The £30,000 exemption

Where a termination payment is not wholly exempt, the first £30,000 is normally free of tax. If you receive both a statutory redundancy payment and a termination payment, the statutory redundancy payment is classed as part of the £30,000 exemption.

There is always the possibility that an *ex gratia* payment may be viewed as an unapproved retirement benefit and so taxable in full with no benefit from the £30,000 exemption. There are no clear cut rules on this, although the general practice of the Inland Revenue is that if the payment is made in connection with your retirement, then it is taxable in full.

Restrictive covenants

When you leave your company, you might be asked to give an undertaking that would restrict your future activities (for example, you may decide to become a consultant in your specialised field but agree with your current employers not to offer your services to certain competitors). Any payment you receive in respect of that agreement is treated as salary in the year it is received. This applies even if the covenant is not strictly legally enforceable.

8.3 SELF-EMPLOYED PEOPLE ABOUT TO RETIRE

The payment of tax by self-employed people has undergone a major upheaval in that the whole basis of assessment is changing. This has an impact on all self-employed people whether they continue to trade or whether they are planning to retire. The following sections provide only an outline and you should get professional advice in specific cases.

8.3.1 Your existing business

The preceding year of assessment basis has been abolished so income and capital gains are assessed on a current year basis. Your accounts are now prepared to reflect your earnings rather than cash received.

8.3.2 Closing down your business

If you are a sole trader then, when you leave the business, for tax purposes the business ends, regardless of whether you sell it, give it away or close it down.

Final year profits

The profit charged to tax in the year in which the business ends is not worked out on the preceding year basis but on the profit (or loss) made in the tax year in which the business ends (ie the year from 6 April to the date on which you leave the business).

Terminal losses

If your business ends up making a loss in its final year, this loss may be carried back against your profits for the previous three tax years. The relief is given against the latest year's profits first.

Other tax considerations

Any item of plant or machinery or other assets on which capital allowances have been granted may have to be re-assessed and made subject to a balancing charge or balancing allowance.

(1) If sold, there may be extra tax to pay in the form of a balancing charge if the proceeds exceed the cost less previous allowances (if the asset is taken over for private use or given away, it is regarded as having been sold at market value).
(2) If the item is scrapped, there may be a balancing allowance.

Your accounts include your stock-in-hand at your year end (unless your accounts are on the cash basis). This stock is normally valued at the lower of cost and realisable value but, when you close your business, any stock must be valued at open market value. This may be higher and this hidden profit is liable to tax.

VAT

If you are registered for VAT, you are regarded as running your business for the purposes of VAT even though you are closing it down. Any disposals of assets, and even the sale or gift of the business itself as a going concern, may be subject to VAT.

Once you have sold or disposed of the business, you must de-register for VAT purposes within 30 days.

8.3.3 Capital gains tax and inheritance tax

If you dispose of your business, you could be liable for capital gains tax on the proceeds and this is covered in 8.6.5.

If you give all or part of the business away, or sell any part of it at less than market value, there are inheritance tax implications (see 9.8).

8.3.4 Partnerships

The profits of a partnership are computed in the same way as a sole trader's profit.

8.3.5 Personal pension schemes

Although you may have retired having sold your business, there may still be scope for continuing to pay contributions to a retirement annuity or personal pension plan by making use of the 'carry back' provisions (see 4.9.2). You may be able to carry back contributions for up to two years to a period when you were in business in order to obtain a tax refund.

8.4 TAXATION IN RETIREMENT

When you retire, you are expected to make returns in the usual way, or at least notify the Inland Revenue of any untaxed income or gains you have received but not accounted for. The Revenue gives you a notice of coding – this goes to your principal pension provider so that they deduct the right amount of tax from your pension payments. This notice of coding also takes into account any state retirement pension you are receiving (which is always paid gross).

8.4.1 Personal allowances

Personal allowances may be claimed by anyone resident in the United Kingdom and also by any British subject. This means that you are able to claim personal allowances on any income you receive in the United Kingdom even if you have gone to live abroad (see Chapter 12).

A claim to any personal allowance must be made within six years of the end of the relevant year of assessment (ie a claim for the 1993–94 tax year may be made up to 5 April 2000). A claim is made on the day it is received by your Inspector of Taxes, not the day it is posted.

The basic personal allowance for 1999–2000 is £4,335. A higher allowance is given to those people who have reached the age of 65 and who are of limited means. Up to age 74, the allowance is £5,720 and rises to £5,980 for those people aged 75 or over. You get the higher allowance for the whole of the tax year in which you attain age 65 or age 75.

However, the higher allowances are reduced by £1 for every £2 by which your 'total income' exceeds £16,800 as follows:

(1) If you are aged between 65 and 74, the £1 for £2 operates on 'total income' between £16,802 and £19,570 (in 1999–2000).
(2) For those aged 75 or over, the deduction operates on 'total incomes' between £16,802 and £20,090 (in 1999–2000).

Your personal allowance can never fall below the basic single person's allowance.

This reduction in age-related personal allowances is quite an imposition and so, if you are a marginal case, it is important to rearrange your investments as far as possible to reduce your 'total income' (see below).

Personal allowances are just that, ie entirely personal to both husband and wife and any reduction in their age-related increases is determined by their individual 'total incomes'.

8.4.2 Total income

Your 'total income' differs from your real income, first because not all your real income counts toward total income, and secondly because certain deductions can be made from your real income in calculating your total income.

(1) Income which does not count towards total income includes:
   (a) Exempt letting income under the 'rent-a-room' scheme (see 6.6.4).
   (b) Interest credited to a TESSA or an ISA (see 6.3.2 and 6.3.3).
   (c) Dividends earned by a PEP or an ISA (see 6.5.6 and 6.3.3).
   (d) Growth in National Savings certificates (see 6.3.1).
   (e) Withdrawals from single premium bonds up to the 5 per cent limit.
(2) The principal deduction that can be made from any other income in arriving at total income is any interest paid on certain types of qualifying loan (though not normally on your mortgage as relief on this will probably have been given through the MIRAS system). However, you may also deduct certain other outgoings such as:
   (a) Contributions paid to an occupational or personal pension plan.
   (b) One-half of any Class 4 national insurance contributions (see 2.2).

8.4.3 Married couple's allowance

The basic rule is that a married man, whose wife is living with him, may claim the married couple's allowance of £1,970 (but relief for 1999–2000 is restricted to 10 per cent). This is increased to £5,125 if either husband or wife is aged between 65 and 74 and to £5,195 if either is aged 75 or over. These higher allowances are for 1999–2000. The additional age-related allowances are also dependent on total income but it is only the *husband's* total income that is taken into account.

The Inland Revenue position on 'living with' can be quite strict. It would rule out circumstances where a separation is likely to be permanent and that has been known to rule out a claim for a married couple's allowance where one of the couple was terminally ill and unlikely to return home.

While the married couple's allowance is normally claimed by the husband, a wife may claim half for herself. Also, a couple may jointly elect for the whole of it to be given to the wife (although the husband could subsequently claim his half back without his wife's consent). Neither of these elections has any impact on the rule that any reduction in the age-related allowance is determined by the husband's total income.

An election must be made before 6 April if it is to apply for the following tax year (although if you have notified your *intention* by the 5 April deadline, you have until 5 May to submit the official forms). Once made, the election stays in force until revoked.

This election to transfer the married couple's allowance applies only to the basic allowance of £1,970; it does not apply to any age-related additional allowance. Also, it is a general right which has been in place for some time and is not a result of the introduction of independent taxation. However, independent taxation also provides a mechanism for transferring the married couple's allowance and this is covered in 8.5.2.

8.4.4 Widow's bereavement allowance

If you are living with your husband at the time of his death, you may claim, in addition to your basic personal allowance, a widow's bereavement allowance of £1,970. The relief for 1999–2000 is given at 10 per cent. This is usually given for the tax year in which your husband died and also for the following year.

The allowance does not qualify for any age-related increase and is strictly for widows, not widowers.

8.4.5 Taxation of pensions

All state retirement pensions are paid gross without deduction of tax. However, if your total income exceeds the basic personal allowance, naturally you will end up with a tax bill. All occupational pensions and personal pensions are taxed under Schedule E and PAYE.

8.5 INDEPENDENT TAXATION

8.5.1 Introduction

All taxpayers, married and single, male and female, are taxed separately on their own income. This means they are required to make their own tax returns, declare their own income and claim their own tax allowances and reliefs. For many married people, it also means that a well thought out rearrangement of assets can result in tax savings.

8.5.2 Married couple's allowance

Both husband and wife have their individual personal allowances and a married couple also has the married couple's allowance which is *usually* claimed by the husband. Over and above the general right for half or all the basic amount of the married couple's allowance to be transferred to the wife (see 8.4.3), if the husband has insufficient income to use the married couple's allowance in full, he may ask for all or part of this allowance (including any age-related increments) to be transferred to his wife.

In assessing your total income for this purpose, you calculate it in the same way as described in 8.4.2 except that you may not deduct the items described in paragraph (2) of that section.

Transferring the married couple's allowance under these rules also has different time limits from those described in 8.4.3; you may request a transfer at any time up to the sixth anniversary of the year of assessment.

8.5.3 Income

Under independent taxation, a husband's and wife's incomes are calculated separately. In the case of a wife, this includes any state retirement pension to which she is entitled, even if this is based on her husband's national insurance contributions. It is her income and she can set her allowances against it.

Income from jointly held assets is normally split equally between husband and wife for tax purposes (the 50:50 rule). However, if the husband's actual entitlement to a jointly held asset and the income from it is different from that of his wife, they may make a joint declaration of their actual beneficial interest in the asset. If no declaration is made, the 50:50 rule applies.

A couple may choose to make a declaration for some of their assets, but not for others. The declaration applies only to the assets listed in the declaration; further declarations can be made at any time in the future.

Income is taxed from the date of declaration. The declaration must be received by your tax office within 60 days of the date of signing. Declarations cannot be backdated and, once made, cannot be withdrawn except in cases of death, marital breakdown or a change in beneficial interest of the assets concerned.

8.5.4 Capital

Just as husband and wife have individual incomes, they can each own individual assets and each may qualify for the annual capital gains tax exemption (see 8.6).

8.5.5 Rearrangement of assets

With the introduction of independent taxation, it immediately became apparent that transferring assets between husband and wife could result in some significant tax savings. Over and above the advisability of dividing up assets for inheritance tax purposes (see 9.4.2), there are, for example, obvious attractions for a husband who is paying higher rate tax on his investment income in transferring some of the income-producing assets to his non-tax paying wife.

However, be warned. The Inland Revenue view is that a transfer of assets is a perfectly legitimate result of the introduction of independent taxation. Nevertheless, it must be an outright gift with no strings attached. While there is nothing whatever to prevent your wife using the capital or income in a way that benefits you, any conditions attached to the gift which *require* her to use the capital or income for your benefit results in the benefit being regarded not as a gift but as a settlement, and therefore taxable (see 11.9).

You need to be careful with any subsequent re-transfers. It could well be that you transferred assets while you were a higher rate taxpayer because it seemed to be the correct thing to do at the time. When you are retired, and perhaps a basic rate taxpayer, those arrangements might not look quite so attractive. But if you attempt to 'unravel' the situation, the Revenue may claim that the first transfer was artificial and treat it as though it never happened, so you could receive a bill for unpaid tax, probably with interest.

8.6 CAPITAL GAINS TAX

Capital gains tax is complex and this chapter only gives a basic outline. More detailed information can be found in the *Allied Dunbar Tax Handbook*.

In general terms, capital gains tax is levied if a chargeable person disposes of a chargeable asset in a way which constitutes a chargeable disposal. Note that it is not simply the *sale* of an asset, it is the *disposal* of an asset.

You are chargeable to capital gains tax if you dispose of assets while you are resident and ordinarily resident in the United Kingdom (see 12.3.1). For most practical purposes, this affects you unless you are planning to go and live abroad.

Gains on virtually all types of assets are potentially liable to capital gains tax. However, certain assets are not regarded as chargeable assets, the main exemptions being chattels sold for less than £6,000, motor cars, gilt-edged securities, shares held in a PEP and your principal private residence.

The most obvious form of chargeable disposal is the outright sale of the asset but, in certain cases, the gift of the assets may also be a chargeable disposal (though not gifts made between husband and wife). There are also other forms of disposal on specific types of asset that would constitute a chargeable disposal.

You cannot be liable for capital gains tax unless your total net gains (for 1999–2000) exceed £7,100. Any gains in excess of that amount are added to your other income and taxed at income tax rates. If your other income is particularly low, you are not allowed to deduct any unused personal allowances from your capital gains in order to reduce your capital gains tax bill.

Since 1998–99, taper relief has applied. The effect of taper relief is that the amount of a chargeable gain is reduced by a percentage that varies according to the length of time (in whole years) up to ten years that an asset is held. A different scale of percentages applies to gains on the disposal of business and non-business assets.

It is important to remember that whether the asset is a business or a non-business asset, there is a residual proportion of the gain that can never be covered by taper relief, no matter how long the length of the period of ownership.

Indexation allowance is frozen as at April 1998 for expenditure prior to that date, and does not apply at all for later expenditure. This means that some disposals will qualify both for 'frozen indexation' in arriving at the amount of the gain, and for taper relief. The order of events is thus:

(1) deduct 'frozen indexation' in arriving at the amount of the gain;
(2) set off any allowable losses against gains as reduced by 'frozen indexation'; and
(3) apply taper relief to the net gain.

The relevant percentages are set out in the following table.

Table 8.1 – Taper relief percentages

Gains on disposals of business assets		*Gains on disposals of non-business assets*	
Number of whole years in qualifying holding period	*Percentage of gain chargeable*	*Number of whole years in qualifying holding period*	*Percentage of gain chargeable*
1	92.5	—	—
2	85.0	—	—
3	77.5	3	95
4	70.0	4	90
5	62.5	5	85
6	55.0	6	80
7	47.5	7	75
8	40.0	8	70
9	32.5	9	65
10 or more	25.0	10 or more	60

This table shows the percentage of the gain which is chargeable according to the number of complete years in the qualifying holding period. It also shows that gains on business assets are written off far more quickly than gains on non-business assets. After ten complete years only 25 per cent of the gain on business assets remains in charge, whereas for non-business assets the comparable figure is 60 per cent. For higher rate taxpayers, the effective tax rate on a gain on a business asset, after ten years, may be reduced to as little as (40 per cent × 25 per cent) = 10 per cent. The comparable effective rate on gains on non-business assets is (20 per cent × 60 per cent) = 24 per cent. Even if a qualifying period is longer than ten years, no further percentage reduction is possible.

Taper relief is advantageous if your assets have a comparatively low acquisition cost (eg shares in newly formed companies). In that case, the taper relief reduces the amount chargeable to a percentage of the gain. Under indexation, the gain was reduced only by a percentage of the acquisition cost.

For acquisitions after 6 April 1998 the qualifying holding period runs from when the asset is first acquired. This is of considerable importance if the asset's value is disproportionately enhanced by subsequent allowable expenditure.

Losses are not tapered. This means that if an asset is held for ten years, all of any loss is allowable, but only 60 or 25 per cent of any net gain is chargeable. Care is needed to ensure that you realise sufficient untapered gains or gains qualifying only for a smaller amount of taper relief in a tax year in which you have allowable losses.

8.6.1 Calculation and indexation

The basic calculation for capital gains tax is that your gain equals the sale proceeds, minus the initial costs.

In calculating your liability to capital gains tax, you are allowed to take into account the costs of buying and of selling the asset. If, for example, you have bought and sold some shares, any commission and stamp duty would be taken into account in computing the overall gain (or loss).

You are also allowed to offset the effects of inflation (ie you are taxable on real gains, not paper gains). Indexation works by inflating the initial cost of the asset by reference to the change in the retail prices index between the date of purchase and the date of sale.

This is the general rule and it applies to all assets acquired since 31 March 1982. All assets owned at 31 March 1982 were, in most instances, revalued as though they had been acquired at 31 March 1982. Assets owned for longer periods of time may be subject to more complex rules.

Indexation allowance is not available on expenditure incurred after 5 April 1998.

8.6.2 Losses

In any one tax year, you are assessable to your total gains made in that year, adjusted by indexation where relevant. You can also reduce your overall gains if you have made any capital losses in the same tax year, ie if you have sold assets at a lower price than you paid for them. The overall impact is that you are only liable to capital gains tax on your overall net gains made during the tax year.

In general terms, indexation relief may only be used to reduce or extinguish a capital gain; it may not be used to create or increase a capital loss.

8.6.3 'Bed and breakfasting'

For many years it has been common practice to enter into 'bed and breakfast' transactions for listed shares and securities. In such transactions, shares were sold and immediately reacquired. The purpose of this was to realise an allowable loss to set against gains on other disposals, or to make a gain to absorb the annual exemption. This facility is effectively removed for disposals after 17 March 1998. For transactions after this date, a disposal must be matched with acquisitions within the following 30 days, thereby assuming that there are no significant fluctuations in price, eliminating the opportunity to obtain a tax advantage. It may be possible in appropriate circumstances to arrange the sale of shares by you and for the repurchase of the shares by your spouse.

8.6.4 Identification of shares and securities

For disposals of shares and securities after 5 April 1998, identification with acquisitions is as follows:

- Same day acquisitions
- Acquisitions within 30 days following the disposal
- Acquisitions made after 5 April 1998 on a last in/first out basis
- Shares held on 5 April 1998
- Shares held on 31 March 1982
- Shares held on 6 April 1965.

Monthly savings plans

Identification would be a nightmare if it was strictly applied to the regular purchase of units in a unit trust or investment trust monthly savings plan. Fortunately, the Revenue accepts a simplified calculation which assumes that you made a single purchase in the seventh month of the trust's accounting year (note, not the tax year) equal to your regular savings in that year plus any re-invested income. You have to elect to use this alternative method and it may only be applied if, in the tax year when you sell units purchased via a monthly savings plan, your total gains exceed the annual exemption or your total *disposals* either exceed twice the annual exemption or result in capital losses.

8.6.5 Business considerations

If you are in business, and decide to dispose of your business or your business-related assets when you retire, then you face a liability to capital gains tax. The two aspects of capital gains tax legislation that affect you are retirement relief and roll-over relief.

8.6.6 Retirement relief

Retirement relief is not a deferral, by roll-over or hold-over, of a charge to tax; it is a permanent relief from tax. The relief is given when, on or before the date of disposal (or, if earlier, the date of cessation of your trade), you are aged 50 or over, or are retiring early on ill-health grounds, and make a disposal of business assets. This is also a disposal of your interest in the assets of a partnership carrying on business; at any time when a business is carried on by a partnership, the business is treated as owned by each individual who is at that time a member of the partnership. You can also claim relief on the disposal of shares in your 'personal' trading company, and on assets that you own but which are used for the purposes of a business carried on by a partnership of which you are a member, or by your 'personal' trading company. In addition, directors, employees and trustees qualify for retirement relief on making a 'relevant disposal' of assets held for the purposes of an office or employment.

For 1998–99, full retirement relief was an exemption for the first £250,000 gain plus relief of 50 per cent of the next £750,000 of gain. With the introduction of taper relief, retirement relief is being phased out over the period from 1999–2000 to 2002–03 so that, in relation to qualifying disposals in a tax year of assessment specified in the first column of Table 8.2, it is as if:

(1) for the references to £250,000 there were substituted references to the amount specified in the second column; and

(2) for the reference to £1,000,000 there were substituted a reference to the amount specified in the third column.

This relief is reduced if the 'qualifying period' is less than ten years or there is non-business use of the asset.

Table 8.2 – Progressive reduction of thresholds during phasing out

Year	100% (£)	50% (£)
1998–99	250,000	1,000,000
1999–2000	200,000	800,000
2000–01	150,000	600,000
2001–02	100,000	400,000
2002–03	50,000	200,000

Except where the relief is claimed on ill-health grounds, the relief is mandatory. That is, it is given without a claim and cannot be disclaimed. This has important consequences in relation to the interaction between this and other reliefs.

It is not normally necessary for you to actually retire in order to claim retirement relief. You can obtain retirement relief on the sale of the goodwill of your business even though you continue as a partner or an employee of the business. You can also set up another business or be employed full-time elsewhere.

Retirement relief is given for each individual who makes a disposal. Husband and wife can each claim the full relief. This can effectively double the relief where the business is jointly owned by husband and wife.

Retirement relief can be available on the proceeds of a liquidation or a distribution made from a company about to be struck off.

Within that apparently simple rule, there is plenty of scope for debate with the Inland Revenue on whether you are selling the business itself (in which case retirement relief is available) or selling assets used in the business (in which case retirement relief is not available). There have, for example, been cases with farmers where the farmer has disposed of part of his land; the Revenue has held that the land is not the business itself but an asset used in the business and retirement relief has been disallowed.

8.6.7 Roll-over relief

In general terms, roll-over relief is available where a person sells an asset which is used by him in a trade and re-invests the proceeds in replacement assets for the same trade. Any gain made is not taxed, but is deducted from the acquisition cost of the replacement asset (ie the future capital gain on the replacement asset now incorporates the gain made on the old asset). This aggregation of capital gains tax to some time in the future is called 'roll-over relief'.

If, as a sole trader or partner, you are selling your business, you may invest the proceeds in a new or existing business and defer any liability to capital gains tax on the original sale. A potentially attractive way in which this might be done is to invest in property bought for the purpose of furnished holiday lettings (see 6.6.3). Under these circumstances, you are regarded as having acquired an asset for the purposes of a trade and roll-over relief may be available.

Re-investment relief

The principle of relief for capital gains tax was further extended in the November 1993 Budget to apply to all individuals who would like to defer a capital gains tax bill. Provided the gain is re-invested into an unquoted trading company that fulfils certain conditions, and provided that you do not emigrate within three years of buying the shares, you can defer the original capital gains tax bill almost indefinitely. You have up to three years after the sale of the asset in which to make the re-investment; you may also claim for an investment that was made up to 12 months before the sale.

However, the fact that the re-investment has to be in an unquoted company makes it a more risky use of funds.

8.7 TAX SAVING AREAS

One of the most frequently quoted rules of investment is never to do something just because it saves tax. Your actions should be based primarily on the merits of the investment in question; tax considerations should be secondary. Nevertheless, within some of the principal areas of investment, the opportunity exists for tax benefits as well and you should take full advantage of these.

The principal guidelines on tax saving are:

(1) Make sure you claim all the tax allowances and reliefs you are eligible for and make sure that the calculations of your tax liability are correct.
(2) Make sure you use the exemptions to which you are entitled.
(3) If you are a married couple, make full use of independent taxation in order to minimise your tax bills, but do bear in mind the following:
   (a) Any transfers must be seen as once-and-for-all gifts with no strings attached. It may even be beneficial to set up separate bank accounts.
   (b) If you are approaching retirement, do bear in mind that your tax position may change, so try not to do anything now that might work against you in the future.
   (c) If you are in your 60s, don't do anything that might jeopardise a claim for age-related higher personal allowances if your income is marginal.
   (d) If a jointly owned income-producing asset is not owned in equal shares, consider applying for the interest to be paid (and therefore taxed) in the correct proportions.
(4) If you hold asset-backed investments, consider investing as much as you can in personal equity plans (see 6.5.6).

(5) Higher rate taxpayers who have used up their ISA allowance might also consider transferring some or part of their investment to single premium bonds.
(6) Assess future income and tax bills when you come to take your pension. If you do not need all the income from your pension now, and if you have the option of deferring all or some of the benefits, you will not be paying tax on 'unwanted' income and your deferred benefits continue to get the benefit of potential growth in a tax-free fund.

9

INHERITANCE TAX

This chapter explains what this tax is, what you can do to limit its impact and how you can best prepare for the often inevitable bill. It explains a tax which has been described as 'a voluntary levy paid by those who distrust their heirs more than they dislike the Inland Revenue' and covers the following topics:

(1) Introduction
(2) A tax on property
(3) The scope of inheritance tax
(4) Tax planning
(5) Life assurance in the mitigation of IHT
(6) Making gifts
(7) The main exemptions
(8) Inheritance tax and businesses
(9) Pension plans and IHT.

One point worth noting is that the Labour Government is very likely to change the existing IHT-avoidance rules to increase the Treasury's catch.

9.1 INTRODUCTION

Inheritance tax was introduced in the Finance Act 1986. It replaced capital transfer tax, which had itself replaced estate duty in 1975. One of the dangers with inheritance tax lies in its very name. The majority of people probably do not regard themselves as wealthy and tend to ignore the things which are associated with 'inheritances' and 'estates'. However, even fairly modest estates can attract the attention of the Inland Revenue because inheritance tax starts to bite at the relatively low level of £231,000 for the 1999–2000 tax year. As a result, for example, of increasing house prices a significant number of older people have built up a potential liability to inheritance tax without realising it and their children may have to pay the bill.

Inheritance tax can be reduced by prudent and sensible planning. Indeed, the Inland Revenue relies on our failure to make sound plans. Without some straightforward sensible planning, it is quite possible that a good proportion of your lifetime efforts may go to the state rather than to your heirs. Of inheritance tax, above all other taxes, it can be truly said that the Revenue is the beneficiary of our inertia.

9.2 A TAX ON PROPERTY

Inheritance tax is a tax on property. The tax liability does not arise merely as a result of the ownership of property (because that would be a wealth tax); the tax liability arises when the property passes from one person to another, ie when you give ownership of the property to somebody else when you are alive or when you die.

'Property' means all your personal possessions of all types. As far as the majority of people who have their permanent homes in the United Kingdom are concerned, it also includes any property situated outside the United Kingdom such as overseas property and overseas bank accounts.

For the purposes of inheritance tax, property can either pass during your lifetime or on your death. During your lifetime, it may pass by gift; on death, it is considered to pass automatically because, being dead, you cannot retain ownership of that property. The ownership must, therefore, pass to someone else. In both cases, inheritance tax is potentially chargeable on this movement of property from you to someone else.

The taxation of lifetime gifts comes as a surprise to many people. They find it hard to believe that, having worked hard and saved money, they do not have total discretion in how they dispose of it while they are alive. The reality is that if you spend it on yourself in a never-to-be-repeated spree in a gambling casino, the Inland Revenue will not bat an eyelid. If you give it to your children and set them loose in a casino, the Revenue may demand its share too.

Overseas assets

If you are domiciled in the United Kingdom, inheritance tax is charged on all your property no matter where in the world it is situated. That does not, of course, mean that you will not also have an inheritance tax liability (or similar liability) in the country where you have assets situated. In some cases, there exist 'double taxation treaties' between the United Kingdom and other countries so this problem is avoided. However, it pays to check and, if necessary, to make arrangements in the country where you have assets. That could mean having a foreign will as well as a UK will. All these matters are covered in more detail in Chapter 12.

9.3 THE SCOPE OF INHERITANCE TAX

'Estate' is simply the legal label that is given to the sum total of everything that you own when you die. It includes your house, your car, your possessions, your bank account, your cash, your stocks and shares, investments and so on. If you have a life assurance policy on your own life then, when you die, the proceeds also fall into your estate.

If you have any outstanding debts (eg a mortgage) then the total of these is deducted from your gross estate to give your net estate. The more common deductions are as follows:

(1) Funeral expenses
(2) Most debts
(3) Legal and professional fees owing at the date of death
(4) Liabilities for income tax and capital gains tax up to the time of death.

It is your net estate which is potentially liable to inheritance tax. Everything that you leave to your heirs over and above the first £231,000 (for 1999–2000) is likely to be taxed. The following example shows how inheritance tax works and is referred to throughout the chapter.

Example – Total net estate

A man's total list of assets is as follows:

House	£215,000
House contents	£42,000
Car	£18,000
Term assurance policy	£18,000
2 weeks' timeshare	£12,000
Savings and investments	£5,000
Mortgage protection policy	£20,000
Bank account/building society	£5,000
Total gross estate	£335,000
Less mortgage	£20,000
Total net estate	£315,000

If he dies he will leave a gross estate of £335,000. The mortgage protection policy would be used to pay off his mortgage, leaving a net estate of £315,000. He therefore 'owns' £315,000 net – but probably regards himself as 'worth' only £10,000 (his bank accounts and savings). After all he cannot spend the house and contents, and the life policy is only there when he is not.

9.3.1 How inheritance tax is calculated

Inheritance tax is currently charged in two bands. The first band, currently (for 1999–2000) £231,000, is charged at the 'nil rate' and no inheritance tax is payable. Everything in excess of that band is chargeable to inheritance tax at a rate of 40 per cent. What that means is that if your net estate totals £331,000 there is a potential liability of 40 per cent of £100,000 (£331,000 less £231,000), ie £40,000. That normally has to be paid, in cash, to the Inland Revenue within six months of death, with an added complication being that (assuming for the moment that the man has no surviving wife) the beneficiaries cannot get access to any of the assets until the tax has been paid.

In the above example, on the assumption that money has been borrowed to pay the inheritance tax bill, the beneficiaries can eventually get access to the savings (of £10,000) and the proceeds of the term policy (£18,000). The beneficiaries are £12,000 short and this has either to come out of their own resources or through selling some of the assets they have been left.

For inheritance tax purposes, your assets are normally valued at their open market value at the date of death. By and large, the Inland Revenue is sympathetic to fluctuating values, particularly where quoted securities are sold for less than their 'date of death' value within 12 months of death. In such cases the people liable to pay the inheritance tax may be able to claim that the sale price should be substituted for the 'date of death' value. If, however, these same people have sold the investments and then reinvested the proceeds, this relief may be lost.

The position on land is rather more complex but, basically, if the person paying the tax on certain land sells it within four years of death for less than its value at the date of death, the sale proceeds can often be substituted in place of the higher value.

9.3.2 Reducing the burden

There are a number of ways in which you can reduce the burden of inheritance tax but they do need to be carefully planned. However, before looking at some of these methods in more detail, there are two important points to make:

(1) The tax on your estate is determined by the law at the time of your death – not the law now. The first important consideration, therefore, in all planning for inheritance tax is to keep your plans flexible. The rules almost certainly change from time to time so you must avoid taking irrevocable actions that are not strictly necessary.

(2) You should be realistic with your plans, and not put tax saving as a

> prime requirement. For example, one possible way to avoid inheritance tax is to dispose of all your capital, but that is hardly a wise thing to do. The prime requirement is to have sufficient resources to live on right up to the date of your death. Inheritance tax planning means doing that – and at the same time trying to ensure that the balance of the proceeds of your life's work pass largely to your family and not to the Inland Revenue.

The next three sections (tax planning, life assurance and making gifts) look in rather more detail at three basic ways either to reduce the amount of inheritance tax that has to be paid on your estate or to provide for the unavoidable inheritance tax bill when you have done everything possible to reduce the amount. There is nothing particularly difficult about any of them and they might have quite a dramatic impact on the way your beneficiaries might remember you.

Once again, it is important to emphasise the need to keep all plans as simple and as flexible as possible. In this way, it may be easier to change them. Although the broad basis of inheritance tax planning has remained unchanged for a number of years now, the Labour Government is likely to make some major changes over the next few years.

9.4 TAX PLANNING

This section covers three of the most straightforward ways of ensuring that the potential inheritance tax bill is kept as low as possible. It also covers a specific form of planning called the will trust plan and looks at situations where planning might not always be to the beneficiaries' advantage. The areas covered are:

(1) Writing a will
(2) Dividing up assets
(3) Writing life assurance policies in trust
(4) The will trust plan
(5) Refusing a legacy.

9.4.1 Writing a will

One of the most important exemptions in the inheritance tax rules is that nothing left to your spouse attracts any liability to inheritance tax at all. If the husband dies first, and leaves his entire estate to his wife, then no inheritance tax is payable. (When, subsequently, the wife dies and leaves the estate to the children, that is when the inheritance tax burden would arise.)

This point is often misunderstood. It is often believed that, because there is no inheritance tax to pay, this therefore means that the entire estate automatically passes to the wife or husband. In reality, it is the other way round. Provided you *guarantee* that everything is left to your wife, then there is no inheritance tax to pay on your death. The only way that a husband can guarantee that everything passes to his wife, and vice versa, is to make a will.

The background

Wills are covered in much more detail in Chapter 10. What follows is a limited description to put wills into context as part of inheritance tax planning.

A will is essentially a very simple and straightforward statement of exactly what you wish to happen to your property when you die. If you die without leaving a will (known as dying 'intestate') it may be that certain of your intended beneficiaries are unable to make a legal claim for any part of your estate, no matter how deserving they may be and no matter what promises you may have made them.

The intestacy rules

Your principal beneficiaries (ie usually your wife and other immediate family) may be protected to some extent because the law provides for your estate to be broken up amongst your family according to the 'intestacy rules'. These rules do not cater for individual needs and requirements and they are not concerned with how you may feel about your family, or how your wife may feel about her in-laws.

The intestacy rules have certain minimum levels so that a small estate (ie up to £125,000 plus personal belongings) passes directly to the spouse. In all other cases, the first to die only inherits everything in certain circumstances. If, for example, a man has not made a will, his wife is guaranteed to inherit everything only if *all* the following conditions are fulfilled:

(1) The couple have no children
(2) The husband's parents are both dead
(3) He has no surviving brothers, sisters, nephews or nieces.

The rules in Scotland are different – and they are likely to work rather more in favour of your close family if you do not make a will. Nevertheless, the basic principle is the same – it is always better if you leave clear, legally enforceable instructions about what you want to happen, ie a will.

Tax planning through wills

As well as ensuring that your property is distributed in the way that you wish, writing a will can often be very effective in inheritance tax planning. Everything you leave to your spouse is free of inheritance tax but you also have the 'nil-rate' band (£231,000 for 1999–2000) which allows property up to that value to be distributed to anybody else without attracting any liability to inheritance tax.

Suppose in the example in 9.3.1 that the man is in fact married. By leaving everything to his wife, her potential estate is increased (which could mean a higher inheritance tax bill when she dies) and a valuable opportunity to reduce her potential estate has been lost. However, the man and his wife might, for example, decide that she will not have any real use for the timeshare if he dies first. By making this a specific gift to their children in his will, there is an immediate potential inheritance tax saving of £4,800 if he is the first to die. The reason is that the estate passing on to the wife is reduced by £12,000 so that, on current figures, the eventual inheritance tax saving when she leaves her estate to her children will be £4,800 (ie, £12,000 × 40 per cent) lower than would otherwise have been the case.

Drawing up a will is a vital part of everybody's financial planning. It ensures that your property is distributed in the way you would wish and can incorporate real inheritance tax efficiency. Not writing a will could result in your property being divided up in a way which you would not wish and at the same time create a tax liability for your beneficiaries which they certainly will not want.

9.4.2 Dividing up assets

Although throughout this book we have concentrated on 'he' and 'him' for simplicity, the statistics confirm quite starkly that there are considerably more widows than widowers. Consequently, most inheritance planning tends to assume that the husband will be the first to die. However, it is dangerous to make this assumption. The wife may die first, but be unable to take advantage of the inheritance tax 'nil-rate' rules if she does not own any property. She would be unable to leave anything to her children, who would face a potentially larger inheritance tax bill when the husband dies.

It can therefore make inheritance tax planning sense for husband and wife to divide their assets between them so as to 'equalise', at least in part, their estates. They are both then able to write their wills in a similar way and to make separate bequests with a view to the potential inheritance tax savings. This is in addition to any tax savings they might make under independent taxation (see 8.5).

9.4.3 Writing life assurance policies in trust

Another way of reducing the inheritance tax burden is through a declaration of trust – and this is particularly relevant to life assurance policies. Many policies are arranged on an 'own life, own benefit' basis which means that the proceeds become part of the policyholder's estate when he dies. His beneficiaries may need this cash to pay the inheritance tax liability but the position is complicated by the fact that the cash itself adds to the inheritance tax problem. If the policyholder's estate, including the policy proceeds, is over £231,000 for 1999–2000, 40 per cent of the policy proceeds end up with the Inland Revenue.

It is possible, however, to have the policy written under a declaration of trust so as to nominate the beneficiaries in advance. If you were to make a stipulation that the proceeds of your life policy were to be paid to beneficiaries (ie it now becomes their property and not yours), the proceeds fall outside your estate and therefore do not attract inheritance tax.

Suppose in the example in 9.3.1, the man and his wife decide that she will have enough to live on after his death without depending on the proceeds of the term assurance policy. He therefore decides to complete a simple declaration of trust – and he makes the children the beneficiaries. When he dies, the proceeds of the policy (£18,000) do not become her property, meaning that the eventual inheritance tax liability on her death is reduced by £7,200.

Writing policies in trust is a very common way of avoiding inheritance tax on the proceeds and many life assurance companies have standard forms drawn up for you to use, often at no charge. Although it is usual to place the policy in trust when it is first taken out, there is nothing to prevent you placing an existing policy in trust (but see 9.7.3).

In the original example in 9.3.1, the beneficiaries were short of £12,000 on an inheritance tax bill of £40,000. By the simple expedient of making a specific bequest in a will (of the timeshare) and asking for an existing life assurance policy to be placed in trust (something that most life companies arrange at no charge), that £12,000 liability has been completely removed.

Many of these aspects of planning are merely devices to rearrange your affairs in the most tax efficient way. In the main, they merely require letters and forms to be filled in. You then make a clear expression of what you wish to happen – and that is what will happen.

9.4.4 The will trust plan

Single premium bonds also offer the opportunity for a specific type of inheritance tax planning. Most married couples leave their total assets to each other on their death. There is no inheritance tax liability at this time but the nil rate band exemption is lost. However, many people may be unwilling to make use of the exemption, either in whole or in part, because of the loss of the assets, and the income from them, to the survivor.

A particular arrangement of single premium bonds can overcome this problem in a comparatively simple way, as follows:

(1) You and your wife each take out a single premium bond of up to the 'nil rate' band limit (£231,000 for 1999–2000). You will both be the joint lives assured on each bond but, individually, you will be the sole owners of your respective bonds.
(2) You each amend your wills so that the first to die leaves their bond to their heirs under the terms of a simple will trust (see 11.1.3).
(3) On the first death, the relevant bond passes into the will trust. As it is within the nil rate band, no inheritance tax is payable.
(4) If the survivor needs to supplement his or her income, they make requests to the trustees (of whom they will be one) for loans from the trust. Such loans, if granted, will be a debt against their estate so reducing the eventual inheritance tax liability when they die.

Under this arrangement, your bonds remain your property to do with exactly as you wish while you are alive; the relevant bonds only become subject to the terms of the trust on the first death.

Single premium bonds are particularly suitable for this kind of arrangement because the fact that they do not distribute income in the form of dividends makes them simple to administer. Also, because they are essentially life assurance products, the trust may be protected. It is often the case that, on the death of the survivor, the value of the residual bonds (less, of course, any units that have been withdrawn to make loans) are never less than the original investment, regardless of prevailing investment conditions.

9.4.5 Refusing a legacy

Just as there are good tax reasons for writing a will, it always pre-supposes, to some extent, that you fully understand the financial position of your beneficiaries. However, it is not unusual for them to prefer that you had left your property, or that you had even drafted your will, in a different way. There are two ways in which the position can be remedied by beneficiaries. They can either disclaim the legacy or arrange for a 'deed of variation' to be drawn up. Both are equally effective in tax planning after the event, ie they do not have an adverse effect on the inheritance tax position and are often undertaken to improve it.

Disclaimer

If you have become entitled to property under the terms of a will, you may disclaim the entitlement particularly if somebody else would benefit as a result of your disclaimer (eg your children). You may also disclaim an entitlement under the intestacy provisions. A disclaimer means that you give up your entitlement; it does not mean that you can re-direct your entitlement to a specific person.

Such a disclaimer is normally effective for tax purposes provided:

(1) you receive no payment for giving up your entitlement; and
(2) you have not already received your legacy either expressly (ie you have started to enjoy the benefit) or by implication (which could occur if you delayed in making your disclaimer).

You should always seek legal advice before making a disclaimer.

Deed of variation

These (sometimes called 'deeds of family arrangement') differ from disclaimers in that, through a deed of variation, you can re-direct the property to a specific person.

The deed must be executed within two years of the death and an election must be filed within six months. In effect, the parties to the deed re-write the dead person's will, and the property is distributed as though the requirements of the deed were the will.

Certain conditions need to be satisfied and you should consult a solicitor:

(1) The deed must be in writing and must specifically refer to the provisions of the will which are to be varied.
(2) It must be signed by everybody who would have benefited under the original will.
(3) Only one deed can ever be effective about a specific piece of property as far as inheritance tax is concerned, so it is important to get the wording right. There could be more than one deed of variation if each one refers to a different item of property in the will.
(4) There must be no payment to a beneficiary as an inducement to enter into a deed of variation.

A deed of variation does not have any untoward implications for the beneficiaries as far as inheritance tax and capital gains tax are concerned. However, the income tax position is not so favourable; all the original beneficiaries are liable for tax on any income that arises from assets in the will up to the time the deed is executed. Also, anybody giving up an entitlement in this way is regarded as a settlor for income tax purposes (see 11.9).

The position in Scotland

Scottish law provides that a person must leave a set part of his estate to his children; their entitlement is called *legitim* (see 10.7.2). If the will does not take account of this, the children can have it set aside. In practice, children often decide to renounce their right to *legitim* particularly where this would result in a larger bequest to the widow. This renunciation does not form a chargeable transfer and the property is treated as passing to the widow under the terms of the will.

There can be potential problems if the children are minors, as children under the age of 18 do not have the legal capacity to renounce their entitlement. Any action taken on their behalf by the executors could have inheritance tax implications when the children reach the age of 18.

9.5 LIFE ASSURANCE IN THE MITIGATION OF IHT

The problem for the executors

Although a certain amount of reorganising of our estates can prevent unnecessary inheritance tax liabilities falling on our children there is a limit to what can be done in this way. The most important requirement for many of us is to ensure that we have enough to live on until the date of our death – and this could mean retaining assets because they produce an income for us. Therefore, we still own some property and there could well be an inheritance tax liability on the death of the surviving spouse that is quite unavoidable.

For the beneficiaries, the first problem they may face is that inheritance tax is payable at the time the executors apply for a grant of probate (see 10.8.1). However, although the estate has a certain amount of cash and liquid assets, the executors cannot get their hands on them until they have obtained the grant of probate. This is a classic case of 'Catch 22'; no grant until the tax has been paid, no money to pay the tax until the grant has been obtained.

The problem might not be quite as bad as it seems because inheritance tax can be paid in instalments but only on certain assets, principally land and buildings, controlling shares in companies and certain other business assets. Rather than having to raise cash through a forced sale, it is possible to pay the inheritance tax by annual instalments over a period of ten years. Under certain circumstances, instalments are free of interest, provided they are paid on time. Similar rules also apply to agricultural property.

The need for cash

However, it is inevitable that some tax will still have to be paid before all the assets are released. The beneficiaries may also have the problem that the total value of the liquid assets could well be lower than the inheritance tax bill. One way or another, if they want to settle the tax bill in total and avoid having to pay interest, they are going to be short of funds. They have three obvious choices:

(1) They may have cash of their own available and be prepared to pay that to the Revenue.
(2) They may be prepared to borrow the money.
(3) They may not have the cash available and may have to sell some of the assets to raise the proceeds. However, it has to be borne in mind that the bill may have to be settled quite quickly and realising assets may take time.

There is, however, a fourth option and that is through a life assurance policy.

The use of life assurance

Life assurance is designed to provide a predictable sum of money at a totally unpredictable time in the future. It is relatively straightforward to look at today's position and estimate the potential liability to inheritance tax and then to take out a life assurance policy to cover it. The principal requirement is for a flexible policy. The tax rules can be guaranteed to change from time to time (as will your personal circumstances) and you will need a policy that is flexible enough to adapt to such changes.

For most married couples, the solution is to take out a 'joint life second death' policy. The policy is written in trust which means that when the second person dies, the proceeds are payable to the beneficiaries and so fall outside the estate. In this way, preparing for a potential inheritance tax problem can be arranged by your life assurance company. Writing a policy in trust can usually be arranged at no extra charge to yourself at all.

However, you may take the view that this life assurance policy is too expensive. You will have to pay the regular contributions out of income and you may well regard this as a high price to pay in order to protect your children. Your children may see things differently and, for them, a more attractive alternative might be for you to start using some of your capital (ie their potential inheritance) in a way which will protect the bulk of it.

Suppose in the example in 9.3 that the couple have not done any planning and have written their wills so that the entire estate passes to the survivor and is retained by the survivor until the second death. That means that there is a potential tax liability on a total net estate of £315,000, ie a potential tax bill of (£315,000 – £231,000) = £33,600. That is 10.67 per cent of the capital and is also the required 'sum assured' currently required for the joint life second death policy.

If the man is in his late 50s and his wife is four or five years younger, the annual premium for such a policy is about £400, ie about 1 per cent of the potential tax bill. On that basis they would have to live for about 100 years to make paying the premiums a less attractive proposition than paying the inheritance tax.

Using capital to preserve capital is one of the most important and most popular ways for families to prepare for a potential inheritance tax liability.

Of course, what you are doing is paying contributions to a life assurance policy where your children will eventually benefit. Consequently, the regular contributions are regarded as a gift. Gifts are the third way in which the burden of inheritance tax can be reduced and these are covered in the next section.

9.6 MAKING GIFTS

The main impact of inheritance tax is felt by our beneficiaries when we die, measured as a percentage of our wealth that we leave behind us. One possible way of avoiding inheritance tax altogether, therefore, is to reduce our wealth by giving our property away while we are alive. Within reason, the Inland Revenue is prepared to go along with this, although you can expect the Revenue to take a keen interest in any large gifts that you make while you are alive.

Of course, there has to be a realistic approach to all of this. To check every single gift would be quite impractical (and unreasonable) and there is a range of exemptions that mean that many gifts fall outside the net. However, even the smaller gifts do have to be watched and planned for, and the next sections cover some of the ways in which you can reduce your inheritance tax burden through your own generosity.

First, though, there are two key aspects to avoiding inheritance tax through gifts:

(1) Gifts with reservation of benefit
(2) Potentially exempt transfers.

9.6.1 Gifts with reservation of benefit

Any gift must be a real gift if it is to avoid inheritance tax; it must be 'absolutely irrevocable'. You cannot put strings on it so that you can ask for it back. For example, if you feel so generous that you are prepared to give away the family home to your children, you might think it sensible to make an arrangement under which your children will let you continue to live there rent free.

Unfortunately, for inheritance tax purposes, this is the equivalent of 'having your cake and eating it'. The technical term labels it as a 'gift with reservation'. You have retained the right to live in the house (ie you have reserved a benefit) which means that you have not really given the house away at all. As far as the Revenue is concerned, it means that the property still belongs to you for inheritance tax purposes and it is included in your estate when you die.

The Revenue can be expected to take an interest in any substantial gifts that you make where there is any possibility of your retaining some kind of benefit. If you give shares to your beneficiaries, but retain the right to receive the income from them, that is a 'gift with reservation' and the shares are included in your estate for inheritance tax purposes.

In order to avoid any problems with gifts, you must make it clear you receive no benefit whatsoever as a result of your generosity; it must be a gift, pure and simple, with no strings attached. Nevertheless, there are some complex ways in which you can continue to receive some kind of benefit but these are for specific situations and beyond the scope of this book.

9.6.2 Potentially exempt transfers

If you suddenly receive grim news about your future life expectancy, you could well have left it too late to do anything much about inheritance tax planning. Although you might have a sudden fit of generosity and decide to reduce your estate in an attempt to reduce the inheritance tax burden, you may not succeed. Timing is all important.

There is one all embracing rule: if death occurs within seven years of making a gift, then all or a proportion of the inheritance tax is payable as though the gift had been included in the estate on death.

'Tapering relief'

If death occurs within three years of making a gift then inheritance tax will not have been avoided at all; the tax is charged at the full rate as though the value of the gift had been included in the estate on death. Provided the donor survives for seven years, the inheritance tax falls away completely. If he dies at any time between the third and seventh years after the gift, then a proportion of the inheritance tax is payable. This gradual reduction of the future tax bill is called 'tapering relief'.

An important point here is that, although the rate of inheritance tax applied to the gift is that applying at the date of death, the value of the gift is the value at the date it was given. Any increase in value belongs to the new owner and is not included in any tax calculations if the donor is unfortunate enough to die within seven years. This can make the gifting of certain types of investment an effective 'hedge' against inheritance tax.

Because of this seven-year rule, a gift which does not benefit from one of the exemptions (see below) carries the potential for an inheritance tax liability within seven years of the gift being made. Consequently, from the Revenue's point of view, the gift is never totally exempt from inheritance tax until seven years have lapsed. The technical term for such a gift, therefore, is a 'potentially exempt transfer' (PET for short) and there are essentially three principal types of gifts covered by this term:

(1) Direct gifts to an individual.
(2) Gifts to what are called 'interest in possession' trusts (which are defined as trusts under which an individual has the right either to the use and enjoyment of the trust assets or to any income from them (see 11.3.1)).
(3) Gifts to what are called 'accumulation and maintenance' trusts (certain kinds of trust which are set up for the benefit of your children or grandchildren, or for the future welfare of a disabled person (see 11.3.5)).

There are other forms of gift which are termed 'chargeable transfers' and these gifts may incur a liability to inheritance tax at the time they are made. Inheritance tax is charged at the time at half the rate payable on death; if death occurs within seven years of the transfer, then further tax may be payable subject to 'tapering relief'.

With considerable aplomb, the legislation defines a chargeable transfer as anything which is not a non-chargeable transfer (ie not a PET or a transfer covered by one of the exemptions).

9.7 THE MAIN EXEMPTIONS

There is a range of exemptions which means that, for most day-to-day gifts, there is not necessarily a tax liability. These are as follows:

(1) Annual exemption
(2) Small gifts exemption

(3) Normal expenditure exemption
(4) Gifts on marriage
(5) Other exemptions.

9.7.1 Annual exemption

You may give away up to £3,000 in any one tax year. That applies equally to husband and wife who could between them give away up to £6,000 to their children without having to face any tax liability at all.

It is also possible to use up any unused amounts from the previous tax year, provided:

(1) it is given away in the current tax year, and
(2) you use up the full exemption for the *current* year first.

Suppose, for example, you have £1,500 left over from the previous tax year. Provided you give away at least £3,000 (ie the current year's exemption), you can make further gifts out of the held-over allowance (ie up to a maximum of an additional £1,500). If you do not give away as much as £3,000, the whole of the held-over amount of £1,500 will be lost as it is not possible to hold it over into a subsequent tax year. If you give away less than £4,500, the balance of the held-over amount is lost.

9.7.2 Small gifts exemption

You can give away as many small gifts as you like to as many people as you like, provided the total value of the gifts to any one individual does not exceed £250. If you have a thousand friends, you could give away £250,000 a year without the Inland Revenue asking you any questions about inheritance tax (though you might be asked where you got the money from in the first place).

9.7.3 Normal expenditure exemption

Many of us give money away on a regular basis. It comes out of our 'after-tax income' and has no overall impact on our normal standard of living. We regard this as 'normal expenditure' – and so does the Revenue – and there is no liability to inheritance tax.

A good example of this is the life assurance premiums paid on a joint life second death policy – the policy written in trust to provide funds to meet your beneficiaries' inheritance tax liability (see 9.5). Because the policy is in trust, the regular contributions are technically a gift. However, because of their regularity and their relatively small size, they generally qualify as 'normal expenditure'.

If they are more substantial and mean you have to draw on capital to provide the contributions then they probably fall within the £3,000 limit. Either way, there is rarely going to be any liability to inheritance tax on the payments themselves.

Existing life assurance placed in trust

However, if you place an existing policy in trust, then you could be making a more substantial transfer. The gift's value is the greater of the gross premiums paid to date or the market value of the policy (which usually means its surrender value). If this value exceeds the exemptions then it is treated as a PET.

9.7.4 Gifts on marriage

If one of your children marries, both husband and wife may each give the child up to £5,000 without incurring any liability to inheritance tax. If one of your grandchildren or great-grandchildren marries you may give them £2,500. If the person getting married is any other kind of relative, or even just a friend, you may give them up to £1,000 without any complications of inheritance tax to think about. However, these gifts are more correctly called 'gifts in consideration of marriage'; they should therefore be made *before* the marriage and should be conditional on the marriage taking place.

For the vast majority of us, therefore, all these exemptions provide a way of giving quite substantial gifts without falling foul of the inheritance tax rules.

It might be the case that the most substantial gift any of us wishes to make is to our children in the event of their marriage. The rules allow the parents of the bride or groom to make gifts of up to £22,000 without any need at all to be concerned about inheritance tax. All it needs is a little bit of careful planning and full use of all the exemptions that are available:

	£
Last year's annual exemption – £3,000 each	6,000
This year's exemption – £3,000 each	6,000
Marriage allowance – £5,000 each	10,000
	22,000

The grandparents could also make gifts so that further marriage allowances of £2,500 each are available. On top of this there could be gifts of £2,500 by each great grandparent and £1,000 each by family friends.

However, despite the fact that these exemptions are there to be used, it is prudent to keep records of exactly how you have calculated the gift in order to avoid any potential problems for you or your beneficiaries.

9.7.5 Other exemptions

In order not to discourage the spirit of giving, successive Governments have ruled that gifts, for example, to charities, for national purposes (eg the National Trust, universities and libraries) and of property for the national benefit are, to all intents and purposes, exempt from inheritance tax.

There is also a certain grim irony in the fact that gifts to the main political parties are also exempt.

9.8 INHERITANCE TAX AND BUSINESSES

Successive Governments have recognised that building up a business can be less than rewarding if its value is to be taxed at high rates when you die. Because of this, what is termed 'relevant business property' qualifies for business property relief, provided that you have owned it for at least two years.

The rules are complex but in broad terms 'relevant business property' includes shares in the business and land, buildings, plant and machinery used for business purposes. The effect of the relief is to reduce the value of that particular property for inheritance tax purposes by 100 per cent or 50 per cent, depending on the type of property being transferred.

For example, if you are a sole proprietor and the business is transferred during your lifetime then it may be regarded as a potentially exempt transfer and business property relief (at 100 per cent) will be available if you die within seven years. However, this relief may be lost if the person to whom you give the property disposes of it before your death unless the proceeds are reinvested in qualifying business property within three years of the sale.

Agricultural property is treated in a similar way. Provided you have occupied the property for agricultural purposes for at least two years (or owned it for seven years with others farming it) at the time of transferring it, then agricultural property relief may be available. If the person making the gift has the right to vacant possession, the relief is 100 per cent. If the person making the gift does not have the right to vacant possession (eg because it is let) then the relief is 50 per cent.

For gifts made within seven years of death, there are rules similar to those for business property.

There are slightly different rules for woodlands. If you have owned woodlands for at least five years or acquired them by gift or inheritance, there is not necessarily an inheritance tax liability on your death. If, however, the recipient sells or gives away the timber, tax is charged on the proceeds or value of the gift. The relief applies only to the standing timber and not the land on which it grows (but the land may qualify for business property relief).

9.9 PENSION PLANS AND IHT

For inheritance tax purposes, the largest single element in a pension plan is the death benefit. Although it is not possible to assign the *pension* benefits as such, it is possible to assign the *death* benefits under a retirement annuity or personal pension plan. There are no adverse inheritance tax implications provided that the death benefit is paid out to the nominated beneficiaries within two years of death.

The same is true of the death benefits paid out by the trustees from an occupational scheme.

10

MAKING A WILL

It is estimated that fewer than three people in ten make a will. Each year a number of cases come before the courts to unravel the problems caused by someone having died 'intestate'. Even people who have taken the sensible step of making a will may leave behind unforeseen problems; the will may not be valid or may not do what they had intended.

In this chapter, wills are covered under the following headings:

(1) The simplicity of a will
(2) When there is no will
(3) Getting advice
(4) Drawing up a will
(5) The formalities
(6) Reviewing your will
(7) The law in Scotland
(8) Administering the estate
(9) The enduring power of attorney
(10) Living wills.

One reason for writing a will is that it can play an important part in tax planning, particularly in relation to inheritance tax (see 9.4.1).

10.1 THE SIMPLICITY OF A WILL

In its most basic form, a will is nothing more than an expression of what you want to happen to your property when you die. Wills have no effect whatsoever during a person's lifetime. This means that a will can be revoked or changed at any time up to the time of death. It also means that as the will only takes effect on death, you are not making any form of gift during your lifetime.

Making a will does not restrict what you can do with your property during your lifetime, nor does it mean that you alter your tax position before the date of your death. In this way, a will is very different from a declaration of trust (see 11.1.1) which *is* effective during your lifetime. This can give rise to some confusion as it is also possible to create a trust in your will. However, any trust that is set up by a will only takes effect on death and, until then, can be revoked or altered, just like any other part of the will.

A will ensures that property passes to someone (the executor) who looks after it and distributes it to the people entitled to benefit under the will (the beneficiaries) in accordance with the instructions of the person who drew up the will (the testator). The role of the executor is generally a temporary one, limited to distributing the testator's assets and paying the testator's debts and any tax bills.

Wills can be revoked by deliberately tearing them up and in some cases by marriage or divorce (see 10.6.1). It is also possible to add to or delete part of a will by means of a codicil (see 10.6.8). The important thing to remember is that a will is not necessarily a 'once and for all' decision and should be reviewed on a regular basis.

10.2 WHEN THERE IS NO WILL

Anyone dying intestate has his affairs administered according to a set of rules laid down by law. These intestacy rules are quite arbitrary and make assumptions about what the majority of people would want to happen to their property on their death. The rules take no account whatsoever of personal choice.

The rules depend on how much your estate is worth and the kind of relatives you leave behind; the rules differ for larger estates and depend on whether you leave behind a spouse or children. There are separate rules for Northern Ireland and Scotland.

Their principal impact can be looked at under five headings:

(1) Who looks after the estate?
(2) Who gets what?
(3) Who looks after the children?
(4) Personal bequests
(5) The tax position.

10.2.1 Who looks after the estate?

If someone dies intestate, the law sets out a list of people who can apply to the courts to do the job of administrator (in Scotland the equivalent is called an 'executor-dative').

In order of priority, the list of potential administrators is as follows:

(1) The surviving spouse.
(2) Any child (or grandchild if the parent has died).
(3) The father or mother (just the mother if the deceased was an illegitimate child).
(4) Any brother or sister (or nephew or niece if the parent has died).

The list then goes on to include more distant relatives. Eventually it includes any creditors of the deceased and even the Treasury Solicitor, who can apply if there are no surviving relatives at all. In Scotland the list of potential executors-dative is different (see 10.7.1).

Of course, there is often a surviving spouse who is entitled to apply to become the administrator, but this may not always be desirable. For example, the survivor may be unable to take on the burden of dealing with financial matters so soon after the death. Equally, the surviving spouse might even have been separated from the deceased at the date of death.

Where there is no surviving spouse, disputes may arise about who is to be the administrator. The right to be administrator can be very important, especially if there are shares with voting rights in a family company which forms part of the estate or there is a valuable asset which some beneficiaries wish to sell and others do not. If there is more than one child, all the children can apply but the first to do so can be appointed as administrator ahead of the others. While there are rules to prevent the administrator taking advantage of the position and to prevent unsuitable people being appointed, disputes usually mean escalating legal costs.

On a practical note, until the uncertainty over who is to take charge is resolved, no one can do anything in relation to the deceased's assets. This can cause considerable difficulties if money is needed urgently or an asset is to be sold.

10.2.2 Who gets what?

Perhaps the largest misconception that people have on this subject is about who gets what if there is no will. Many married couples assume that the surviving spouse receives all the family property but this is often not so. The following tables set out the position for deaths after 20 November 1993.

Table 10.1 Intestacy table – England and Wales

MARRIED COUPLE – WITH CHILDREN	
Spouse receives:	All the personal belongings (car, furniture, jewellery, etc.)
	£125,000 absolutely*.
	A 'life interest' (ie the income only) in half the balance, for the rest of her life.
Children receive: (shared equally):	Half the balance when they attain the age of 18 or marry, if earlier.
	The remainder of the estate when spouse dies
MARRIED COUPLE – NO CHILDREN	
Where there is a living parent, brother, sister, nephew or niece:	
Spouse receives:	All the personal belongings.
	£200,000 absolutely.
	Half the balance absolutely.
Relatives receive:	Half the balance to parents but, if no living parent, to brothers and sisters (with nephews and nieces stepping into their parent's shoes if the parent is dead).
Where there is no living parent, brother, sister, nephew or niece:	
Spouse receives:	Everything absolutely.
SINGLE PERSON	
Estate passes to:	Children; but if none:
	Parents; but if none:
	Brothers, sisters (nephews and nieces step into parent's shoes); but if none:
	Grandparents; but if none:
	Uncles and aunts (cousins step into their parent's shoes); but if none:
	The Crown.

*Absolutely = without condition or limitation.

Table 10.2 Intestacy table – Northern Ireland

MARRIED COUPLE – WITH CHILDREN	
Spouse receives:	All the personal belongings (car, furniture, jewellery, etc).
	£125,000 absolutely.
	Half the balance, where there is one child, or one-third of the balance, where there is more than one child.
Children receive: (shared equally)	Half or two-thirds of the balance depending on whether one or more child survives.
MARRIED COUPLE – NO CHILDREN	
Where there is a living parent, brother, sister, nephew or niece	
Spouse receives:	All the personal belongings.
	£200,000 absolutely.
	Half the balance absolutely.
Relatives receive:	Half the balance to parents, but if no living parent to brothers and sisters (with nephews and nieces stepping into their parent's shoes if the parent is dead).
Where there is no living parent, brother, sister, nephew or niece	
Spouse receives:	Everything absolutely.
SINGLE PERSON	
Estate passes to:	Children; but if none:
	Parents; but if none:
	Brothers, sisters (nephews and nieces step into parent's shoes); but if none:
	Next of kin; but if none:
	The Crown.

There are separate rules for England and Wales and for Northern Ireland; the position in Scotland is dealt with later (see 10.7). Which rules apply depends upon the person's domicile (see 12.3.2) at the date of death.

The intestacy rules represent different attempts at an 'average' which is suitable for the majority of cases. The rules are updated periodically, the last changes having been made in England and Wales in 1993 (the time before that was 1987). The changes are normally to the monetary limits rather than the basic principles. In England and Wales, these principles have remained largely unchanged since 1925 (although a fundamental review did take place in Scotland as recently as 1964). The rules do not take account, for example, of any tax advantages that can be achieved by writing a will in a particular way, nor indeed do they reflect the social changes that have occurred in recent years. For example, it is much more common nowadays to leave property to a widow outright than it was in 1925.

10.2.3 Example – Intestacy rules

A has died, leaving behind his widow, B and two teenage children, a daughter aged 13 and a son aged 16. At the date of his death, A owned the following assets:

Family home (half share)	£80,000
Share portfolio	60,000
Life assurance (not in trust)	75,000
Building society account	15,000
Car	10,000
Investment property	25,000
Bank accounts	4,000
Total	£269,000

There was a mortgage of £75,000 on the family home but this will be repaid by another life assurance policy assigned to the mortgage company.
The house was held as a 'joint tenancy' (see note below) so that it now passes automatically to B and can be left out of the calculations. Removing the half share of the family home (£80,000) leaves a figure of £189,000. Out of this the car (£10,000) and any other personal effects will pass to B along with £125,000. This leaves a balance of £54,000 which is divided into two halves. One half will be held in trust and invested so that B will receive the income for her life with the capital passing to the two children when she dies. The remaining £27,000 will be divided between the children and held in trust so that they will each receive £13,500 (plus any investment growth) when they reach 18.

All this may appear reasonable until you analyse it in more detail. First, a large part of the investments is now tied up in trust so that B does not have complete control over those assets. Secondly, the children receive a large sum of money at an early age, which may not be what A would have wanted. If the son decides to spend some of his £13,500 on a powerful motorcycle on his 18th birthday, B is powerless to stop him. In addition, A's favourite charity, which had been receiving a regular amount each month under a covenant, does not receive a penny because the covenant has been cancelled by his death.

Joint tenancy

This is the most common way of owning a property but it is not always used. Sometimes the property is held by a couple as 'tenants in common' so that it does not go to the surviving spouse. Where this applies, the deceased's share in the property forms part of his estate and, if no will has been left, is subject to the intestacy rules. If you do not know which applies to your home you should check with the person who did the conveyancing when you purchased the property; alternatively your lender or a solicitor can advise you.

Simultaneous deaths

Statistically, the likelihood of a husband and wife dying at the same time or within a brief period is very small. Unfortunately, however, such tragedies do happen and when a couple leaves behind young children the consequences can be serious.

The rules that apply in these situations are complicated. This is especially true where it cannot be established which of the couple died first, as occasionally happens in car accidents, for example. The general rule in such cases is that the younger is treated as the last to die with the assets of the elder first of all being subject to the intestacy rules and then passing to the younger's estate with the intestacy rules applying again if the younger one has left no will.

One effect of this is that, in England and Wales, the rules which apply to the estate can exclude entirely the parents and other relatives of the spouse that dies first (or is treated as having died first). In this case, all the property could pass to the other set of parents, for example. In Scotland, this problem is avoided by presuming that, in the case of a married couple, neither survives the other with the rules applying to each estate separately.

10.2.4 Who looks after the children?

If you have children under the age of 18, making a will is a 'must', if only to appoint a guardian to look after them should both you and your wife die. Few people even think of this and those that do often assume that the grandparents will be there to look after them. They may be willing to undertake the job but if they are elderly they may not be a suitable choice. Without a will, the matter may be left to the authorities to determine.

If there is no will the courts have the power to appoint a guardian (called a 'tutor' in Scotland). In choosing the most suitable person, the courts must have regard to the best interests of the child and, in many cases, there will be an obvious candidate, perhaps the grandparents or an aunt and uncle with children of a similar age. However, this may not always be the case and the only option may be for the children to be placed in the care of the local authority.

Another problem which can arise as a result of the operation of the intestacy rules is the possibility of relatively large sums of money passing to the children at an early age. Few18-year-olds have the maturity to deal with large sums of money and this, together with the loss of their parents' stabilising influence, can be a cause for concern.

10.2.5 Personal bequests

If you wish to make specific gifts to individuals or to charity on death, the only means of doing this is by a will – the intestacy rules do not stretch to individual gifts to your family or friends or to charities. If you die without leaving any living relatives, your estate can pass to the Crown; hundreds of thousands of pounds are 'given' in this way every year.

10.2.6 The tax position

The final point about dying intestate is that many of the ways of avoiding inheritance tax (see 9.4.1) are totally lost. Not only could your family suffer emotionally as a result of your failure to leave a will, they could also eventually find themselves paying a larger than necessary inheritance tax bill to the Inland Revenue.

10.3 GETTING ADVICE

10.3.1 Do you need advice?

The answer to this is inevitably 'Yes' although there is no law preventing you from drafting your own will. However, there are sound reasons why you should seek advice from someone who can give clear guidance on the contents.

(1) If your will is not correctly witnessed (see 10.5.4) it may be completely invalid so that none of your wishes can be carried out.
(2) Even comparatively simple words can lead to complex legal disputes. For example, in two instances that led to court cases, the word 'pictures' was given two different meanings in relation to a stamp collection.
(3) If you choose words that are not sufficiently certain there could be an unexpected tax bill to pay. This can happen where, for example, property is given to charity and the words used to describe the charity are not clear, with the result that the charity does not benefit and the tax man does.
(4) If you are divorced, you might still have obligations to a former spouse and this can affect what must go into your will.
(5) You may want to leave your Porsche to your son but, if you replace it with a Ferrari at a later date, the gift could lapse.

DIY wills are possible, but are not to be recommended.

10.3.2 Where to get advice

Solicitors

A solicitor is a common choice for someone thinking of making a will. As cost is a consideration for many it is wise to obtain quotations from several solicitors before committing yourself.

Will writing companies

Recently, a number of companies have started to provide wills. They normally charge about the same as solicitors for simple wills, although in general they are not able to deal with the more complicated wills that only a solicitor should handle. Most of these companies use a computer program (similar to that used by many solicitors) to produce the will based on information that is supplied in response to a questionnaire.

In recent times, a number of insurance companies have begun to offer a will writing service. These offer the advantage of a visit to your own home to discuss your requirements; the company may also offer a storage facility so that your will is always kept in a safe place.

Will kits

For the brave, there are a number of books and 'will kits' that provide you with guidance on how to draft a will. In very simple situations it should be possible to use this type of book to draw up an adequate will. However, the leading legal textbook on the subject runs to two volumes and over 1,700 pages so, unless you have *some* legal experience, it is probably best to get professional help.

10.4 DRAWING UP A WILL

The first step is to make a list of the people whom you wish to benefit and the type of gifts that you wish to make.

10.4.1 Who must benefit?

English law, unlike the law of many other countries including Scotland, does not impose too many rules regarding those to whom you must make gifts. In many countries, you are obliged to make gifts to your children and your spouse and these must be a certain percentage of your estate. Under English law, you are not obliged to make gifts of any specific amount, but the law does attempt to ensure that your family and dependants are reasonably provided for.

This arises under the Inheritance (Provision for Family and Dependants) Act 1975, which allows members of your family to apply to the courts if they consider that they should have received more from your estate than your will provides. Those who can apply include your spouse, an unmarried former spouse, any of your children (including any who, although not strictly your children, you treated as such) and any person whom you maintained immediately before your death. In drafting your will, you should think carefully about how much you want to give to members of your family, because the court can override your will if you have not made reasonable financial provision for them. When considering the case, the court will look at all the relevant factors, such as the claimants' other resources and their ability to take care of themselves.

The law in Scotland is very different (see 10.7).

10.4.2 The appointment of executors, guardians and trustees

Executors

You will have to appoint executors to administer your estate. It is sometimes thought that a solicitor (or a firm of solicitors) must be appointed to act as executor, but this is not a legal necessity. It is perfectly acceptable to appoint a spouse, relative or friend, and although the role of an executor can be quite demanding, especially in complicated cases, the advice of a solicitor can still be obtained if needed at the time. If the will leaves everything to the surviving spouse, it is normally advisable to appoint her as the sole executor (though the will can also make provision if the surviving spouse is unable or unwilling to act for any reason).

Guardians

If you have children under the age of 18, the most important decision is your choice of guardian for your children, should both you and your wife die. Normally, two people are appointed as joint guardians and a couple of similar age to yourselves would be considered preferable if it is felt that the child needs the support of a 'normal' family.

Trustees

If your will is one which sets up a trust (see 11.1.3), perhaps for your minor children, you have to consider who are to be the trustees. One point to note is that the trustees do not have to be the same as the executors although this is the normal position. However, if your trust is for a minor child, you might want to appoint someone other than the child's guardian as the trustee, as this separates the responsibility for the financial affairs from the day-to-day welfare of the child.

10.4.3 Drafting the will

The next step is for your will to be drafted. If it is to be drafted by a solicitor or a will drafting company this may take a few days – more if the will is complicated.

You should read the will carefully and check that everything is in order. Pay particular attention to names and addresses because mistakes in these are easily made. If you do not understand why a particular clause is in the will, you should ask the person drafting it for an explanation of what it means.

A 'model' will is included at the end of this book as Appendix 3.

10.5 THE FORMALITIES

A will has to satisfy certain formalities before it is valid. These are intended to reduce the risk of a will being forged or fraudulent alterations being made to it and to help reduce the chances that a person could be forced to make a will against his wishes. The main legal requirements for wills are as follows:

(1) They must be in writing.
(2) They must be signed.
(3) The testator must intend to make a will and must be of sound mind.
(4) They must be validly witnessed.

10.5.1 Wills must be in writing

A will must be written, but under English law (the position is slightly different in Scotland) they do not have to be handwritten. You can use any language, although you should be careful that there is someone who will be able to understand the significance of the will when it comes to light after your death.

If your will consists of more than one page, the pages should be firmly stapled or preferably bound together so that they do not become separated. You must not add a new page after the will has been executed because this is not valid. You should not staple anything to the will because this could cause problems later.

10.5.2 Wills must be signed

You should sign with your normal signature but there is no need to write your full name as long as you use your usual signature. If you cannot sign, perhaps because of some physical incapacity, you can ask someone to sign on your behalf as long as you are physically present when they do so.

If there are any minor alterations (eg to correct spelling mistakes) these should be signed and witnessed, but this should only be done *before* the will is finally signed. If there are any major alterations, a completely new will is probably best. A will should not be altered in any way once you have signed it; the proper course is to amend the will using a suitable codicil (see 10.6.4) or to have a completely new will drawn up.

In Scotland, if you cannot sign the will personally, it must be notarially executed before a notary public, a solicitor, justice of the peace or the local parish minister. Also, except in the case of a 'holograph' will (one which is in the testator's handwriting or is typewritten or printed but signed as 'adopted as holograph' by the testator), the testator must also sign each page of the will if it is written on more than one piece of paper.

10.5.3 The testator's intentions must be clear

Normally, there is no doubt that in signing a will the testator intends to validate the *entire* will. However, there can be situations where there is some doubt. For example, if the signature does not come at the end of the will, there can be doubt whether the testator intends that all the will is to be valid, or just the part before the signature.

A valid will can be made only if the testator is of sound mind. If the testator is incapable of understanding that he is signing a document which gives property to certain beneficiaries after death, the will is invalid. In addition, the will can be challenged if it can be proved that the testator was acting under the undue influence of another person, for example where the testator is very elderly and influenced by a person who was looking after him.

10.5.4 Wills must be validly witnessed

This is the area that causes most of the problems in practice and it is particularly important to meet all the requirements. In outline, the normal rules are as follows:

(1) There must be two witnesses.
(2) The testator must sign the will in the presence of both witnesses.
(3) The witnesses must sign the will intending to witness the signature of the testator.
(4) Except in Scotland, the witnesses must sign in the presence of the testator and each other.
(5) The witnesses or their spouses must not receive any benefit under the will.

In Scotland there is a special rule that holograph wills do not need to be witnessed at all (although the normal case is for the will to be witnessed).

Most of the problems arise from the rule that a witness (or spouse of a witness) must *not* benefit from the will. The safest way to ensure that the will is executed properly is to have two completely independent witnesses who are not mentioned in the will in any way (whether as executors, trustees or beneficiaries). The witnesses do not need to know what is in the will and it is quite common for the will to be witnessed by neighbours or members of the solicitor's staff. If a will is witnessed by a person who takes any benefit under the will, it is still valid, but the witness will *not* be able to receive his gift.

10.5.5 Challenging the will

If the will is properly drafted, signed and witnessed and any dependants entitled to a claim on the deceased's estate have been adequately provided for, there should be little danger of the will being challenged. However, challenges to wills do occur and are sometimes successful.

There are several grounds on which a will can be challenged. The main ones are as follows:

(1) A claim under the Inheritance (Provision for Family and Dependants) Act by a dependant or relative for whom reasonable provision was not made in the will (this does not apply in Scotland).
(2) A claim that the testator was not mentally capable of making a will.
(3) A claim that the testator was forced to make the will against his wishes or was subject to undue pressure at the time the will was made.
(4) In Scotland, a child born after the will was made but not included in it may claim that the will is invalid.

It should be possible to avoid all these pitfalls by taking proper advice at the time the will is made. For example, it is more difficult to claim that someone was pressurised into making a will if that person was advised by a solicitor of his own choosing. Similarly, if there is likely to be any doubt that the testator was mentally capable, it may be desirable to have the will witnessed by the person's doctor, who could later testify that the person was capable at the time.

10.6 REVIEWING YOUR WILL

The best advice is to review your will on a regular basis. If tax is a concern to you, then the annual Budget speech is often a good time for a review of the way you intend to leave your property (particularly as the impact of inheritance tax will be according to the tax rules at the date of death, not the date you drew up your will). Apart from that (and apart from the fact that you may wish to amend your will simply because you have changed your mind) the events that should trigger off a review of your will are as follows:

(1) Marriage and divorce
(2) Changes to people mentioned in your will
(3) Disposal or acquisition of assets.

10.6.1 Marriage and divorce

Marriage

Except in Scotland, the general rule is that the entire will is revoked by the marriage of the testator after the will was made. This does not apply where the will is made 'in expectation of marriage', ie where an engaged couple make wills which clearly envisage that they are to get married.

To be certain, it must state clearly that it is made in anticipation of the marriage *to a specific person* and that it is not to be revoked by the marriage.

Divorce

For divorce a slightly different rule applies. Again with the exception of Scotland, the will remains valid but any gift to the former spouse lapses. The former spouse's appointment as an executor also lapses. However, the need to review the will remains for two reasons.

(1) The effect of the lapse of gifts may mean that the will does not deal with who is to receive any property left to the former spouse.
(2) There could be a liability to make reasonable provision for a former spouse who is a dependant, perhaps because they are receiving maintenance.

The position in Scotland is dealt with later on (see 10.7.5).

10.6.2 Changes to people mentioned in your will

Birth of children or grandchildren

The will may be drafted in such a way as to refer to all future children and grandchildren, but it is wise to check that the will covers all the children and not just those named specifically. In Scotland the law goes further than this and a will which does not provide for children born after the will was made may be challenged by any child who was born subsequently.

Death of a beneficiary

The effect of the death of a beneficiary of the will depends upon the way in which the gift to them is drafted. If the will makes a specific provision for what is to happen, no change may be required. If it does not cover the situation, the will should be reviewed and a new one drafted or a suitable codicil made.

Changes to executors, trustees or guardians

You should review regularly whether the people you have chosen as executors, trustees or guardians are still suitable and available to act. Again, any changes can be made by a suitable codicil.

10.6.3 Disposal or acquisition of assets

If you make a specific gift of property in your will and then sell that asset, the gift is not valid, even if you use the proceeds of the sale to purchase new assets (unless the will includes a specific clause which says this is to happen). Similarly, if you acquire new assets, the general rule is that the assets pass to the person entitled to the residue of your estate and, unless this is what you intend, you need to revise your will.

10.6.4 New will or codicil

Whatever the reason for the change to the will, you have a choice of using a codicil or making a new will. A codicil is suitable where the change is relatively simple; for example, if you want to change your executors or make a further specific gift of some property you have recently acquired. However, in most cases, a new will is preferable as it ensures that all your wishes are contained in one document. In either case you need to get advice on the contents.

If you decide to add a codicil you need to go through the formal process of signing and witnessing again because the rules are identical to those for a new will, except that the existing will remains valid subject to any changes that are made.

10.7 THE LAW IN SCOTLAND

The law in Scotland differs substantially from the law in the remainder of the United Kingdom and these differences are particularly marked in the areas of wills and the laws of intestacy.

10.7.1 What happens when there is no will?

The first question is who will deal with the estate and see to the payment of debts and the distribution of the estate. This person is called an executor-dative and the list of potential claimants for this role is broadly as follows:

(1) The surviving spouse (who has the sole right to be executor where she is entitled to the entire estate by virtue of 'prior rights' – see below)
(2) Any child, grandchild or great grandchild
(3) The father or mother
(4) Aunts, uncles and nieces and nephews.

The full list also includes remoter relatives and also creditors, judicial factors (in the case of a bankruptcy) and the procurator-fiscal. The key point is that, in the absence of a will naming the person to administer the estate, the choice is very wide.

10.7.2 Prior rights and legal rights

A key element of the Scots law relating to wills is the system of 'prior rights' and 'legal rights'. These are the rights of a person's spouse and children to a specified share of the estate after death. These rights apply not only to the estates of persons who die without making a will but also act, with certain modifications, to supplement or, indeed, override the terms of any will that has been made. The effect of these rules is to restrict the freedom of testators to make a will in the way that they choose and to ensure that provision is always made for the spouse and children.

Prior rights

Prior rights are the rights of the surviving spouse to certain property, furnishings and money from the deceased's estate. These rights have, as their name suggests, priority over all other claims over the estate other than debts and expenses. They apply where there is no will or if the will does not cover all of the deceased's property.

Legal rights

These are the rights of the deceased's spouse and the children to a share of the deceased's property (the children's legal rights are known as *legitim*). They apply not only where there is no will but also where there is a will. Legal rights apply only to the deceased's 'movable property' (basically any property, including investments and life assurance policies, other than land and buildings) and cover the value of the moveable property after prior rights have been paid.

10.7.3 The free estate

Once the prior rights and the legal rights have been paid, the balance of the movable estate is added to the deceased's 'heritable property' (any land or buildings that belong to the deceased). This balance is called the free estate and passes in the following order:

(1) Children (including illegitimate and adopted children, but not stepchildren)
(2) Parents, brothers and sisters

(3) The surviving spouse
(4) Uncles and aunts
(5) Grandparents
(6) Brothers and sisters of the grandparents
(7) Remoter ancestors
(8) The Crown, if no relatives can be found.

It is worth noting that the spouse (being protected by the system of prior rights and legal rights) only appears third in the list of potential beneficiaries of the free estate.

10.7.4 Effect of wills

Unlike the law in the remainder of the United Kingdom, a Scots-domiciled person who leaves a spouse or other dependants is restricted in the way that he can write a will. The will can only apply to a person's free estate, ie a Scots testator can only have a will that deals with any land or buildings (his heritable property) and the share of his movable estate which is not affected by the legal rights (prior rights do not apply where there is a will unless the will does not deal with all the deceased's property for some reason).

10.7.5 Reviewing wills

Reviewing a will is just as important in Scotland as elsewhere in the United Kingdom but there are important differences in the law.

The first difference is that a will is not revoked by a subsequent marriage. This is because the system of legal rights automatically ensures that the spouse is provided for at least to some extent. In addition, there is no rule that gifts to a divorced spouse lapse. Although the divorced spouse's legal rights cease to apply, gifts in the will are still valid after a divorce unless it is made clear in the will that the gift to the spouse is conditional on the marriage existing at the date of death.

Perhaps the most significant difference between English and Scots law is the rule that a will which does not include children born after the will is made can be ruled invalid. There is no equivalent rule elsewhere in the United Kingdom but, in Scotland, unless it is clear from the will or the surrounding circumstances that the will is to remain in force, the birth of a child who is not provided for in the will could mean that the child could challenge the will at a later date. In all cases, the birth of a child should prompt a review of your will to ensure that it is kept up to date.

A final point is that many people overlook the importance of ensuring that the will can be found when it is needed. In Scotland this is doubly important as a lost will is presumed to have been revoked unless it can be proved that the loss of the will was not due to its destruction by the testator.

10.8 ADMINISTERING THE ESTATE

All deaths must be registered (with the local Registrar of Births, Deaths and Marriages) within five days (eight in Scotland) by a relative or the person who is making the funeral arrangements. The Registrar issues a Certificate of Registration of Death for social security purposes, and a Certificate for Burial or Cremation which needs to be given to the funeral directors before the funeral can proceed. He can also issue, for a fee, as many copies of the death certificate as the executors need for probate, pension claims, insurance policies etc.

10.8.1 Paying inheritance tax and obtaining the grant of probate

The grant of probate (or confirmation in Scotland) is the formal authority that is needed to allow the executors to deal with the assets of the deceased. The grant is obtained by an application to the appropriate Probate Registry (or, in Scotland, to the local sheriff court), and involves the completion of various forms which give details about the will and the assets of the estate. Without the formal authority of probate or confirmation, banks, insurance companies, company registrars etc who hold the deceased's assets are perfectly within their rights to refuse to deal with the executors.

Sometimes, especially where the estate is small, insurance companies and banks etc may be prepared to make small payments without a formal grant of probate. However, before a grant of probate can be obtained, the executors must pay any inheritance tax that is due on the value of the estate. This may mean that the executors have to borrow the money to pay the inheritance tax unless there are funds readily available elsewhere, such as from an insurance policy that was written in trust (see 9.5).

10.8.2 Duties of the executors

The executors have an important role to play. In short, their duties are to pay the deceased's debts and any tax and then distribute the balance of the estate in the way specified in the will. The exact duties of the executors vary from will to will.

(1) The first task is usually to find out exactly what the deceased owned and whether there are any outstanding debts that need to be paid. This information is also needed by the Inland Revenue to assess any tax that may be payable. All of the deceased's debts and liabilities need to be identified as part of the inheritance tax calculation and they need to be paid before the estate is wound up.
(2) The next step is to collect in all the assets of the estate. For example, with shares, the executors can apply to the company registrars for the estate to be registered as a shareholder or, if the will provides, for the shares to pass to a beneficiary. The grant of probate or confirmation allows the executors to close accounts and transfer the proceeds to a special bank account which should be set up for this purpose in the name of the executors.
(3) The debts of the deceased, including any unpaid income and capital gains tax, must be paid before the final balance of the estate is transferred to the people entitled to the residue. Once it is clear that there is sufficient in the estate to pay all the debts, the executors can pay out any specific gifts of money or assets that are provided by the will. Where gifts of money are concerned, this is usually done by selling assets to raise the money. If the beneficiary consents, assets can be transferred rather than being sold to pay cash.
(4) The next stages are to formalise the accounts of the estate and to ascertain how much money is available to be paid to the beneficiaries who are entitled to the residue. This may result in an adjustment to the inheritance tax bill that was previously paid if new assets have come to light during the administration of the estate or if any assets have fallen significantly in value before the date of death. The final accounts also deal with the expenses of the administration such as the funeral and any solicitors' or other costs incurred. There may also be some income tax to pay in respect of any income received during the period when the estate is being administered. Once the accounts have been finalised and all remaining debts settled, the residue of the estate can be transferred to the beneficiaries (or to the trustees if the residue is to be held in a trust).

10.8.3 Intestacy

If no will can be found and there is no evidence that a will was drawn up, then the deceased is assumed to have died intestate. In this case, if you are entitled to administer the estate under the intestacy rules (see 10.2.1), you may apply for a grant of letters of administration.

The position in Scotland is different (see 10.7.1).

Letters of administration have the same authority as a grant of probate, but it is the *only* authority held by an administrator. An executor, on the other hand, derives authority from the will itself and can, even before the grant is issued, perform certain acts which do not require proof of his authority (eg pay debts or put a house on the market).

10.9 THE ENDURING POWER OF ATTORNEY

Mental disability can affect anyone, whatever his age. It can arise as a result of illness, such as a stroke, or accident, and is not confined to those in extreme old age. Whatever the cause, the effects are the same, with the sufferer left incapable of dealing with the financial and other matters that most of us would take for granted.

People who are mentally incapable of dealing with their business affairs are legally prevented from taking any action in relation to their property and investments. While there are special legal procedures to deal with the problems, these are by no means always satisfactory.

10.9.1 What happens when mental disability strikes?

In practical terms, the effect is very similar to the position on death. At death, the law provides that someone will take over the administration of the estate and, if there is no will, there are always the intestacy rules to fall back on. Where mental disability strikes there are several possibilities. One is that dealings with the property are simply suspended until the person dies, at which point the person's executors or administrators can take over and distribute the assets in accordance with the will or the intestacy rules.

A further alternative is that an application is made to the Court of Protection, a special court that looks after the affairs of people who are incapable of looking after their own affairs because of mental disability. The procedure is usually for the court to appoint a receiver to administer the estate. This means that the receiver (normally a near relative or a solicitor or accountant) can receive the person's income, pay debts and deal with most day-to-day matters. Larger transactions, such as the sale of the family house or significant investment decisions, require specific approval from the court, who will then need to be satisfied that they are in the best interests of the individual before letting the transaction go ahead.

Although there are special procedures for smaller estates of less than £5,000 in total value, the costs can be very significant. In addition, the limited personal attention is one reason why the Court of Protection may often not be suitable.

10.9.2 Powers and enduring powers

A power of attorney is simply an authority to a named individual, called the attorney, which allows the attorney to act on behalf of the person who is giving the authority, called the donor. Normal powers of attorney are quite commonplace but have the disadvantage that they come to an end if the donor ceases to be able to look after his own affairs as a result of mental incapacity.

The enduring power of attorney was introduced in England in 1985. It allows people to choose someone to look after their affairs should they become unable to do so themselves. As its name suggests, it endures *after* the donor becomes incapable, and may even be worded in a way that it only takes effect once incapacity strikes. (The position in Scotland is slightly different. Anybody appointed to act on your behalf since 1 January 1991 can continue to do so even if you become unable to look after your own affairs as a result of mental illness.)

10.9.3 What are the advantages of enduring powers?

Compared with an application to the Court of Protection, an enduring power of attorney offers many advantages.

(1) They are inexpensive. The only fee is a small registration fee if the power has to be used and there are no annual fees.
(2) They enable you to choose who is to be your attorney, rather than having to rely on a court-appointed receiver. You are free to choose whoever you want, usually your spouse, a relative or friend, or a professional adviser.
(3) A degree of advance planning is possible. You are able to execute an enduring power at any time, as long as you are able to understand the nature and effect of the document.
(4) There are standard forms for enduring powers and a solicitor can help you with these. The documents are relatively simple with detailed explanatory notes and require only to be signed, by both the donor and the attorney, and be independently witnessed. In the standard form, the attorney can be given wide powers that are usually enough to cope with most situations that arise.
(5) Once the power needs to be used, the procedures are very simple. When the donor becomes incapable of managing his affairs, the attorney must give notice to the donor and to certain relatives of the donor and any co-attorneys. If no objection is made, the attorney can register the power with the Court of Protection, allowing it to be used.

10.9.4 Wills and enduring powers

It is advisable to consider executing an enduring power at the same time as you make a will. One thing that the attorney cannot do for you is to make or amend your will, except with the approval of the Court of Protection. However, the combination of a will and an enduring power covers most situations that could arise, ensuring that your affairs will be looked after in all eventualities.

10.10 LIVING WILLS

A living will is a statement, in writing, made by an adult outlining the steps that should or should not be taken in the event of terminal illness. Essentially they are an expression of a wish that medical treatment should be withdrawn if there is no hope of improvement or if the treatment becomes a burden.

They are not legally binding and can only be an expression of your wishes. In the final event, your doctor has the right to decide whether treatment is withdrawn. The benefit of having a living will drawn up is that your doctor is at least aware of your wishes.

There is, of course, a considerable difference between, on the one hand, the withdrawal of treatment which is keeping somebody alive and, on the other hand, actively helping somebody to die (which is technically murder). However, doctors are allowed to withdraw treatment in certain cases where recovery is impossible and this was confirmed by the Government in May 1994. Despite this, there is no specific legislation on living wills and there is no reference to living wills in any existing legislation.

Nevertheless, it is important that a living will is drawn up in a legal form not only to make sure your wishes are clear and unambiguous but also to give protection to those people whom you expect to respect your wishes and withdraw treatment when the time comes. Details of a suitably drafted living will can be obtained from the Voluntary Euthanasia Society.

11

TRUSTS

Among the great military adventures of the last thousand years were the Crusades. For any wealthy land-owning knight, setting out from England on such a hazardous mission, a worry had to be what would happen to his land whilst he was away and, more importantly, if he were killed. It became the custom for the knight to leave his land with trustworthy friends and ask them to look after it for the benefit of his son until he returned. If he were killed, the friends could continue to use the land for the son's benefit until the son reached 21, at which point the land would become his.

As the alternative was for the land to go to the Lord of the Manor, you can see that trusts (or 'uses' as they were called) were an early but effective form of tax planning. From such simple beginnings, trusts have evolved to become a very useful way of arranging your affairs so that things happen in the way that you want them to happen. That was true for the knights of the Crusades and it is true for a great many people today.

This chapter looks at trusts under the following headings:

(1) What is a trust?
(2) Why trusts can be a good idea
(3) The principal types of trust
(4) Setting up a trust
(5) The appointment, retirement and removal of trustees
(6) The duties and responsibilities of trustees
(7) The rights of beneficiaries
(8) Trusts in practice – an example
(9) Anti-avoidance legislation.

11.1 WHAT IS A TRUST?

11.1.1 The basic workings of a trust

A will is a straightforward statement of your wishes regarding what happens to your property when you die. If you want your nephew to receive

£1,000 then you put that in your will and it will happen. A trust is similar to a will in that it allows you to dispose of your property in the way that you wish. One difference, however, is that a trust allows you to give your property away while you are alive and, at the same time, retain a degree of control over it.

Suppose you would prefer your nephew to get the money while you are alive. If you give him £1,000 in cash for him to spend, it is an outright gift. You have immediately handed over the £1,000 and you have no further say in what happens to it. In legal terms, you (the donor) have made a gift to your nephew (the beneficiary) absolutely.

But you may not wish to make an absolute gift; your nephew may be young and unused to handling money. Trusts allow you to make a gift now in such a way that the full benefit may not take effect until some time in the future. Instead of making an outright gift to the beneficiary, you give it instead to a person or group of people who looks after the property on behalf of the beneficiary. These people (the trustees) have to follow your instructions regarding the eventual handing over of the property, and its treatment in the meantime and those instructions (the trust deed) are carefully drafted to eliminate doubts over what you want to happen.

The obvious question, of course, is why not wait until the nephew *is* old enough and give him the money then? Tax could play a part in this, particularly inheritance tax. You might wish to make use of the annual exemptions to make gifts (see 9.7.1) but you might not wish to make an outright gift.

11.1.2 A simple example

A couple have been married for some years and have two teenage children. The husband has invested with some success and has built up a portfolio of shares and unit trusts. He keeps a close eye on these and manages his portfolio as best he can. His wife isn't particularly interested in the detail of this type of investment but the income from them is a useful addition to the household budget.

The husband wants to ensure that his children eventually benefit from his investment success. However, he has to think of what would happen if he died first:

(1) Will his wife want to look after the portfolio?
(2) If the children inherit the portfolio while they are still young:
    (a) how will they know what to do with it?
    (b) will his wife miss the income?

His solution is to set up a trust and hand over his portfolio to a person or group of people he can trust (the trustees) to look after the portfolio (and there is no reason why he cannot appoint himself as a trustee for as long as he is alive). The trustees have to act at all times in the interests of the beneficiaries (the people who will benefit from the trust) and he will make quite sure that the trust deed spells out what they can and cannot do – and he will use a solicitor to get the words right.

The basis of this particular type of trust is that, on his death, his wife receives the income from the portfolio for as long as she is alive. On her death (or later, if they are still young), the portfolio passes to the children and the trust is 'wound up'.

11.1.3 Wills versus trusts

A key point about trusts is the difference between a trust and a will. They are both concerned with giving away property but wills only take effect on death. You can change a will as often as you want while you are alive. Trusts, on the other hand, take effect as soon as they are set up and can be very difficult (or even impossible) to change.

Will trusts

Wills and trusts can be combined. It is possible, for example, to make a gift via a will that is not an outright gift but one which is controlled until the beneficiary is of a suitable age. This is what is called a will trust and, in effect, gives you the best of both worlds. You can look after and enjoy your property while you are alive but you can make the necessary arrangements to make sure that, in the event of your death, the interests of your beneficiaries are looked after until they are old enough to look after themselves. In fact, this is probably what the husband would have done in the previous example.

11.1.4 Setting up a trust

When you set up a trust (or, as it is often put, 'declare' a trust) you are making a gift; you are transferring the property. However, it is not a simple gift, as would be the case where, for example, you give some property to your son. In this case, your son would be the outright owner of the property or assets and could do with them whatever he wished. If you make a gift of the same property or assets through a trust, the arrangements would be somewhat different.

There are, in fact, two types of ownership of property: legal ownership and beneficial ownership. If you own something absolutely, you have both legal and beneficial ownership and this, for most of us, is the usual state of affairs. However, it is possible to separate legal from beneficial ownership and this is what happens when a trust is set up.

For example, if you make a gift of property or assets to your child through a trust, your child becomes the *beneficial* owner of the property or assets but there would be a new body of people, the trustees, in place as the *legal* owners. The trustees must always act in the child's best interests and their actions are usually controlled by the terms of the trust deed.

11.2 WHY TRUSTS CAN BE A GOOD IDEA

11.2.1 The general advantages of trusts

There are a number of general advantages of making large lifetime transfers by putting money into trust rather than making outright gifts. The main ones are:

(1) Trusts are a very effective way of giving property away 'with strings attached'. You may want to make sure that the capital you give away is applied for specific purposes or, at any rate, is not frittered away. You must, however, be wary of making a gift under which you could benefit yourself (although there are a few *limited* circumstances in which you can benefit under the terms of your own trust without falling foul of the Inland Revenue).
(2) You can retain a measure of control either by appointing trustees who pay due regard to your views and wishes, or even by being a trustee yourself.
(3) You can make provision for your spouse to benefit at some time in the future after your death should her financial circumstances change for the worse.

Trusts also enable you effectively to have control over the management of your assets after your death.

11.2.2 Typical uses of trusts

The following are typical ways in which trusts are put to everyday use:

Giving property away

Rather than leave a large amount of money in your will which could have inheritance tax implications you could give away smaller sums of money over a number of years (see 9.7.1). By declaring a trust you can dispose of the money without making outright gifts of it to a particular individual. In this way, trusts can be an important part of your long-term tax planning.

Looking after your beneficiaries

Your intended beneficiary could be too young to hold the property or assets. There is no objection, however, to property or assets being held on trust for such a beneficiary. The beneficiary might not be considered responsible or mature enough to hold the property or assets outright, so you might not wish to make an irreversible decision as to who is going to get the benefits. You could even give the trustees discretion as to the amount which they would be allowed to pay over to the beneficiary or beneficiaries at any given time.

Benefiting future generations

A trust could be used to ensure that your property will benefit certain persons in succession. If you were to make an outright gift to a married son or daughter, you could not be certain that, on their death, the property would go to your grandchildren. If you were to make a gift to trustees to hold upon trust for that parent for life, with the property going to the children on the parent's death, you would know that your grandchildren will ultimately benefit from the gift.

Life assurance in the right place

Trusts can be very flexible indeed. You may wish to leave the proceeds of a life assurance policy to your heirs without giving rise to any inheritance tax liability and without any probate delay. If the policy was written under a suitable trust it would not form part of your estate (thereby avoiding inheritance tax) and the proceeds could be paid to the trustees (for them to pay to the beneficiaries) without any need to wait for the grant of probate (see 9.5).

11.3 THE PRINCIPAL TYPES OF TRUST

From the above ways in which trusts can be used, it is clear that they can be extremely flexible. Quite simply, you can make a trust do more or less exactly what you want it to do and there are different kinds of trusts for different purposes. However, there are three particular types of trust that crop up over and over again:

(1) Interest in possession trusts.
(2) Discretionary trusts.
(3) Accumulation and maintenance trusts.

Of course, there is nothing so certain as death and taxes, and trusts do not escape. Consequently, it is important to have a basic understanding of the way trusts are taxed. However, it is a complex area, and the following notes are not intended to be anything other than an introductory guide.

Trusts involve a transfer of property (so there are inheritance tax implications), the assets may earn income (so there are income tax implications) and assets may be bought and sold (with implications for capital gains tax). Furthermore, there could be tax implications for the settlor (the person setting up the trust), the beneficiaries and the trustees.

11.3.1 Interest in possession trusts

In the example in 11.1.2, the husband put his investments into trust so that:

(1) he could look after them while he was alive;
(2) after his death, his wife received the income for as long as she was alive; and
(3) his children inherited the capital when his wife died.

This is an interest in possession trust and the basic principle behind this type of trust is that the income is treated separately from the capital. Under such trusts, one or more of the beneficiaries enjoys the right to any income arising from the trust fund for a certain period – usually during their lifetime. These beneficiaries are the 'life tenants' and are said to have a 'life interest' under the trust. After the death of the life tenant (or the last surviving life tenant, if there is more than one) the capital then passes to those people that you wish to benefit from the capital. These people (the 'remaindermen') are said to be entitled to the reversion and have a 'reversionary interest' in the trust.

You could also write such a trust under the terms of a will. You might be concerned about leaving capital to your surviving spouse when you die. By setting up an interest in possession trust under the terms of your will, you can ensure that your surviving spouse receives the income from the capital but not the capital itself (unless, of course, the trustees have the power to distribute capital and decide to exercise that power).

11.3.2 The taxation of interest in possession trusts

Inheritance tax

When you set a trust up during your lifetime, the life tenant is regarded as receiving a gift of the value of the trust fund; he or she has the benefit of the fund which is producing an income. The inheritance tax position depends on the relationship between you and the life tenant:

(1) If the life tenant is your spouse, there will be no inheritance tax payable because of the inter-spouse exemption (see 9.4.1).
(2) If the life tenant is anyone else, the gift will be a potentially exempt transfer (see 9.6.2).

The death of the life tenant gives rise to inheritance tax implications for the life tenant's estate (as it includes the value of the trust property) and there are also inheritance tax implications if the life tenant renounces his or her entitlement to the income (as the property is handed back to the trustees and this is a potentially exempt transfer).

If you include yourself in the class of beneficiaries, the property transferred into the trust is still included in your estate on your death for inheritance tax purposes under the gifts with reservation of benefit rule (see 9.6.1). This should not prevent your spouse from benefiting under the trust after your death.

Income tax

The trustees are liable for income tax (at the basic rate) on any income earned by the assets of the trust. This income (after deducting any expenses incurred by the trustees) is then paid to the life tenant. Any tax paid may be reclaimed by the life tenant if he or she is a non-taxpayer. If the life tenant is a higher rate taxpayer he or she may be liable to pay an additional 15 per cent (at current rates).

If you or your spouse (or your minor children) could benefit under a trust set up by you, the trustees' income is taxed as if it were yours. This could mean your facing a liability to higher rate tax even though the income is actually paid to someone else. You are allowed to claim the tax back from the trustees but the underlying point is that the tax due is based on your overall financial position and not that of the trust (ie there is no overall tax advantage). There are details of further anti-avoidance provisions in 11.9.

Capital gains tax

Capital gains tax is payable by the trustees usually at the same rate as they pay income tax on the trust's total gains for the tax year after deducting the annual exemption, which for trusts is usually half the individual exemption (see 8.6). If either you or your spouse could benefit under the trust, now or in the future, the trust gains are treated as your gains, though you have the right to recover the tax paid from the trustees.

11.3.3 Discretionary trusts

Stripped of legalese, a discretionary trust usually provides something like this:

> The trustees will hold the trust fund until [a fixed day in the future] and will use the income to make payments to any one or more of a defined class of beneficiaries as they shall, in their absolute discretion, decide. The trustees may also distribute capital if they wish. At the appointed day, the trust fund will be distributed as follows . . .

Discretionary trusts can therefore be extremely flexible. The appointed day may often be a date up to 80 years after the trust was created. The class of beneficiaries may be very narrowly defined (eg, 'my wife and daughter') or it may be very widely defined (eg, 'any lineal descendant of my great grandfather'). The trustees have the power to accumulate income for a limited period (ie not to pay it out but to reinvest it) and they may or may not have power to distribute capital before the appointed day.

Such a trust requires careful thought. On the one hand, it is a very flexible vehicle giving the trustees wide powers to apply your money to meet changing circumstances and needs. On the other hand, it is giving considerable powers to the trustees and you have to choose them carefully.

11.3.4 The taxation of discretionary trusts

Discretionary trusts are known as 'settlements without an interest in possession'. The tax position is quite different from that of interest in possession trusts.

Inheritance tax

Because of the wide powers given to trustees, they can delay the distribution of capital almost indefinitely. In order to prevent this delay of potential inheritance tax, there are special rules designed to collect it 'on account'.

(1) There is an immediate liability to inheritance tax (at 20 per cent) whenever property in excess of the nil rate band is transferred to a discretionary trust.

(2) There is a ten-yearly 'periodic charge' (at reduced rates) on property remaining in the trust.
(3) There is a proportionate 'exit charge' when property is transferred out of the trust.

Income tax

The trustees are normally liable to income tax at the special rate of 34 per cent on all the income which the trust receives.

Where the trustees distribute income to beneficiaries, the amounts received by the beneficiaries are treated as being net of tax at 33 per cent. The beneficiaries may reclaim part or all of this tax if their incomes are low enough. If the beneficiaries are higher rate taxpayers, however, they may be liable to a further tax charge.

If you or your spouse is named as a beneficiary of a trust set up by you, you yourself are assessed for income tax on all the income of the trust at both basic and (where appropriate) higher rates, though you can claim back the tax paid from the trustees.

The position with your minor children is slightly different. The trust may have been set up for them and, as the underlying structure is that it is a 'settlement without interest in possession' (ie the income is generally accumulated, not distributed), you only face a tax liability if the income is distributed to your minor children.

Capital gains tax

The trustees are normally charged to capital gains tax at the special rate of 34 per cent on any gains arising within the trust. The annual exemption is half the individual exemption (see 8.6). Once again, if either you or your spouse could benefit under the trust, now or in the future, the trust gains are treated as your gains, though you can claim back the tax from the trustees.

Overall, discretionary trusts offer you considerable flexibility in arranging your financial affairs and looking after the family money but this has to be balanced to some extent by the rather more complicated tax position.

11.3.5 Accumulation and maintenance (A & M) trusts

An accumulation and maintenance trust is a special type of discretionary trust set up for a stated class of beneficiaries. They are popular trusts for family purposes as the trustees are given a fair amount of control and discretion and, at the same time, the tax treatment is considerably more favourable than for normal discretionary trusts. There are four conditions which must be satisfied:

(1) The trust must have a life of not more than 25 years or it must be a trust for the benefit of grandchildren of a common grandparent.
(2) All the beneficiaries must be below the age of 25 when the trust commences. There must be at least one beneficiary alive when the trust is set up but the beneficiaries could include unborn children (eg future grandchildren).
(3) One or more of the beneficiaries must become entitled to an interest in possession (ie the income) on or before reaching a specified age not exceeding 25 years. In practice, these trusts often provide that the beneficiaries become entitled to the income at the age of 18 or 21.
(4) Prior to this, the income must be either accumulated or distributed for the maintenance, education or benefit of one or more of the beneficiaries.

The trustees can postpone applying the *capital* for the benefit of the beneficiaries almost indefinitely. This makes these trusts popular because, although the beneficiaries are bound to benefit from the income, the trustees decide when they may benefit from the capital.

11.3.6 The taxation of accumulation and maintenance trusts

Inheritance tax

A transfer of property into such a trust is a potentially exempt transfer (see 9.6.2). Unlike a normal discretionary trust, there is no immediate liability to inheritance tax and there are no periodic or exit charges. Also, there is no inheritance tax liability:

(1) when a beneficiary becomes beneficially entitled to an interest in possession in the trust property; or
(2) on the death of a beneficiary before attaining the specified age; or
(3) when a beneficiary becomes absolutely entitled to trust property.

Income tax

Income received by the trustees is subject to tax at the basic rate plus a surcharge of 10 per cent (15 per cent in the case of dividends). When a beneficiary becomes entitled to the income, the rate of tax goes down to the basic rate. The beneficiary may reclaim tax (if a non-taxpayer) or be liable for additional tax (if a higher rate taxpayer).

Capital gains tax

The trustees are liable for capital gains tax (at the special rate of 34 per cent) on any chargeable disposals. The annual exemption is half the annual exemption for individuals. If you or your spouse could benefit under the trust now or in the future, the trust gains are treated as your gains, though you can claim any tax paid back from the trustees.

There may be a deemed disposal for capital gains tax purposes when:

(1) a beneficiary becomes entitled to an interest in possession; or
(2) when the trustees make an advance of capital to a beneficiary; or
(3) when a beneficiary becomes absolutely entitled to trust property.

The significance here is that, with an A & M trust, the actual or effective transfer of property to a beneficiary gives rise to a liability to capital gains tax, not inheritance tax.

11.3.7 Other types of trusts

The three types of trust described above are those most commonly found in practice and the majority of financial planning situations can be resolved by one or other of these. However, they are not the only types available.

Bare trusts

A bare trust (also known as a simple trust) arises where a trustee simply holds the trust property but has no active duties to perform. For example, if property is left to a minor by way of gift, that property is held by a bare trustee (usually a parent or guardian) until the child reaches the age of 18.

Special trusts

A special trust is one where the settlor appoints a trustee to carry out specific purposes. For example, the trustee might be asked to collect the income arising from the trust property and pay such income to a life tenant.

Precatory trusts

A precatory trust is one where the trust instrument uses such phrases as 'I hope' or 'I wish'. Precatory trusts are not legally binding and would be appropriate where you are undecided as to who should receive your property after your death but have full confidence that one person will carry out your wishes. With a legally binding trust, you would need to execute a new will or codicil every time you changed your mind. With a precatory trust, one supreme beneficiary can be chosen to distribute the property in accordance with your wishes, with your instructions being amended from time to time by informal notification to the beneficiary.

Offshore trusts

A trust is treated as UK-resident unless the general administration of the trust is carried on outside the United Kingdom and the trustees (or at least the majority of them) are not resident or ordinarily resident in the United Kingdom (see 12.3.1). Offshore (or non-resident) trusts may provide tax advantages for UK expatriates; however, anybody who is considering sheltering their investments from the Revenue must consider very carefully the anti-avoidance legislation which is complex and beyond the scope of this book.

11.4 SETTING UP A TRUST

Declaring a trust is a significant step. Unlike a will (which only comes into effect on your death and which can be changed as often as you like while you are alive), a trust takes effect immediately. If you subsequently find that it is not achieving its purpose, it can be very difficult indeed to change. It is therefore vital to obtain competent legal advice.

11.4.1 The three certainties

In order for a trust to be valid, it must fulfil requirements known as the three certainties:

(1) The words used in the declaration must express sufficiently clearly the intentions of the settlor. The word 'trust' is not absolutely necessary if the settlor's intention is clear.
(2) The beneficiaries should be clearly ascertained even if the list of beneficiaries includes as yet unborn beneficiaries.
(3) The property which is going into the trust must be clearly identified: for example, you need to specify which shares, how much money, which life assurance policies etc.

11.4.2 Capacity to declare a trust

Any individual over the age of 18 and of sound mind is able to declare a trust. A minor could declare a trust but such a trust would be voidable by the individual when he reached the age of 18 (ie he could declare that the trust no longer exists).

11.4.3 Choice of trustee

The choice of trustee is of great importance to everyone involved with the trust. Unless you have appointed yourself as trustee (or otherwise reserved powers for yourself in the trust deed), you will have handed complete control over the property to the trustees. It goes without saying, therefore, that the trustees must be honest, be prepared to look after the trust property, understand your wishes and understand the terms of the trust. Unless the trust specifically permits the payment of fees to the trustees, they must act without any payment.

If you wish to appoint an individual as trustee, you might consider appointing someone who knows you and your financial affairs, such as your accountant or solicitor. If you are considering appointing a friend or relative as a trustee, somebody with no experience of financial matters at all is not likely to be a suitable choice.

The location of your trustees is also important. Your trustees should be readily accessible – a delay in obtaining a trustee's signature might prejudice the interests of the beneficiaries.

People often choose their spouse as trustee; after all, your spouse is the person who knows and probably understands your wishes better than anyone. In the majority of cases there is no doubt that this is a wise choice. Nevertheless, some marriages do fail and, if the split is acrimonious, life is not made any easier by your spouse being the trustee or co-trustee of a trust that you have set up. After all, the trustees can only act unanimously, a trustee cannot be forced to resign, and legal action (which is usually expensive) would need to be taken to have an uncooperative trustee removed. It is, however, possible to include, within the trust deed, the power to have a trustee removed in certain circumstances.

11.4.4 Who can be a trustee?

Any individual, limited company or other corporation may be appointed as trustee. There is nothing to prevent a beneficiary being a trustee, although it would perhaps be sensible to ensure that a beneficiary was not a sole trustee.

Trust corporation

A trust corporation is a company that is empowered to act as a trustee; it is likely to charge a fee for accepting the appointment and for managing the trust, and may also charge a fee when assets are withdrawn from the trust.

Public trustee

The public trustee is a public corporation whose main function is to administer private trusts; it can be appointed to act in the same way as a private individual. The public trustee always imposes a charge for acting, its remuneration being based on the value of the trust property.

Custodian trustee

A custodian trustee's function is simply to hold the legal title to trust property, leaving the administration of the trust in the hands of managing trustees. A custodian trustee (eg a bank) is usually appointed so that there is no need for any further appointment of new trustees to look after the trust deeds and securities.

11.5 THE APPOINTMENT, RETIREMENT AND REMOVAL OF TRUSTEES

Statutory provision is made in the Trustee Act 1925 for the appointment and removal of trustees.

11.5.1 The appointment of trustees

Trustees must be appointed on the creation of a new trust and may also be appointed during the continuance of an existing trust. The appointment of trustees is always made by deed (ie it is not sufficient merely to write a letter appointing someone as trustee). Sometimes the court will have to make the appointment itself when there is no-one else capable of making the appointment.

You, as the settlor, usually appoint the first trustees. You could declare yourself the sole trustee of the trust or you could appoint yourself and others to be the first trustees. Also, you may want to retain the right to appoint future trustees.

If new trustees need to be appointed, there may be provision for this within the trust instrument itself; if not, there is statutory power within the Trustee Act.

The total number of trustees must not exceed four. Where a trustee wishes to retire, but there is no proposal to replace him as trustee, he can retire if there are at least two trustees remaining. As a rule of thumb, a minimum of two trustees is desirable, to give the beneficiaries adequate protection.

11.5.2 Retirement of trustees

It is possible for trustees to retire from office. They could do so under the terms of the trust itself, under the statutory powers of the Trustee Act, by obtaining the consent of all the beneficiaries (who must be over 18 and absolutely entitled to the trust property), or by obtaining the consent of the court. Trustees may retire provided there remains a minimum of two trustees (or a trust corporation) after their retirement and provided they obtain the consent of the remaining trustees.

11.5.3 Removal of trustees

A trustee may be removed from office either under a power within the trust itself, under a statutory power within the Trustee Act or by the court. A statutory power of removal can be used where trustees remain outside the United Kingdom for more than 12 consecutive months, where they refuse to act, or where they are either unfit to act or are incapable of acting.

11.6 THE DUTIES AND RESPONSIBILITIES OF TRUSTEES

If you accept an appointment as a trustee, you are bound to participate in the administration of the trust and you will, of course, have to take on certain responsibilities:

(1) You must become familiar with the terms of the trust. If you undertake a transaction which is not permitted under the terms of the trust, this would constitute a breach of trust. It is clearly important, for example, that you do not distribute trust funds to the wrong beneficiary.

(2) Where you are a new trustee appointed to an existing trust, you must be satisfied that there has been no prior breach of trust. Although you cannot be held to be liable for such a breach, you could be acting in breach of trust yourself by not enquiring.

(3) In the administration of the trust (as an unpaid trustee), you must use as much care as any prudent person would use in the management of their own affairs.

(4) On occasions, the trustees may not be sure how they should act. In such cases, they should apply to the courts for guidance or direction.

(5) All acts and decisions of the trustees must usually be unanimous – unless the trust specifically allows it, it is not possible for a decision of the majority to bind all the trustees (although this is the case in Scotland).

(6) Trustees are responsible for keeping the Inland Revenue informed about the trust and for making annual returns.

11.6.1 Investment policy

On matters of investment policy, the trustees' bible is the Trustee Investments Act 1961 (although its provisions are often expressly varied by the trust itself). The main principles laid down by the Act are:

(1) Trustees must consider the interests of the beneficiaries at all times. If, for example, there is a life tenant and remaindermen then, as well as taking steps to preserve the income of the life tenant, trustees must also take account of the need to preserve the capital for the remaindermen.
(2) Trustees could be in breach of trust if they do not take all practicable steps to reduce risk by diversification.
(3) Trustees must take proper advice about specific investments.
(4) The Act states that at least half the trust fund should be invested in 'narrower range' investments (eg bank and building society deposits, gilt-edged securities, most National Savings products and certain debentures) with the balance in 'wider range' investments (such as unit trusts and also ordinary shares that meet certain criteria).

Usually, trust deeds give express powers of investment overriding the provisions of the Act but that does not remove from trustees a duty of care over the investments in the trust, ie the principles in the Act still hold true. If the terms of the trust do not override the provisions of the Act then the only investments you may consider are those certified as 'trustee investments'.

11.7 THE RIGHTS OF BENEFICIARIES

Generally speaking, as a beneficiary, you cannot interfere in the administration of the trust; all you can do is anticipate the benefits which the trustees will eventually forward to you. However, that is not the final word as the law does give beneficiaries some rights outside the strict wording of the trust.

(1) Beneficiaries often wish to have some say in the control of the trustees' discretion, particularly in the field of investments and the allocation of discretionary trusts. The trustees are bound to take note of any representation that is made to them by the beneficiaries, although ultimately any decision has to be taken by the trustees alone.

(2) It is possible, in certain circumstances, for the beneficiaries to bring a trust to an end. Put simply, if there is a sole beneficiary under the trust who is of a sound mind and over the age of 18, or if there are two or more such beneficiaries who are all in agreement, they can bring the trust to an end irrespective of the wishes of the trustees or the settlor.
(3) If you consider that the trust is not being properly administered, you may apply to the courts either for the determination of a specific question or for an action for general administration of the trust.
(4) You are entitled to inspect deeds and documents relating to the trust and to be provided with information about the trust including copies of the accounts.

11.8 TRUSTS IN PRACTICE – AN EXAMPLE

A couple have three adult children and seven grandchildren. Their house is worth about £200,000, they have investments (mainly in shares and unit trusts) totalling approximately £40,000 and they have about £20,000 in a building society deposit.

The husband is a successful businessman who has built up a small printing business of which he is the principal shareholder; the company is worth something in the region of £500,000. He has a good pension plan and a lot of personal life assurance.

He has decided that he would like to make arrangements for the following:

(1) To make effective provision for his wife on his death (she has already made it clear that she is not interested in the business).
(2) To prepare for any inheritance tax that might be payable on his death.
(3) To ensure that his business is divided fairly between his children in a tax-efficient way.
(4) To help with the education and future careers of his grandchildren.

Providing for the family

He has agreed with his wife that, in view of the amount of personal life assurance already arranged, she will only require the income from the investments and capital that he was going to leave. He therefore creates a trust in his will giving her the right to receive the income from the total investments for as long as she is alive and then, on her death, for the portfolio to pass to the children. This will come into effect on his death; until then, he continues to own the investments outright.

The type of trust is an interest in possession trust with the life interest belonging to his wife and the reversionary interest belonging to the children.

Preparing for inheritance tax

He intends to provide the funds to pay any eventual inheritance tax bill in the future, rather than gifting all of his property during his lifetime (he also has to take account of the fact that his life assurance will provide capital on his death and this will almost certainly increase the estate of his wife on *her* death). He arranges this through a joint life, second death, whole-of-life policy on the lives of himself and his wife and, to ensure that the proceeds do not fall into the deceased's estate at the second death, the policy is written in trust with the children as beneficiaries.

Looking after the business

A large part of the husband's wealth consists of his shares in his business. He understands that one way of reducing his inheritance tax bill (and at the same time helping his family) would be to transfer some of his shares to his children now. However, like many proprietors of family businesses he does not wish to relinquish control.

He puts the shares into a discretionary trust for the benefit of his children, appointing himself and/or his professional advisers as trustees. Provided the value does not exceed the nil rate band, there will be no inheritance tax liability at the time. Of course, as trustee, he must act in the interests of his beneficiaries and not just himself (this is doubly important to avoid any suggestion that he has retained an interest or is deriving some benefit from the shares).

Educating the grandchildren

He is also keen to help with the education and future career developments of his grandchildren. By transferring a block of his shares in his company to an accumulation and maintenance trust of which his grandchildren are the beneficiaries, the dividends received by the trustees could then be used to cover their school fees. The personal allowances of the grandchildren may well mean that no income tax is ultimately paid on these dividends. The shares will, of course, become the property of the grandchildren at some time in the future but the trustees have absolute discretion over when that happens.

11.9 ANTI-AVOIDANCE LEGISLATION

Setting up a trust can be very beneficial from the point of view of tax planning, particularly in relation to inheritance tax. There may also be some benefits from the point of view of income tax and capital gains tax. Here, however, there is a range of anti-avoidance provisions in place to make sure that the trust is a genuine settlement and not one from which you may benefit. It is an area where you need professional advice; the broad thrust of the provisions is as follows.

(1) If you set up a trust where you and your wife *may* benefit, then you may be liable to income tax on income earned by the assets of the trust. If the trust wording is not clear on whether you may benefit, the Revenue may well tax you on the income if it believes you *could* benefit. The effect of this legislation is that the benefits of independent taxation (see 8.5) are not obtained by putting capital in trust for your wife. The legislation also has implications for deeds of variation (see 9.4.5).

(2) Setting up a trust for your unmarried minor children, including adopted and illegitimate children, means that, in most cases, you will be liable to income tax on the income (though this does not apply in the case of bare trusts if the income is not distributed before the child reaches the age of 18).

(3) You may also be liable for income tax (even if you are expressly excluded from benefiting from the income) if you receive capital payments from a trust set up by you which has undistributed income.

(4) If you set up a trust where there are any circumstances whatsoever whereby you or your wife could benefit from capital or income then you will be liable for paying the capital gains tax on any gains made by the trust. This could have a significant impact as the retention of only a very small interest in the trust could make you liable for tax on possibly considerable gains that you did not (and perhaps could not) enjoy.

In the vast majority of cases, you can claim back any tax that you have paid from the trustees. The underlying point is that the tax is based on your personal circumstances (eg it takes your allowances and other income into account) with the overall objective being to ensure that you cannot set up a trust in order to 'shelter' income or capital gains from tax.

12

RETIRING ABROAD

The growth in foreign travel over the last 30 years has led to an increasing number of people buying property abroad, usually for holidays. This became a veritable flood when exchange control restrictions were lifted in 1979. Today, a considerable number of people own property abroad, with France and Spain being two particularly popular areas. Many of these people are retired; for them, the opportunity to get away from the long British winters has proved to be irresistible.

There is, of course, considerably more to retiring abroad than indulging in a warmer climate. This chapter looks at the following areas:

(1) The emotional factor
(2) Buying property abroad
(3) Domicile and residence
(4) UK taxation
(5) Pensions
(6) Tax in a foreign country
(7) Investment considerations
(8) Health and social security
(9) Returning home
(10) Conclusions.

12.1 THE EMOTIONAL FACTOR

This might seem a slightly odd way to start this chapter but the fact is that some people do seem to make decisions about living abroad or buying property abroad for entirely emotional reasons, without really considering any of the practical problems. After a pleasant holiday or two in an area with which they have become familiar, people have been known to make, in the warmth of the afternoon sun, a decision which will affect their lifestyle for some years to come and over which they would deliberate for many weeks if they were at home. The decision to sell up and move to another part of the United Kingdom would be a long and carefully thought-out process. The decision to sell up and move to, say, Spain, has been taken over a few drinks.

Many people do successfully transport themselves to another country and adapt to a new way of life. Others do not and discover that they have made an expensive mistake, finding themselves unable to come to terms with a different culture, different laws, different taxes, different standards, different health systems and different attitudes towards retired people – all conducted in a different language. After many years of experience, they know how the United Kingdom works. They know how to get things done, how to complain if things go wrong and how to sort out an incorrect gas or electricity bill. In a foreign country, they have to learn new tricks of social survival and a fair proportion of them find that it is too much hassle.

The overall message is to explore your own thoughts about why the prospect of retiring abroad is so attractive. If you are really enthusiastic about learning new skills and absorbing new ideas, then you may well be suited to life in a warm climate. But if it is just the climate that attracts you, then it might be an idea to think again.

12.2 BUYING PROPERTY ABROAD

The growth in overseas property buying in recent years has been quite staggering and not just from the point of view of the United Kingdom. The general increase in prosperity throughout Europe has meant that more and more people from northern Europe are looking for a holiday or retirement home in the sunnier parts of southern Europe. The Mediterranean coastline is now dotted with apartments and villas, with Spain being a favourite spot.

Compared to buying property in the United Kingdom, buying property abroad seems to be simplicity itself. There are no end of people in the United Kingdom eager to sell you property abroad and they may even fly you out there and put you up in an hotel at their expense. Provided you are prepared to limit your search in this way, there are a number of reputable agencies that will provide you with an excellent service. But be warned; buying a property in, for example, Spain, may appear to be little different from buying property in England when you are having it explained to you at an hotel seminar in Tunbridge Wells. However, the reality is:

(1) You are buying a house in a foreign country.
(2) The contract may be in a foreign language.
(3) The legal system is totally different.
(4) The bureaucracy in some foreign countries can seem almost medieval at times.
(5) Different countries have different tax systems.

Provided you follow the rules, you will have no problems but you can more or less guarantee a layer of extra complication which will occasionally make buying a house in the United Kingdom look like child's play. Things will obviously be easier if you learn some of the local language.

The golden rules are not to cut corners and be prepared to pay for expert advice and help. If you were buying a house in the United Kingdom, you would expect to pay a solicitor to ensure that all the legalities were tied up, but some people still buy houses abroad without a thought for the legal niceties.

12.2.1 A home for retirement

It is not at all uncommon, of course, to buy property now with a view to using it as a retirement home when you finally do retire. The important thing to bear in mind, if this is your aim, is to ensure the property is suitable for you when you do retire. On the rushed inspection flight, it is all too easy to buy the perfect property now but one which could well become a problem for you in the future. If you intend to buy property in the sun for use as a home when you retire, you should consider it from all manner of viewpoints to make sure it will be the kind of property that will suit you when you retire.

Two very important considerations are the weather and maintenance. If you go out to look for your retirement home in the fine weather, it is tempting to believe that it is fine all the time. But the coastline at the western end of the Mediterranean, whilst it can have fine warm days in winter, can also have some very cold days, some very wet days and some very windy days. People who have built houses in more exposed positions (eg on hillsides to get those wonderful views) have found to their cost that log fires, and even central heating, to keep warm in the winter have been of more value than air conditioning to keep cool in the summer.

Also, do keep a very careful eye on future maintenance. Do not believe that just because you have a home in the sun, it will not require looking after. Those white houses look lovely in the sunshine, but they soon get dirty and start to look shabby. They are going to need painting about once every three years.

On the plus side, membership of the EU has meant a general raising of building standards and houses throughout the EU tend to be of much better quality than, say, ten years ago.

12.2.2 The key steps

Unless you know the area where you are going to look for property, you will probably do what most buyers do and go and look 'on spec'. The choice of property is often very wide and, if you are buying new property, you may find the sales pitch more than enticing. Clearly, you can make your own mind up about the property itself but you should also reassure yourself about the nearest shops, the access to English speaking doctors and dentists, local bus and taxi services, likely future development in the area and so on.

Having decided that you like the area and that the property is also to your liking, you can then start thinking about the steps to be taken in actually purchasing the property.

The first thing to do is to engage a lawyer and the general advice is to find a solicitor in the United Kingdom who has experience in property transactions in the area in which you wish to live. The Law Society can advise you on solicitors who can do this. This is a significantly better option than using a local lawyer because there is no guarantee that he will do the job with anything like the attention to detail you are entitled to expect from your UK solicitor. Your powers of redress in the event of problems may be limited and very difficult to pursue.

Do not be tempted by the deals which appear to save you money, the most popular one being to organise the purchase in such a way as to save you tax. The chances are it will not save you tax in the long run and the immediate benefit may be to the seller.

Do not over commit yourself on the purchase price or running costs. Remember that in addition to coping with domestic inflation you now have to cope with a fluctuating exchange rate and a foreign inflation rate which could be higher than that in the United Kingdom.

Do not overlook the tax and rates position. If you own a second house in the United Kingdom you will have to take due regard of capital gains tax, inheritance tax and, if you let your property, income tax. The same will probably be true in a foreign country so you will need to make yourself fully familiar with their tax rules as well. You will almost certainly have some taxes to pay when you buy your property and also when you own it.

Finally, do take care and do not sign anything or pay over any money at all until you have sought professional advice. A number of people have lost money in overseas property deals and not just at the hands of foreign companies. Your legal title to property in some foreign countries is considerably weaker than it is in the United Kingdom and the only way to prevent yourself from falling into the many traps is to use competent legal advice.

12.3 DOMICILE AND RESIDENCE

As soon as you decide to spend any length of time outside the United Kingdom, you are faced with questions of your domicile and residence. These are important because they decide the basis on which you are to be taxed. Throughout this chapter, residence refers to your *tax* residence – ie to which Inland Revenue you will be obliged to make tax returns. This is a quite separate concept to your *legal* residence, ie gaining the necessary authority to live in the country of your choice. It is, for example, perfectly possible, in any one tax year, for you to be a legal resident of Spain (because you comply with their requirements to live there permanently) and be a tax resident of the United Kingdom (because of the amount of time you have spent in the United Kingdom in the tax year in question). It may also be possible to be a tax resident in more than one country at a time.

For the purposes of UK taxation, the 'United Kingdom' means England, Scotland, Wales and Northern Ireland. It does not include the Channel Islands or the Isle of Man.

12.3.1 Residence and ordinary residence

These concepts are not defined anywhere in tax law. There are a number of factors which are regularly taken into account when the Inland Revenue determines your tax status but, in complex cases, a final decision depends on the facts of the case in question.

Residence

You are resident in the United Kingdom if you fulfil one of two basic requirements.

(1) If you are physically present here for 183 days or more in the tax year. There are no exceptions to this rule. It does not matter if the time is taken up in one long visit or several visits (though the days of arrival and departure are normally not counted).
(2) If you average 91 days or more here per annum over a period of four tax years.

Ordinary residence

If you are resident in the United Kingdom year after year (ie you regard the United Kingdom as your habitual home) then you are ordinarily resident here. It is quite possible to be ordinarily resident here but resident elsewhere, eg by going on a long holiday and not setting foot in the United Kingdom for a complete tax year.

If you claim that you are no longer resident or ordinarily resident, then it is up to you to prove it. Inland Revenue booklet IR 20 (*Residents and non-residents – liability to tax in the United Kingdom*) states as follows:

> . . . you will normally be asked for some evidence that you have left the United Kingdom permanently – for example, that you have taken steps to acquire accommodation abroad to live in as a permanent home, and if you continue to own property in the United Kingdom, the reason is consistent with your stated aim of permanent residence abroad. If you can provide this, you may be treated as *provisionally* not-resident and not-ordinarily resident from the day after the date of your departure. Normally, this provisional ruling is confirmed after you have lived abroad for a whole tax year, as long as your visits to the United Kingdom since leaving have averaged less than 91 days a tax year.
>
> If you do not have this evidence, a decision is postponed for up to three years. The decision will be based on what has actually happened since you left the United Kingdom. Until then you are provisionally treated as remaining resident in the United Kingdom. You continue to receive tax allowances and reliefs. Your tax bill may be adjusted when the final decision has been made.

12.3.2 Domicile

The implication of domicile is that if you are of UK domicile, you are liable to inheritance tax on your worldwide assets, *regardless* of your residence or ordinary residence (as distinct from income tax and capital gains tax where your liability depends on your residence and ordinary residence).

Domicile is a concept of general law and is determined by a range of factors. Broadly speaking, domicile is where you have your permanent home. It is distinct from nationality or residence. You can only have one domicile at a time. You normally acquire a domicile of origin from your father when you are born, though this may have changed if the person on whom you were dependent at the time changed his domicile before you were aged 16.

Women who married before 1974 automatically acquired their husband's domicile, though they may now change it to a domicile of their choice.

Anybody over the age of 16 has the legal power to apply for a new domicile of choice. However, it is not easy to do and usually requires proof that you have severed all connections with your existing country and intend to settle permanently in a new country.

12.4 UK TAXATION

The UK income tax system is very wide-ranging. If you are resident in the United Kingdom for tax purposes, then it sets out to tax you on any investment income that arises in the United Kingdom or that is remitted to the United Kingdom. 'Arising' income is income that is actually earned in the United Kingdom, eg interest on a bank account. 'Remitted' income means it could arise outside the United Kingdom but is actually paid into the United Kingdom. Non-residents are liable to UK income tax on investment income that arises in the United Kingdom.

The most common types of investment income are:

(1) Interest from banks and building societies
(2) Interest from government securities
(3) Rental income
(4) Dividends.

Pensions are regarded as earned income, not investment income. They are dealt with in 12.5.

12.4.1 Double taxation relief

As a tax resident of a foreign country, you also have to make tax returns to the fiscal authorities of that country for any income you receive. However, it is not generally the purpose of governments to tax people twice and so the UK Government has entered into agreements with the governments of other countries for the purpose of preventing double taxation on the same income. Under double taxation conventions, certain types of income are taxable in only one of the countries and that is generally the one in which you live.

Even where there is no double taxation agreement, the UK authorities generally give you a credit (called 'unilateral relief') for any foreign tax which has been deducted from income which you have earned. Fortunately, the United Kingdom has concluded double taxation treaties with the principal countries which people retire to. However, the terms and the taxes covered vary considerably from country to country so it is essential to check on the rules for your particular country of interest.

12.4.2 Income tax

Personal allowances

Under normal circumstances, you are entitled to claim certain allowances that can be deducted from gross income to arrive at the actual level of income on which tax will be levied. The most important of these are personal allowances which are of particular interest to the retired expatriate as it is possible to continue to claim them even though you are no longer resident in the United Kingdom for tax purposes. This is particularly useful if you have income arising in the United Kingdom that you cannot or do not wish to rearrange.

Independent taxation

There could be a good case for dividing up income-producing UK assets in order that both husband and wife can fully offset their individual personal allowances against income arising in the United Kingdom.

Interest from banks and building societies

If you are not ordinarily resident in the United Kingdom and receive interest from a UK bank or building society, you can apply to have the interest paid gross without deduction of tax. You have to provide a declaration to your bank or building society that you are not ordinarily resident and all future interest will be paid gross (declarations cannot be backdated). If you have a joint account, both account holders must be able to sign the declaration for income to be paid gross.

Note that the fact that you are receiving gross interest does not of itself mean that you are not obliged to pay tax. You are (because of your domicile) but, by concession, tax is not charged if you are non-resident for the whole of any tax year for which you received gross interest.

Another point to bear in mind is that the need for compliance with Inland Revenue rules is an extra responsibility for the banks and building societies and this is occasionally reflected in high minimum levels of deposits or lower rates of interest for non-residents with onshore accounts. Some even refuse to pay gross interest and always deduct tax.

Offshore accounts avoid all this as the interest is paid gross anyway.

UK Government securities (gilts)

Interest paid on certain British Government 'FOTRA' securities is exempt from income tax provided you are neither resident nor ordinarily resident in the United Kingdom. This applies *only* if you hold a stock at the date that the interest is actually paid (ie it does not apply if you have sold the stock even though the sale may have been 'ex-dividend'). The Inland Revenue applies a strict interpretation of this rule.

Rental income

If you are living abroad, but own property in the United Kingdom which is being let, there are tax implications for both you and your tenants. Anybody who rents UK property is required to deduct basic rate tax from any rents paid to a non-resident landlord and pay the tax to the Inland Revenue. This is the case even if the rent is paid into a UK bank account. In addition, the obligation to deduct basic rate tax applies to the gross amount of the rent so that if the landlord incurs expenses, he is obliged to make a repayment claim.

The only way of avoiding these problems is for the rent to be collected by a UK agent. Rent paid to an agent is paid gross and the agent then becomes liable for assessment. However, the assessment is on the net amount after deducting allowable expenses, so this provides a valuable cashflow benefit.

The usual allowable expenses are agent's fees, 10 per cent of the net rents for wear and tear to furniture, and interest on mortgages and similar loans (but not overdrafts). The relief on mortgage interest is not limited to interest on the first £30,000 only of the loan provided the property is let for six months of the year and is available for letting all year round.

Dividends

If you are resident in the United Kingdom, you are entitled to a tax credit when you receive dividends (see 6.4.6). If you are a non-resident, you only get the benefit of the tax credit if you are claiming your UK allowances. If you are not in this position, you do not get the tax credit even though the tax has been withheld from the dividend payment. As the income is potentially liable to tax in the country where you are now a tax resident, there is the real chance of double taxation.

This can be avoided if the other country has a double taxation treaty with the United Kingdom as, under these circumstances, you may be entitled to a tax credit.

12.4.3 Capital gains tax

You are liable to capital gains tax if you are either resident or ordinarily resident in the United Kingdom, ie the rules are tighter than for income tax. If you leave the United Kingdom during a tax year and cease to be resident and ordinarily resident then, by concession, you are not taxed on gains you make after your date of departure. Provided you remain a non-resident and non-ordinarily resident for the whole of the following 36 months, you are only liable for capital gains made after your return to the United Kingdom.

The net effect is that if you have assets that are 'pregnant' with capital gains, moving abroad for at least three years potentially removes all liability to UK capital gains tax (though you still have to abide by the residence rule – see 12.3.1). However, this depends on the Inland Revenue applying the terms of the necessary extra-statutory concession and the general Inland Revenue view is that such concessions are not applied in cases where people seek to take advantage of them for tax avoidance. The Revenue practice is, therefore, to charge tax on certain gains realised very shortly after an individual moves abroad if those gains fall in the same tax year.

You may, of course, have a liability to capital gains tax in your new country of residence but you could avoid that if you time your arrival correctly (see 12.6.1).

Double taxation agreements also cover capital gains tax to prevent you being taxed twice on the same disposal. You are generally taxed in the country where you were resident at the time.

Sale of property

If you are intending to sell your home when you retire abroad, there are not usually any implications for capital gains tax (on the basis that it is your main residence). However, if you have other property to sell then it is beneficial to time the sale to take place after your departure and, preferably, in a different tax year. Bear in mind that it is usually the date contracts are exchanged that is the crucial date, not the completion date.

Sale of a business

You face no liability if you dispose of your shares in a private limited company after you have ceased to be resident or ordinarily resident. However, if you are a sole proprietor or a partner, you may find it more difficult. The chances are you will want to sell it as a going concern which means that the price may well contain a sizable element of goodwill. Unfortunately, even if you are neither resident nor ordinarily resident in the United Kingdom, you are still liable to capital gains tax if you dispose of business aspects whilst the business is still active. You may be unable to convince the Revenue that the business is not active if it is being sold as a going concern in order to maximise the price and the end result might be that you just have to pay the tax.

12.4.4 Inheritance tax

Domicile can have a major impact on your liability to inheritance tax. If you are UK-domiciled then all of your assets, wherever they are situated in the world, fall into the UK inheritance tax net. This is a major liability and needs to be quantified rather than trusting to luck that you will not have a problem. Even if you become non-domiciled, you still have a liability to inheritance tax on assets that are physically situated in the United Kingdom, such as property or investments.

Writing a will

Under international law, where there is a will, the passing of assets from your estate to your heirs is governed by the law of your country of domicile in the case of 'movable' property (such as bank deposits or securities) and by local law in the case of 'immovable' property (such as a house). It is therefore quite possible that the decision of, say, an English court relating to your overseas home is not effective in the other country until it has been approved by a court there. A further point to bear in mind about overseas assets is that not all countries allow you complete freedom to dispose of your property as you please. In many countries, your children are entitled to inherit a minimum portion of your estate (and often get priority over your wife) and it is often the case that the incidence of estate duties is according to the kinship of the heirs and the value of their existing assets.

From all this it follows that the administration of an overseas estate can be very complex. One thing is certain; the trouble and expense (in the way of legal fees payable both here and elsewhere) incurred in sorting matters out properly in advance will be a fraction of the time, trouble and expense your heirs might be put to if you do not make a will in the country where you intend to retire to.

12.5 PENSIONS

The tax treatment depends on the type of your pension and the country you have chosen to retire to.

State retirement pension

This is always paid to you gross and it forms part of your worldwide income on which you normally have to pay tax in your country of residence. Living abroad does not normally affect the amount of your pension (but see 12.8).

Occupational pension or personal pension

This is normally paid to you net of tax at the basic rate but once you have been accepted as a non-ordinarily resident pensioner, you can apply to the Inspector of Foreign Dividends to receive your pension gross (or net at a lower rate of tax) when it is taxable solely in your country of residence. However, if you move to a country that does not levy taxes, you may find that the Inland Revenue will tax your pension at source.

Your decision to move abroad could also have an impact on the timing of taking benefits if you have not already done so by then. Some countries, for example, do not recognise the concept of the 'tax-free' lump sum and will tax it along with your pension.

Government pensions

Civil service, NHS and armed forces pensions etc are always paid net of UK tax regardless of your country of residence. If there is a double taxation agreement between that country and the United Kingdom, there is usually no further tax to pay.

12.6 TAX IN A FOREIGN COUNTRY

The main purpose of this chapter is to help you with the UK considerations you must take into account when planning to retire abroad. However, it is clear that tax and investment considerations in your chosen retirement country are equally important. Clearly, a book of this nature cannot deal in any detail with taxation in even the most popular retirement countries but the following are some general principles which will hold good for most countries. If your affairs are complex, you should get advice from a competent financial adviser.

Many countries on the European mainland, principally Spain and Portugal, used to be tax havens. This was not only because tax rates were low but also because the administration was somewhat inefficient. Tax evasion was a way of life and almost to be encouraged. This is no longer the case. Although some tax rates are still lower than their UK equivalent, others are more severe. Also, the authorities are significantly more efficient than they used to be and now insist that you pay your dues.

Tax returns are often designed to be filled in by the taxpayer or his representative and, from the form, it is usually possible to calculate your tax liability. Consequently, when you send in your forms, you send in your cheque at the same time.

12.6.1 Tax status

Domicile

There is no direct equivalent of the UK concept of domicile in most other countries. In inheritance tax matters, your nationality often (though not always) stands in its place. This is certainly the case in most of Europe where, if you are a national of the country concerned, you are subject to inheritance tax on your worldwide assets but, if you are a non-national, you are subject to the tax on your locally sited assets only.

It follows that if you are UK-domiciled and therefore subject to UK inheritance tax on your worldwide assets, you are probably liable for both British and foreign inheritance taxes on your foreign assets. The burden is alleviated slightly by the fact that unilateral relief (see 12.4.1) may be granted in the United Kingdom for that part of your estate which has already been subjected to foreign taxation. This does not mean, of course, that foreign inheritance taxes can be ignored.

Residence

Most countries in the world operate a 'six-month rule' so that if you spend 183 days or more in that country during the tax year, you are resident there for tax purposes. However, you should remember that although the UK tax year runs from April to April, in most other countries the tax year is the same as the calendar year. This means that it is perfectly possible to be resident in two countries at the same time by virtue of the same rule, although the potentially damaging effects of this are usually alleviated by double taxation treaties.

It could also be that timing your departure and your arrival could work to your advantage because the same rule could mean that you are not tax resident in either country for a period of time. By leaving the United Kingdom before 5 April means that you have given yourself the means to be non-resident in the United Kingdom for the whole of the following tax year. By not arriving in your new country until after 1 July, you are also not regarded as a resident there for the tax year ending on 31 December.

You should also find out if the definition of residence is covered by other factors. Until recently, for example, you would have been regarded as a resident of the United Kingdom if you had accommodation 'available for your use' there (and 'available' was given a very liberal interpretation by the Inland Revenue). This rule was dispensed with in 1993 but other countries are starting to introduce it.

Ordinary residence

There is no direct equivalent to ordinary residence in most foreign tax systems though many have some provision for recognising a degree of permanency in your residence arrangements.

12.6.2 Tax liabilities

Income tax

Unlike the United Kingdom, which taxes resident foreigners differently from (and sometimes more favourably than) its own citizens, most countries make no distinction in their tax treatment between locals and immigrants. Quite reasonably, the tax authorities take the view that if you decide to live in their country, you must expect to be asked to pay the same taxes as their own citizens. As a result, once you move abroad, you can expect to be asked to pay tax on your worldwide income (and usually your capital gains also) whether remitted to that country or not, though you will, of course, be protected by any double taxation treaties.

Capital gains tax

As is now the case in the United Kingdom, it is common in many tax regimes to tax capital gains as income in the year that they are made. Most also take account of the effects of inflation to ensure that only 'real' gains are subject to taxation. This means that, in the majority of cases, redemption of a capital holding gives rise to a lower overall rate of tax than would the equivalent income.

However, not many countries follow the UK practice of allowing you to realise a proportion of your annual gains free of capital gains tax.

Inheritance tax

In many countries (particularly most continental countries), inheritance tax applies to lifetime gifts as well as transfers at death. More importantly, there is often no inter-spouse exemption as we have in the United Kingdom. This means that if you keep substantial assets abroad, your death could result in your partner receiving a sizable tax bill at a time when there are likely to be problems enough. The rate of tax levied usually depends on the blood relationship between you and the recipients of your estate, with the lowest rates applying to your immediate family and the highest to remoter relations and friends.

You may be able to mitigate the effects of the tax if you keep as much of your estate as possible outside the country by arranging your investments elsewhere, ie in one of the offshore 'tax havens' for example.

12.7 INVESTMENT CONSIDERATIONS

The overall investment strategy outlined in Chapter 6 is still valid regardless of where you live. The position on living abroad is, however, complicated by the interplay of three factors:

(1) UK taxation
(2) Foreign taxation
(3) Exchange rate movements.

Currency movements are an important factor in planning retirement income abroad. As all your living expenses are going to be in a currency other than sterling, there is something to be said for perhaps increasing the amount of short-term cash and have rather more of it immediately accessible so that you can convert it quickly into your local currency if exchange rates move in your favour.

A number of banks and building societies operate expatriate accounts which enable you to have the benefits of a bank or building society account and to receive the interest gross (but see 12.4.2).

With your other investments, you will want to organise these in the most tax-efficient way. You can make use of some of the tax-efficient short to medium-term investments (eg TESSAs, ISAs and National Savings) with the one exception of personal equity plans which are only available to UK residents.

If you wish to invest in gilt-edged securities, then it may be appropriate for you to invest in one or more of the exempt gilts.

If you decide to invest in any form of asset-backed, income-producing investments, then there is some merit in investing in UK-based funds but only up to the extent that you are able to claim back tax paid on any income arising from them (ie up to the extent of your personal allowances). In all other cases, it may be more appropriate for you to invest in offshore funds so as to avoid the problems of withholding tax.

In the same way, it might be beneficial to set up an offshore bank account (in the Channel Islands, Isle of Man and the Dublin International Financial Centre) as the means of receiving all income. This then enables you to control the flow of money into your new country without having to reclaim tax paid on UK bank or building society deposits. Clearly, you will also require a bank account in your new country but you may find it helpful to arrange that through a bank with offices in both your new country and your offshore choice.

Finally, do not forget that you have to make tax returns in your new country. Some people find it simpler to engage a local accountant to do this for them (although in Spain, for example, you can use the services of a *gestor* – literally a 'form filler' – to do the job for you).

Do be advised that the tax collection agencies of most countries to which you are likely to retire to are very much stricter than they may have been. Do not be tempted to cut corners, no matter how much the locals tell you it is the done thing.

12.8 HEALTH AND SOCIAL SECURITY

Social security payments (particularly pensions) and medical treatment (particularly the availability of free medical treatment) are important considerations for anybody planning to retire abroad. For the purposes of your entitlement to the various benefits, the world is divided into three areas:

(1) The European Union, which currently consists of the United Kingdom, Austria, Belgium, Denmark, Finland, France, Germany, Greece, the Republic of Ireland, Italy, Luxembourg, The Netherlands, Norway, Portugal, Spain and Sweden.

The United Kingdom (for the purpose of health and social security benefits only) includes Gibraltar, but not the Channel Islands or the Isle of Man.

Members of the European Free Trade Area are also covered. Most now belong to the EU but also included are Iceland and Liechtenstein.

(2) Countries with which the United Kingdom has reciprocal agreements. These are currently Australia, Barbados, Bermuda, Canada, Cyprus, Israel, Jamaica, Jersey and Guernsey, Malta, Mauritius, New Zealand, the Philippines, Switzerland, Turkey, the USA and former Yugoslavia (including the newly independent former republics). However, the agreements with Australia, Canada and New Zealand do not include annual upratings in the state pension.

(3) Any other country.

12.8.1 The European Union

Pensions and social security benefits

If you are drawing any kind of benefit in the United Kingdom, you should get specific advice on the implications of a move to another country.

In general terms, if you retire to a country covered by the EU requirements, you are under the same obligation to pay national insurance contributions as though you had retired in this country. This would mean that if you took early retirement, it could be in your best interests to pay Class 3 voluntary contributions (see 2.2).

When the time comes for you to receive your pension, you should claim this in the normal way. It is paid to you in the usual way but normally only either four weekly or quarterly. Payments can be either sent direct to you, or paid into a foreign bank account (or UK bank or building society).

You will qualify for indexation increments and also increased payments for dependants (see 13.2).

In general terms, if you have been receiving any special allowances (for example, attendance allowance and invalid care allowance) then these do not continue to be paid, but you may be able to qualify for a similar benefit in your new country. If you are widowed in your new country, you can claim widow's benefit in your new country. (A full description of all relevant UK social security benefits is given in Chapters 13 and 14.)

Health

If you are below state retirement age, you do not automatically qualify for free medical help in your new country (though you may qualify if you are receiving certain allowances in the United Kingdom). You may be able to contribute voluntarily to the state sickness scheme of your new country; alternatively, you may have to take out private medical insurance in the United Kingdom before you leave (some countries insist on this anyway).

Once you qualify for your retirement pension (or widow's benefit), then you and your dependants are generally entitled to the health services of the state sickness insurance scheme of your new country.

In all cases, you only qualify for health care in the United Kingdom if you are living in the United Kingdom. The fact that you continue to pay UK national insurance contributions does *not* entitle you to health care in your new country at UK expense.

Most important of all, you should consider what will happen to you if you become seriously ill. Clearly, hospital treatment is available but, for more elderly people, nursing and residential homes may be both limited and expensive in other countries.

12.8.2 Non-EU countries

Pensions and social security benefits

You are obliged to continue to pay Class 3 national insurance contributions in order to qualify for your full benefits. An important point (for men) to note is that you do not get any contributions credited to you when you reach age 60 for any tax year you are a non-UK resident, ie you may have to pay contributions up to age 65.

Your pension can be paid to you in the usual way but you do not get any cost of living increases unless you remain ordinarily resident in the United Kingdom or you go to live in one of the countries with which the United Kingdom has reciprocal agreements (with the notable exceptions of Australia, New Zealand and Canada).

In the case of other social security benefits or allowances, you may be able to continue receiving these if there is a reciprocal arrangement with the country concerned.

Health

It is most inadvisable to rely on the health services of any country outside the EU and you should always make private arrangements in the United Kingdom before you leave. There is no claim against the NHS for any treatment you receive abroad.

12.9 RETURNING HOME

If it was odd to start this chapter on the emotional aspects, it may seem even odder to end it with a section on returning home. In many ways, however, facing up to the problems of returning home is one of the most important aspects of taking the decision to go abroad in the first place.

For all its faults, Britain is home to most of us. It is the place where we feel most comfortable, particularly when things start to go wrong. Increasing frailty, old age and illness can turn a foreign idyll into a nightmare, and in all the advertisements for overseas property, there will always be a fair sprinkling of 'distress' sales, instances where the dream has gone sour and the people concerned want to get home literally at any price.

Living abroad does present problems in particular for your family if you suddenly need their help. A 100-mile car drive may be a nuisance; a 1,000-mile flight may be impossible. The general advice on housing is to think the next stage well in advance. If your current house is getting too big, it makes sense to move into a smaller house while the move is still a relatively simple problem. This is even more true for overseas property. There are plenty of advertisements for overseas property but most of them are developers selling new property. Selling second-hand property in a foreign country is never easy and it is extremely difficult indeed to do it successfully from the United Kingdom.

Plan your departure carefully – but plan your return with even greater care and give yourself both time and room to manoeuvre.

Many people, for example, really do pull up their roots and move away only to wish they had retained a base in the United Kingdom to which they could return. It is no good relying on sons and daughters to keep a room open for you – a new arrival in their family may mean the room being taken up for more immediate purposes. Retention of property may well be the best option; even a small property in the United Kingdom is likely to maintain its value in real terms. If you sell up and move away completely, you might find it very difficult to return at a later date and get back into the property market.

12.10 CONCLUSIONS

Overall, moving from the cold winters of the United Kingdom to the warmth of, say, the Mediterranean has a lot of attractions for many people – but it is certainly not a decision which should be taken hastily. If you have been going on holiday to the same part of Europe for many years, you will have grown used to it and it could just be the place for you to retire. But retiring there and living there full time is significantly different from spending a few weeks once a year there. Providing you can cope with the overall changes, life in a warm climate can be very motivating and extremely pleasant. But if you are just going for the cheap drink and low taxes, it might be best to think again.

USEFUL READING MATTER

The Allied Dunbar Expatriate Tax and Investment Guide gives more detailed information on investment and other matters affecting expatriates. It can be obtained through any bookshop.

Inland Revenue leaflet IR 20 (Residents and non-residents) gives detailed guidance on the taxation implications of living abroad. A copy can be obtained from your local tax office.

DSS booklets SA 29 and NI 38 give information on social security matters within the European Community and outside the Community respectively.

13

THE PAYMENT OF STATE PENSIONS

In this and the next two chapters, the topics covered are those affecting people approaching or at retirement age. This particular chapter looks at the various factors that can affect the amount of state retirement pension that may be claimed by people of state retirement age, and the way in which certain other state benefits may have an interaction with their state pension. The subject is dealt with under the following headings:

(1) Introduction
(2) Increases to state pensions
(3) Deferring your state pension
(4) Married women
(5) Widows and widowers
(6) The impact of other benefits on your pension.

13.1 INTRODUCTION

When the time comes to draw your state pension, there are a number of factors which could have an influence on the amount you are eligible for. There are even circumstances under which you may decide not to start drawing your pension or even to stop it once you have started to draw it and to restart it at a later date. In addition, you may be claiming certain other state benefits as you approach retirement age and you will have to decide whether to continue with these other benefits or to stop them and start drawing your pension instead.

As with everything else in the social security system, the position is not at all straightforward and it takes some digging around to find out all the relevant facts. Some benefits affect your entitlement to other benefits, your entitlement to some benefits is affected by your level of other income (and, in some cases, the income of your wife or partner). Some benefits are taxable, others are not.

What follows can only be taken as an outline guide to the benefits on offer and the conditions that have to be fulfilled if you are to claim any of them. What is important are the options that may surround what appears to be, at first sight, a straightforward situation. It may, for example, seem obvious to take your state pension when you can. However, in certain circumstances, that may not be the best thing to do because, by doing so, you may lose other benefits that are of better value.

This is certainly an area where you have to ask the way and, such is the complexity of the system, the DSS has had to ensure that a small army of people is gainfully employed, up and down the country, in doing nothing more than answering questions. You may also find the answers to most of your questions in the array of booklets and brochures published by the DSS. You may well need a handful to answer more complex questions because the level of cross-referencing and cross-dependency between benefits is quite high. Age Concern also publishes a useful booklet which helps to explain the benefits entitlement of older people.

13.1.1 The terminology and other background points

Category A pension

At retirement age, you are entitled to the basic retirement pension and, possibly, an additional pension (eg SERPS). The basic pension (plus, if relevant, the additional pension) is called the 'category A' pension. It is based on your own national insurance contributions.

In addition, if you have been contracted-out of SERPS at any time, you receive a pension from your contracting-out scheme coupled, of course, with a correspondingly lower additional pension. (Throughout this chapter, there are a number of references to the effect of contracting-out of SERPS and the influence of either the guaranteed minimum pension or the 'contracted-out deduction' on any additional pension you might be eligible for. All these are defined in 2.8 and 2.9.2.)

Category B pension

Married women, widows and widowers may also qualify for a basic pension (and, where relevant, an additional pension) based on the contributions of their husband or wife. This is called the 'category B' pension.

In short, your category A pension is based on your own contributions; your category B pension is based on those of your spouse.

13.2 INCREASES TO STATE PENSIONS

Increases to state pensions can occur in one of five ways.

13.2.1 Indexation

All state pensions (with the exception of the age addition – see 13.2.5) are reviewed annually in line with any increase in the rate of inflation. The increase takes place in April of each year.

13.2.2 Graduated pension

If you are eligible for this benefit (see 2.5), you receive an extra pension dependent on the number of units you have accumulated. The total weekly benefit is the number of units multiplied by the unit price and this price is also re-valued each year.

13.2.3 Dependency increases

Children

If you are responsible for a child, and claiming child benefit (see below), then you may claim an addition to your category A or B pension. Any increases are affected by the earnings of your wife or partner living with you if these earnings exceed certain prescribed limits. In this context, 'earnings' includes any occupational or personal pension.

There are also certain limited circumstances when you can get an increase if someone is looking after the child on your behalf.

Child benefit is a tax-free weekly cash payment for anyone who is responsible for a child (or children) regardless of income or national insurance contribution record. It is payable for any child aged under 16 (or up to 19 if they are in full-time education). The rates for second and subsequent children are slightly lower than the rate for the first child.

Being responsible for a child means that, in normal circumstances, the child is living with you and is dependent on you. This would mean, for example, that child benefit could be claimed by grandparents.

Your wife

You can get an increase in your category A pension for your wife. The amount depends on whether she herself gets a category A pension (or any other state benefits), whether she is living with you, and also whether she has earnings of her own above the prescribed limits.

If you are unable to claim a dependency increase for your wife because her earnings are too high, it might be that you would still be better taking your pension so that she can claim her category B pension on your contributions.

Your husband

You can get an increase in your category A pension for your husband, but only if his earnings are below the prescribed limits and you were getting an increase of sickness benefit, unemployment benefit or invalidity pension (see 13.6) for him immediately before you qualified for your pension.

In all the above three cases, the prescribed limits on earnings levels are different.

13.2.4 Invalidity allowance

If you are getting invalidity allowance shortly before you reach pensionable age, your basic retirement pension is permanently increased (see 13.6.3).

13.2.5 Age addition

At the age of 80, you qualify for an additional 25p a week. This has been the same for many years and is not indexed.

13.3 DEFERRING YOUR STATE PENSION

There is no obligation on you to start drawing your pension when you reach state retirement age and there is even a facility to stop drawing your pension and restart it at a later date. In both situations you eventually get a higher pension as a result of 'increments'.

13.3.1 Delaying your state pension

If you put off drawing your state pension beyond state retirement age, then it will be increased by 'extra pension increments'. You must put off receiving your pension for at least seven weeks; your pension will increase by one-seventh of 1p for every £1 of benefit for every six days (not including Sundays) that you do not claim it. You will not, however, be credited with increments for any period during which you are claiming any of the other regularly paid benefits covered in this chapter. Increments do not apply to the age addition or for any increases for dependants (see 13.2.3).

The overall rate of increase is about 7.5 per cent for each full year that you do not claim it. You may not defer drawing your pension beyond age

70 (for men) or age 65 (for women) which means a total maximum increase of around 35 per cent. The level of increments is due to change in 2010 to coincide with the move to equalise state pension age (see 2.11.1). The rate will rise to around 10 per cent a year and it will be possible to defer your pension indefinitely.

You will also be able to delay taking any pension you are entitled to as a result of contracting out of SERPS. You may be entitled to certain increments, except in the case of money purchase schemes where your eventual pension depends on the value of the underlying fund.

13.3.2 Stopping and starting your state pension

Once you have started to draw your pension, you may give it up temporarily and start again at a later date. You will earn increments during this period, but you may only stop and restart your pension once (and you may not back-date your request). If your wife receives a category B pension as a result of your past contributions, you will need her written permission to give up your pension because she will have temporarily to give up her pension as well (although she will get increments).

It will not usually be possible to suspend any pension you are receiving as a result of contracting out. However, if you are receiving a guaranteed minimum pension from your employer and you return to work with the same employer, it may be suspended and will benefit from increments.

If you temporarily give up your pension because you have returned to work, you will not lose your entitlement to sickness benefit, invalidity benefit or unemployment benefit if you subsequently fall ill or lose your job.

13.4 MARRIED WOMEN

Married women can qualify for a category A pension in their own right and may also be able to claim (at some point) a category B pension based on their husband's contributions. What you actually receive and when depends on your respective ages and when you decide to claim your pension.

You cannot claim a pension until you reach age 60. If you are not entitled to a category A pension or graduated retirement benefit, you do not get any benefit at all until your husband reaches 65 or until he actually decides to take his pension.

If you are only entitled to claim a category B pension on the basis of your husband's contributions, you may put off drawing your pension and get increments even though your husband decides to draw his category A pension. If, however, your husband decides to defer his pension then you cannot draw your pension in the meantime, though you do, of course, qualify for increments. It was taken by the DSS that you would disqualify yourself from increments if you started to draw any graduated retirement benefit to which you were entitled but the courts have ruled that this is not the case.

If you are entitled to a category A pension in your own right, you may take it, but your category B pension is not payable until your husband decides to take his own pension and does not benefit from any increments in the meantime. If your own pension is small, therefore, it might make sense to forgo it, so that you can earn increments on the category B pension based on your husband's contributions.

If you wish to give up your pension temporarily, you must give up all your pension, including any category B pension (although your husband does not need to give up his category A pension).

13.5 WIDOWS AND WIDOWERS

In considering the potential benefits for a husband and wife, there is a range of conditions that could exist.

(1) Either could qualify for a basic retirement pension in his or her own right though the exact amount depends on their past contribution record.
(2) Either could qualify for an additional pension and either may at some time in the past have contracted out of SERPS and so be eligible for a guaranteed minimum pension or the benefits from a money purchase scheme.
(3) Either could potentially qualify for a category B pension based on the contributions of the other.
(4) Either could qualify for graduated retirement benefit.

If one of them dies, then the pension payable to the survivor could be a mixture of all these elements. The legislation sets out to ensure that the survivor does not lose out on any benefits but is also designed to ensure that they do not profit. The effect is that some, but not all, of the deceased's benefits will go to the survivor with the greatest impact being on any additional pension that they might be eligible for.

13.5.1 Widows

Widows are entitled to a basic pension, but the precise rules depend on whether they were widowed before or after age 60. They are also entitled to additional pensions and benefits not only from their own past contributions, but also from their husband's past contributions. There is a range of benefits payable to widows (see 13.6.4) but none of these are usually paid if you take your retirement pension.

Widowed before age 60

At age 60, you have a choice of doing one of three things:

(1) you may claim your pension; or
(2) you may continue to receive any widow's benefit until you wish to claim your pension (or until you reach age 65); or
(3) you may put off your pension, give up widow's benefit and get increments on your pension until you do decide to claim it (or until you reach age 65).

You may be entitled to your own category A pension and also a category B pension from your late husband's contributions. You can qualify for both but only up to the amount of a single person's pension.

You are also eligible for an additional pension if either you or your husband had contributed to SERPS. If, in the past, you have contracted out of SERPS you get your own benefit from your own contracted-out scheme and you suffer a contracted-out deduction from your additional pension.

If your late husband had contracted out of SERPS, you get a benefit from his scheme as follows:

(1) If he was a member of a scheme paying a guaranteed minimum pension, you get half the guaranteed minimum pension to which he would have been entitled.
(2) If he was a member of a money purchase scheme, you get the widow's pension from that scheme. If you yourself are a member of a contracted-out scheme, the value of the benefit you receive from your husband's scheme is added to your own contracted-out deduction, ie your own additional pension is reduced.

You get your own graduated retirement benefit, if relevant, and half of your late husband's entitlement, if relevant.

You also qualify for a widow's payment (see 13.6.4).

Widowed after age 60

You are entitled to a category B pension based on your late husband's contributions. If you are also entitled to a category A pension in your own right, the two basic pensions are combined but may not exceed the single person's basic pension.

You are also entitled to the relevant proportion of your husband's entitlement to any contracted-out benefits or graduated retirement benefit (see above).

If your husband was not entitled to a pension when he died, you get a widow's payment (see 13.6.4).

13.5.2 Widowers

If your wife died before you were aged 65 (or after you were aged 65, but before your wife was aged 60), and your own category A pension is not at the full rate, it may be possible for your late wife's contributions record to be taken into account. You are also entitled to a proportion of her benefits from a contracted-out scheme. Normally, these benefits are not be deducted from your own additional pension.

If your wife died when both you and your wife were of pensionable age, you may be entitled to a category B pension (based on your wife's past contributions) in addition to your own category A pension but only up to the level of a single person's pension. You are also entitled to half of any of her graduated retirement benefit.

If she was receiving benefit from a contracted-out scheme paying a guaranteed minimum pension, you are entitled to half the benefit and this is added to your own contracted-out deduction. If she was receiving benefits from a money purchase scheme, you are entitled to a pension from the scheme but the amount is not included in your contracted-out deductions.

13.6 THE IMPACT OF OTHER BENEFITS ON YOUR PENSION

There is a range of other state benefits that you may be receiving when you reach state retirement age and that could be affected if you start to take your state pension. Under certain circumstances, you may be better off not taking your pension immediately.

The benefits covered in this section are as follows:

(1) Jobseekers' allowance
(2) Incapacity benefit
(3) Widows' benefits
(4) Invalid care allowance
(5) Miscellaneous aspects.

13.6.1 Jobseekers' allowance

In October 1996, jobseekers' allowance (JSA) replaced unemployment benefit. The eligibility rules are much tougher – for example you must be available to work at least 40 hours per week and be actively seeking work. After an initial search of up to 13 weeks for suitable work you must accept virtually anything.

13.6.2 Incapacity benefit

From April 1995 sickness benefit and invalidity benefit were replaced by incapacity benefit which covers two contingencies:

(1) Short-term incapacity benefit is payable for the first 52 weeks of incapacity. The rate for the first 28 weeks is equivalent to the basic rate of sickness benefit with a higher rate being paid for the following 24 weeks. Payment continues beyond state retirement age only if the incapacity started before state retirement age.

(2) Long-term incapacity benefit is payable after short-term incapacity benefit but not beyond state retirement age. The basic rate is equal to invalidity benefit but the additional pension is to be withdrawn for all new cases.

The first 28 weeks of incapacity is based on incapacity for your own occupation; after that, eligibility depends on your incapacity to carry out any occupation.

The overall effect is a tightening of the rules for eligibility and a general reduction in the amount of state help for longer-term incapacity. This reduction is most marked in the 24 weeks following the initial 28-week period.

13.6.3 Widows' benefits

The overall range of widows' benefits depends on whether you were widowed before, or on or after 11 April 1988.

Before 11 April 1988

If you are currently widowed, and were widowed before 11 April 1988, you could well be claiming either the widowed mother's allowance or widow's pension (you cannot claim both at the same time). Both benefits depend on your late husband having paid or having been credited with the required number of Class 1 national insurance contributions at the date of his death.

You qualify for the widowed mother's allowance by having at least one child on whom you are entitled to claim child benefit (see 13.2.3). Once you cease to qualify because you no longer have a dependent child then, provided you are under the age of 60, but not under the age of 40, you qualify for a widow's pension.

The widow's pension is payable when you are widowed or when you cease to be eligible for the widowed mother's allowance provided you are over 40 at the time. You get the full rate of pension if you were 50 or older when your husband died and a reduced percentage if you were between 40 and 49.

Both the widowed mother's allowance and widow's pension are taxable.

In addition to these benefits, you may also be receiving an additional pension based on your late husband's earnings from employment since 1978. This is reduced if, because of your age, you qualify for only a reduced rate on widow's pension.

On or after 11 April 1988

If you are widowed on or after 11 April 1988, you may qualify for widow's payment and either the widowed mother's allowance or the widow's pension. All the benefits are dependent on your late husband having paid or been credited with the required number of Class 1 national insurance contributions at the date of his death.

The widow's payment is a single tax-free lump sum benefit payable if you are under the age of 60 when your husband dies or if he was not entitled to a category A pension when he died.

The widowed mother's allowance is payable if you have a child for whom you are entitled to claim child benefit or if you are expecting a baby. Once you cease to be eligible for the widowed mother's allowance then, provided you are under the age of 60 but not under age 45, you may be eligible for a widow's pension.

The widow's pension is payable when you are widowed or when you cease to be eligible for the widowed mother's allowance provided you are at least aged 45 at the time. You get the full pension if you were 55 or over at the date of your husband's death. You get a reduced percentage if you were between 45 and 54.

You may also qualify for an additional pension based on your husband's earnings from employment since 1978. This is reduced if, because of your age, you qualify for only a reduced rate of widow's pension.

13.6.4 Invalid care allowance

Provided you qualify for invalid care allowance when you reach state retirement age, you can continue to claim it for a further five years (and sometimes more). It is reduced by the amount of your basic pension, but not by any additional pension or graduated retirement benefit.

If your wife or partner is receiving invalidity benefit (see 13.6.2), he or she is entitled to a dependency increase for you, but not if you are receiving invalid care allowance. Under these circumstances, and depending on the figures, it might be worth both of you not drawing your pension and also giving up invalid care allowance. Your wife or partner then gets an increase in invalidity benefit and, in the meantime, your retirement pensions benefit from increments.

Invalid care allowance is covered in more detail in Chapter 14.

13.6.5 Miscellaneous benefits

Reduced earnings allowance

This is a special allowance to which you may be entitled if you cannot return to your regular type of work because of disablement due to an accident which occurred before 1 October 1990. If you take your pension, you lose your entitlement to it, but you may qualify for a retirement allowance, equal to 25 per cent of the reduced earnings allowance that you were previously entitled to.

Severe disablement allowance

This is a tax-free benefit payable to people who cannot get sickness benefit or invalidity benefit because they have not paid enough national insurance contributions. You can go on claiming this provided you are still entitled to it, but it is reduced by the amount of any basic pension you receive. It is not affected by any additional pension or graduated retirement benefit.

Other aspects

Normally, any benefits you receive from the DSS or any other government department has an impact on your basic pension. In the same way:

(1) any benefits paid to dependants affects any increases you might claim on your pension; and
(2) any benefits paid to you have an effect on any increase to the pensions of those on whom you are dependent.

In every case, it is worth doing the figures because it might be better to claim the dependency increases and leave the pension to gain increments until it is needed.

USEFUL READING MATTER

For a list of useful DSS and Benefit Agency booklets, see Appendix 2.

14

HELP AT HOME

Many elderly people have to try to manage without the income from an occupational or a personal pension scheme. Their sole source of earnings is a state pension and the income from their savings. This is not always enough and, particularly if they start to succumb to the physical problems of old age, they may start to need increasing levels of financial assistance.

In addition, as they get older, they require practical help and they may well become increasingly dependent on you, their children. Planning for your own retirement may, therefore, be further complicated by increasing demands from elderly relatives and you need to know the ground rules.

This chapter looks first at the range of financial and other benefits that are available either from the state or from local government to support people on low incomes and then looks at the position of the carer. The following topics are covered:

(1) Sources of financial help
(2) Income support
(3) Housing benefit and council tax benefit
(4) The social fund and other sources of help
(5) State benefits for the disabled and housebound
(6) Caring for the elderly
(7) Financial help for carers.

14.1 SOURCES OF FINANCIAL HELP

14.1.1 Introduction

The three main benefits available to people of limited means and whose income is below a level set by Parliament are income support, housing benefit and council tax benefit. In addition, certain help can be obtained from the social fund.

All the three main benefits are non-taxable and do not depend on the past record of national insurance contributions. They are all means-tested benefits. The general way in which they all work is as follows:

(1) If the individual believes himself to be eligible, he submits a detailed claim containing information about his personal circumstances.
(2) His weekly income needs are expressed as a combination of allowances and premiums for various circumstances. The personal allowance is an amount towards day-to-day living expenses and is determined by the claimant's age and whether he is single or has a partner. Each person applying for benefit is individually assessed to see which allowances and premiums are applicable in his case. The total of these premiums and allowances (the 'applicable amount' – see 14.1.4) is his weekly assessed need.
(3) The individual's savings are taken into account. If they are above a certain limit, he gets no benefit. Savings below a certain level are ignored; savings between the lower and upper levels are taken to produce a level of notional weekly income (called the 'tariff income' – see 14.1.5).
(4) The individual's total income (including any tariff income) can then be calculated. If his total weekly income is above the applicable amount, he gets no benefit; if it is below, he gets weekly benefit to make up the difference.

However, the detailed rules covering eligibility for benefits are extremely complex. In addition, the various benefits inter-relate and claiming one may rule out a claim to another. The following pages contain an overview of the key benefits; full details can be found in the various DSS or Benefits Agency leaflets and booklets.

14.1.2 Making a claim

Claims for income support are made to the local DSS office; if housing benefit and council tax benefit are also required, they are claimed at the same time. If income support is not being claimed, claims for housing benefit and council tax benefit are made direct to the local council.

All claims require the disclosure of a good deal of information about the claimant, particularly his financial circumstances. A claim may also involve an interview. All claims are assessed and a decision made; there is an appeals procedure for disputed decisions.

The period covered by a claim for benefits normally begins on the date the claim is made but, in some cases, claims can be backdated. Benefits are paid for as long as the claimant is eligible and there is an absolute responsibility on the claimant to notify any changes in his personal circumstances that would increase or reduce his entitlement to benefit.

14.1.3 Who can claim?

The family

The group of people in a claim is called 'a family'. This includes the claimant, his spouse or partner, and any children under the age of 19. If a claimant is unmarried, he is treated as a single claimant. If he is married, or lives as though he were married with someone of the opposite sex, they are regarded as a couple. Only one person in the family can claim benefit.

Non-dependants

Non-dependants are people who normally live with the claimant. These are usually relatives but the term does not include members of the family as defined above. Some benefits may be affected if a non-dependant lives with the claimant.

14.1.4 The applicable amount

The total amount of assessable needs (the applicable amount) is a combination of allowances and premiums.

Premiums are additional amounts paid to people with special needs:

(1) A carer premium is paid to people who are caring for people and who qualify for invalid care allowance (see 14.7.2).
(2) The pensioner premium is paid to people aged 60 and over (or to a couple, where one of them is age 60 or over) and is paid at three rates:
    (a) a basic rate if either person is aged 60 to 74;
    (b) an enhanced premium if either person is aged 75 to 79;
    (c) a higher premium if either person is over age 80. This is also paid if either person is over 60 and claiming certain disability benefits.
(3) There are also certain disability premiums for people claiming disability living allowance or attendance allowance (see 14.5.3).

14.1.5 Capital and income

The assessment of any of these benefits takes into account any resources owned by the claimant and, where relevant, his partner. These resources are split into capital and income. The first major test is on the total amount of capital:

(1) If it exceeds £8,000, it rules out any claim to income support.
(2) If it exceeds £16,000, it rules out any claim for housing benefit or council tax benefit.

Tariff income

Any capital or savings between £3,000 and the upper limit is taken to produce a weekly 'tariff income' of £1 for every £250 of capital or part of £250. For example, capital of £4,000 is taken to produce an income of £4 a week, capital of £6,000 is taken to produce an income of £12 a week, capital of £6,000.01 is taken to produce an income of £13 a week and so on.

Capital includes all money held in whatever form (but does not include the surrender value of life assurance policies). It does not include the value of a home lived in by the claimant unless part of the premises could reasonably be sold off. Ninety per cent of the value of any second home (including overseas property) counts as capital unless it is occupied by the claimant's partner, family member or elderly, sick or disabled relative.

If the claimant is owed money, this may also count as capital as does any capital that has been disposed of for a purpose not connected with the claimant's personal welfare. Any capital given away to bring the claimant within the benefit levels is taken into account. Personal possessions are also normally disregarded unless items have been bought specifically to reduce the amount of capital for the purposes of claiming benefits.

Total income

The assessment of total income is not straightforward. Depending on the type of income, some of it is ignored totally, some of it is ignored partially (the 'disregards') and some is taken fully into account.

Most social security pensions and benefits are taken fully into account (with the exception of the three benefits covered here and certain disability benefits). Occupational and personal pensions are also taken fully into account. Any earnings from part-time or casual work are generally taken into account if they exceed the disregarded level.

Actual income from savings and capital is ignored; instead, the tariff income is taken fully into account (and any income arising from the capital is regarded as capital when it is due).

14.1.6 Hospitalisation

If the claimant (or his partner, or both) has to go into hospital, they may be able to claim additional allowances to help with continuing household costs such as standing charges. There is generally no impact on benefits for the first six weeks of hospitalisation but there may be adjustments to benefits paid for up to the following 46 weeks.

After 52 weeks, the claimant is generally reassessed and treated as a single claimant.

There are different rules for residents in a residential care or nursing home (see 15.7).

14.2 INCOME SUPPORT

Income support is generally available to a wide range of people whose resources are below certain levels. For the purposes of this chapter, however, income support is covered in the context of people aged over 60 and also for people who have to stay at home to look after elderly relatives (see 14.7). In these circumstances the claimant does not have to sign on as available for work.

Income support is paid only to UK residents but it continues to be paid during temporary absences abroad, eg for a holiday.

In addition to the allowances and premiums, the applicable amount for income support can also take into account housing costs not covered by housing benefit. These are generally related to mortgage interest payments (ie not capital repayments nor premiums on endowment policies or pension plans) and interest on loans taken out for essential repairs and improvements (eg damp proofing, insulation etc). Benefits may be reduced if it is considered that the housing costs are excessive, for example, that the house is unnecessarily large or located in a particularly expensive area.

Any allowance for housing costs may be reduced if there are non-dependants living with the claimant. The amount deducted depends on the number and age of non-dependants but no deduction is made if the claimant or partner is getting either attendance allowance or the care component of disability living allowance (see 14.5.3).

14.3 HOUSING BENEFIT AND COUNCIL TAX BENEFIT

These are social security benefits schemes to help pay for rent and council tax. They are assessed and paid by local councils. They are similar in treatment to income support but the minimum capital levels to qualify for benefit are different. Someone who is not entitled to income support because of the level of their savings may still be able to claim for housing benefit or council tax benefit.

If the claimant does qualify for income support, he usually qualifies for the maximum housing benefit and council tax benefit.

14.3.1 Housing benefit

Housing benefit helps with the cost of rent for accommodation lived in by the claimant. It does not cover mortgage interest payments – these are covered by income support.

The form that housing benefit takes is determined to some extent by the type of accommodation. For private rented accommodation it is paid as an allowance; for council accommodation, it results in a reduction in the rent.

In general terms, housing benefit does not apply to owner-occupied houses though some assistance may be granted towards ground rent and service charges on leasehold properties if the original lease was for less than 22 years.

It does not just apply to fixed property; it can also apply to houseboats, mobile homes and caravans.

Housing benefit can only be claimed if rent has to be paid to a landlord; it does not apply if the landlord is a close relative and lives in the same property.

Eligible rent

Housing benefit can be claimed on the amount of rent paid for living accommodation. The local council will want to assure itself that the accommodation is suitable and that the rent is reasonable. If it decides that the house is too large then it may regard it as unsuitable and restrict the amount of benefit. Benefit may also be reduced if the council believes the rent to be excessive.

'Eligible rent' is the money the council considers is paid for actually occupying the house, ie it would not include any fuel costs and would also exclude certain service charges. Housing benefit is always related to eligible rent and can never exceed 100 per cent of this figure.

14.3.2 Council tax benefit

Council tax benefit is a rebate scheme to provide help with up to 100 per cent of the council tax.

14.3.3 How the benefits are calculated

The maximum benefits that may be claimed are 100 per cent of the eligible rent and 100 per cent of the council tax. If the claimant is on income support, he qualifies for the full rate of housing benefit and council tax benefit.

The applicant's total needs (the applicable amount) and assessable income are calculated in the usual way. If the total assessable income from all sources (including any tariff income from savings) is less than the applicable amount, then housing benefit and council tax benefit are paid in full.

If his assessable income is greater than the applicable amount, then lower benefits are paid. The reduction is based on the difference between the assessed income and the applicable amount and a percentage of this difference is deducted from the maximum benefit. It follows that, above a certain level of assessed income, no benefit is payable.

Housing benefit

If the assessable income is less than the applicable amount, then the eligible rent is paid in full. If the assessable income is greater than the applicable amount, then the amount of benefit is reduced by 65 per cent of the difference.

There may be an impact on housing benefit if a non-dependant is living in the same property. If the council believes that arrangements have been made to take advantage of housing benefit and that the non-dependant has greater resources, then it is the non-dependant's resources that are taken into account. There is no impact on housing benefit due to non-dependants if the claimant or partner is receiving either attendance allowance or the care component of disability living allowance.

Another important point is that, in certain circumstances, the net income from a home income plan (see 6.6.2) may be regarded as part of the claimant's assessable income.

Council tax benefit

If the claimant's assessable income is higher than the applicable amount, then the amount of available benefit is reduced by 20 per cent of the difference.

As with housing benefit, council tax benefit may be affected if non-dependants are sharing the same accommodation (but not if the claimant or partner are receiving disability benefits). There is a non-income related reduction of council tax benefit equal to £1 per week if there are non-dependants living in the same accommodation rising to £2 per week if they are in remunerative work (defined as working for 16 hours a week or more).

14.4 THE SOCIAL FUND AND OTHER SOURCES OF HELP

14.4.1 The social fund

This exists to help people with exceptional expenses which are difficult to pay out of regular income.

Cold weather payments

These are special payments made to people on income support and qualifying for the pensioner premium. They are paid automatically.

Community care grants

These are discretionary grants available to a range of people who are trying to rehabilitate themselves in the community. They are, for example, occasionally granted to people who are trying to move back into the community after a period of residential care; they could even be granted to help people try to avoid having to go into residential care in the first place.

The grants are not easy to obtain and the means-testing is tighter than that for income support (only capital under £500 is totally disregarded).

Budgeting loans

These are interest-free loans obtainable by people on income support to help spread the payment of large one-off expenses over a longer period.

Crisis loans

These are interest-free loans available to cover emergency short-term expenses. They are also available to people not receiving any other social security benefits and could, for example, cover the period while a claim for income support was being assessed.

14.4.2 Other sources of help

People on income support are eligible for the following NHS benefits:

(1) Free prescriptions
(2) Free dental treatment
(3) Free eye test, prescription and vouchers toward the cost of glasses
(4) Free travel to hospital
(5) Free NHS wigs and fabric supports.

Unless they are on income support, people of state retirement age qualify only for free prescriptions. They may also be able to qualify for a whole range of local services available via their local social security office, but there is normally a charge for these (see Chapter 15).

14.5 STATE BENEFITS FOR THE DISABLED OR HOUSEBOUND

The two principal benefits that are payable to disabled or housebound people are either disability living allowance or attendance allowance. The qualification is essentially based on age. Both benefits are tax free, are unaffected by the past record of national insurance contributions and are normally unaffected by the level of income or capital resources.

Both also offer a basis of self-assessment in that a medical examination is not normally necessary to support a claim. However, in assessing a claim, information may be required from the claimant's doctor.

14.5.1 Disability living allowance

This allowance is for individuals who are either under 65 years of age or who are over 65, who started to require help before they were 65 and who claimed before their 66th birthday. It consists of a care component (for people who need help with personal care) and a mobility component (for people who need help in getting around).

To qualify for the allowance, the need for help must have existed for at least three months and must be expected to continue for a further six months. Once granted, the allowance can be paid for as long as the conditions of entitlement are met.

The waiting period is usually waived for people with a terminal illness.

The care component

The care component is paid to someone who is so severely disabled (physically or mentally) that he is unable to carry out some of the essential tasks of daily living without assistance. There are three rates (lowest, middle and highest) depending on the level of attention or supervision required. Somebody unable to cook themselves a main meal, for example, would be on the lowest rate; somebody requiring frequent attention, day and night, would be eligible for the highest rate.

Terminally ill people automatically qualify for the highest rate.

The mobility component

The mobility component is paid to someone who is either totally or virtually unable to walk without restriction either because of a direct incapacity (such as physical disability) or because of an indirect incapacity (such as being both blind and deaf). There are two rates (lower and higher). The lower rate is payable to someone needing assistance in unfamiliar places. The higher rate is payable to someone who is unable to walk, an amputee, deaf and blind or mentally impaired and qualifying for the highest rate of the care component.

Hospitalisation

The mobility component of disability living allowance is not affected by hospitalisation but the care component may be withdrawn after 28 days.

For the position relating to residential or nursing home care, see 15.7.

14.5.2 Attendance allowance

This allowance is for individuals whose need for care begins after their 65th birthday, or who do not claim for assistance until after their 66th birthday. An important point is that the benefit is potentially payable to people who can demonstrate that they have a *need* for help with personal care; they are not disqualified from benefit if they are not actually receiving the help they need.

To qualify for attendance allowance, claimants must be so severely disabled that they either need frequent attention throughout the day in connection with their bodily functions or need prolonged or repeated attention at night. Also, they must have needed help for at least six months. People with a terminal illness can get financial assistance immediately.

There are two rates of allowances; the lower rate is paid to people who need frequent help with personal care day *or* night, the higher rate is paid if help is needed both day *and* night.

14.5.3 Impact on other benefits

Disability living allowance

If a person claiming income support, housing benefit or council tax benefit is also receiving disability living allowance, his applicable amount includes the higher pensioner premium.

If he is a single claimant, and qualifies for the middle or higher care component of disability living allowance, he also qualifies for the severe disability premium. Couples can only get the severe disability premium if both fulfil these requirements. A person receiving the care component of disability living allowance will not have his housing benefit (or any housing costs incorporated with income support) affected if he shares his house with a non-dependant (see 14.1.3).

Attendance allowance

If a person claiming income support, housing benefit or council tax benefit is also receiving attendance allowance, the applicable amount includes the higher pensioner premium. If he is a single claimant, he also qualifies for the severe disability premium but only if:

(1) nobody is claiming invalid care allowance for him (see 14.7.2); or
(2) there are no non-dependants living with him.

If he has a partner, they only get the severe disability premium if both qualify.

Any reduction in housing benefit (on housing costs incorporated as part of income support) due to non-dependants does not apply if the claimant is receiving attendance allowance.

14.6 CARING FOR THE ELDERLY

14.6.1 Helping the elderly to care for themselves

Many elderly people would prefer the independence and quality of life available through living in their own home and there is a range of services and resources to help them do this. Indeed, the workings of the Community Care Act (described in more detail in Chapter 15) means that, if care is required, local authorities set out to provide as much help as possible at home, with residential care being very much a last resort.

The level of help varies across the country, so that first port of call is the local social services office to find out what help is available. Home help, meals on wheels, chiropodist services etc are usually available (although, nowadays, at a cost). Elderly people with specific medical problems might also be able to get access to district nurses and health workers, physiotherapy and occupational therapy. In particularly serious cases, nursing (even night nursing) facilities may be available.

If alterations to the home are needed for people with mobility problems, there may well be advice available through the local authority on how the alterations might best be done.

If substantial alterations are required to a home to make it suitable for an elderly person to remain living there, the local authority may be able to help in a number of ways:

(1) Home improvement grants may be awarded to help people with mobility problems adapt their home to make it more suitable (eg installing a stairlift or wheelchair ramps).
(2) Some councils (and building societies) offer interest-only loans to help with home adaptation with the capital being repaid when the house is sold.
(3) Some councils will install relatively minor safety aids themselves (eg safety rails for baths, or light fittings at low level).
(4) Elderly people receiving income support or housing benefit can apply for grants to cover the cost of fitting insulation or draught proofing to their homes.

14.6.2 Caring at home

It is estimated that over five million people in the United Kingdom provide long hours of care for someone, usually a relative, who is elderly or disabled. Carers tend to come from the age range of 45–65, tend usually to be women and most of them look after people of 75 or older.

Help for carers is much more readily available than it used to be. There are specific social security benefits aimed at carers and there is a growing band of support groups and organisations set up to help.

However, it scarcely needs saying that the decision to take a dependent person into your home and provide them with full-time care is not an easy one to make. The Government is, of course, trying to increase the level of help from within the family and to make people less dependent on state resources; the Community Care Act is evidence of this. However, any decisions you take in this regard have to be looked at from the emotional and physical viewpoint as well as the financial.

The emotional implications

If your elderly relative has become so frail that he needs constant care, your immediate reaction may be that home care is preferable to residential or nursing home care and not just from the financial viewpoint. However, that immediate reaction does need to be tested against a fairly objective review of the implications.

Whilst you may get on extremely well with your relative on the basis of infrequent meetings and visits, that is not the same as having someone living in your home for 24 hours a day, seven days a week. Also, he will be there not on the basis of a visit or holiday, but because he needs care and attention and probably on an increasing basis.

Even close relatives draw apart in terms of their likes and dislikes and having to take a middle course can be stressful to both sides. Your loss of independence will not help.

You also need to think about the impact on your own family. Their needs can often be overlooked, yet the strain on them could be almost as great as the strain on you.

The physical implications

Your decision on whether to accept an elderly relative into your home could hinge on purely physical aspects. Your home may simply not be suitable, due to lack of space, or it could be that changes have to be made. Many elderly people have difficulty with stairs or getting in and out of the bath.

You also have to consider your own physical limitations. You have to be sure that you are strong enough to help an elderly person, possibly with mobility problems, and that you can cope with the inevitable disruption to your sleeping patterns. Also, whilst there are resources available to help with aspects of personal care, you have to face the fact that, at sometime or other, you may be called upon to provide a level of personal care that you last faced with your own infant children.

14.6.3 Help for carers

When you come up against the problem of caring for an elderly relative, it is often surprising just how much help is available. The first step is to talk it through with your local social services department – your GP is in a position to give you an introduction if you need one. Many of the resources available to elderly people are available regardless of whether they are living on their own or living with you.

The **Carers National Association** is a nationwide organisation which gives help and advice to carers through a network of branches and carer support groups. It has been established for nearly 40 years and has been active in promoting the needs of carers at local and national level. It produces a bi-monthly journal and operates CarersLine, a telephone advice and information service.

Help the Aged sets out to provide support to the elderly, particularly those who are frail or living on limited means. It helps with the funding of day centres and hospices (to give respite to carers) and it is also active in home safety and community alarms for elderly people living on their own. It runs a SeniorLine telephone information service for elderly people, their relatives, friends and carers.

Counsel and Care provides a nationwide service for older people and their carers. It offers a free advice and information service and issues a series of fact sheets. In certain cases, it is able to offer financial assistance to elderly people who require care and may be able to help with one-off payments for such things as telephone installation, household goods and respite care.

14.7 FINANCIAL HELP FOR CARERS

14.7.1 Introduction

The financial implications of living with an elderly person are more than just an extra mouth to feed. Old people need more resources and money and their needs increase as they get older. You will be faced with extra fuel costs, more travel costs and so on.

In addition, a relative moving into your home may end up costing more overall because his entitlement to any social security benefits will be reassessed and your financial circumstances may be taken into account.

14.7.2 Invalid care allowance

Invalid care allowance is paid to those people who are ‘regularly and substantially’ engaged in looking after a disabled person and who are not gainfully employed (and who are unable to get a job because of their commitment to the disabled person).

You may be able to qualify for invalid care allowance if you meet all of the following conditions:

(1) The person you are caring for is getting either attendance allowance (see 14.5.2) or the care component of disability living allowance at the middle or highest rate (see 14.5.1).
(2) You are aged under 65.
(3) You spend at least 35 hours a week looking after the person.
(4) You normally live in the United Kingdom.

The benefit is taxable. You cannot claim invalid care allowance if you earn more than £50 a week after allowance for certain expenses (and this applies if you were being paid to look after the disabled person).

Once you have received the allowance for 22 weeks, occasional weeks of non-caring do not disqualify you from receiving the allowance, ie you (or the disabled person) could go on holiday for up to four weeks in every 26 without the allowance being stopped.

The allowance stops once the person you are caring for goes into hospital or residential care and ceases to receive attendance allowance or the care component of disability living allowance.

14.7.3 The impact on other benefits

If you yourself are receiving income support, housing benefit or council tax benefit, then your benefits will be affected if you start to receive invalid care allowance, ie they will be reduced as invalid care allowance counts as your income. However, you will also get the benefit of the carer premium in assessing your applicable amount.

If the person you are caring for qualifies for the severe disability premium, then he loses this when you start to receive invalid care allowance.

Your maximum entitlement to invalid care allowance is also affected if you are claiming certain other benefits (eg invalidity benefit or widow's benefit). However, it may still be worth claiming it. If, for example, the other benefit is a widow's pension, you are credited with national insurance contributions for each week you are claiming invalid care allowance (though not if you have kept the right to pay reduced rate contributions).

14.7.4 Home responsibilities protection

Home responsibilities protection (HRP) is a system for reducing the number of qualifying years you need to work in order to qualify for a basic retirement pension (see 2.3). It applies to both men and women who are carers.

If you are a carer, you get HRP if you fulfil one of the following two conditions for at least one complete tax year:

(1) You have stayed at home for at least 35 hours a week to look after a person who, for a minimum of 48 weeks in the year, got either attendance allowance or the middle or highest rate of the care component of disability living allowance.
(2) You are able to claim income support on the basis that you are looking after a sick or disabled person.

In the first case, you have to apply for home responsibilities protection; in the second case, you qualify for it automatically.

If you are a married woman or widow, you cannot get HRP for any tax year when you have exercised the right to pay reduced contributions, though you may cancel this right if you still have it.

USEFUL READING MATTER

The following DSS booklets provide more information on the topics covered in this chapter.

FB 2 – Which benefit? A guide to Social Security and NHS benefits

IS 20 – A guide to income support

RR 2 – A guide to housing benefit and council tax benefit.

FB 31 – Caring for someone?

CF 411 – Home Responsibilities Protection

15

CARING FOR THE ELDERLY

With increasing age and frailty, the need to turn to residential care of one sort or another for the future support of an elderly person becomes ever more likely. Although there is a wide choice of residential care and nursing homes, finding the one that suits a particular individual is not so simple. Added to that, there is the matter of cost. Residential care is not cheap and the introduction of the Community Care Act has meant that anybody looking to the state (or, more likely, their local authority) for help will find some rigorous means-testing in place. This chapter covers the following topics:

(1) Introduction
(2) Care in the community
(3) Financial aspects of community care
(4) Sheltered housing
(5) Residential care homes and nursing homes
(6) Long-term care insurance
(7) State benefits and residential care
(8) Sources of help.

15.1 INTRODUCTION

One of the biggest social changes in the United Kingdom is taking place right before our eyes. It is often called the 'demographic time bomb' which, although now something of a cliché, underlines the extent of the change. The balance of the UK population is slowly changing as, with increased standards of health care, more and more people are living into their 80s and 90s. The projected shift over the next 30 years means that, by the year 2025, there will be a 25 per cent increase in the number of people of state retirement age, ie age 65 and over.

One measure of the changing balance of the population is the 'age dependency' ratio. This is the proportion of the population aged 65 and over (ie those most likely to be looking for state help) expressed as a percentage of the population aged 15 to 64 (ie those earning the income out of which the state help is funded). At present, it is 23 per cent. It will dip slightly over the period to 2010 but will rise to over 25 per cent in the year 2020 and to over 30 per cent in the year 2030. At present, the United Kingdom has one of the highest age dependency ratios and this almost certainly is one of the reasons which has led to the intended equalisation of state pensions at age 65. Other countries fare better at the moment but stand to do less well in the future (in Germany, for example, the age dependency ratio could be nearly 45 per cent by the year 2030).

What is even more significant is the proportion of people aged over 85 and their expected rate of increase. At present it is one in 60 of the population. By the year 2010, it will be one in 45.

This has considerable implications for some people planning for retirement as they may well face not only the problem of providing for their own long-term future, but also the prospect of elderly parents or other relatives becoming increasingly dependent on them as well.

Changes in financial support

Hand-in-hand with this development has gone the realisation by the Government that it cannot continue to fund long-term care out of the public purse. In recent years, the level of support for the payment of residential care and nursing home fees has simply exploded; it is estimated that in the ten years up to 1993 (ie the implementation of the Community Care Act), the level of support increased by a factor of 100, from £2.5m a year to over £2bn. The Community Care Act pushes the responsibility for this funding on to local authorities and it is quite clear that, in future, the resources are going to have to come increasingly out of our own pockets with public funds providing only a safety net.

In simple terms, the *automatic* provision of services for those people who are too frail to look after themselves is a thing of the past. Some services may not be there and, if they are, they may only be available at a cost. The fact that the service is available is no guarantee that it will become available in any specific case; needs are now assessed by local authorities and their decision is final. If an alternative level of care is felt to be desirable, we may have to arrange it ourselves and pay the full cost.

The financial implications are covered in more detail in the next section but, in broad terms, if there is a need for residential care, support from the local authority will only start to become available if the resident's income (including any pension) does not cover the fees and their total capital (which may include the value of their home) is below £16,000.

15.2 CARE IN THE COMMUNITY

Broadly speaking, community care covers the following areas:

(1) Providing accommodation and welfare services for disabled people (which would include the blind, the deaf and the mentally ill).
(2) Promoting the welfare of older people, mothers and young children.
(3) Providing certain after-care and home help services.

The Community Care Act (or, to give it its full name, the National Health Service and Community Care Act 1990) introduced a new regime for the care of needy people with effect from 1 April 1993.

The practical implications of the Act are that the responsibility for arranging community care for vulnerable people now lies with local authorities. Local social service departments now have financial control over expenditure incurred in arranging this care and it is they who decide on the type of resources to be provided in any area and for deciding who qualifies for help. This means that those in need, and of limited means, no longer have the right to automatic state support. The provision of care is now dependent on local budgets and the type of care offered may, at times, depend on the political persuasion of the local party in power.

Added to that, the new regulations are a major change for local authorities and, as with any new rules, they take time to settle down and are not always applied in a fair and consistent way.

15.2.1 Local authority assessments

As all care services are to be provided by local authorities, it is they who decide who is in need of these services. The local authority has the power to assess someone whom it believes has needs, but it has no legal obligation to assess anyone who asks to be assessed. There are circumstances where the local authority is within its legal rights to refuse an assessment (eg some authorities may decline to assess somebody who does not habitually live in the area).

A key part of the Act is that the assessment of needs and the provision of services to meet those needs are quite separate. If a local authority is made aware that someone may have special needs, it is obliged to assess those needs. However, it is not obliged, unless legally required to do so, to provide the services that will meet those needs.

An equally important point is that the financial resources of the claimant or his family are not relevant at the assessment stage. The local authority must first establish the need and then decide whether it can provide the service to meet the needs. If it can, then and only then do the claimant's financial resources come into contention.

The overall approach of local authorities is to find the most cost-effective package of services that meets the need, taking into account the personal preferences of the claimant or carer. The route followed is to look first at providing the service in the claimant's own home wherever possible and then to consider other alternatives as follows:

(1) A move to other accommodation, such as sheltered housing
(2) A move to another private household, eg with relatives or an adult fostering scheme
(3) Residential care
(4) Nursing home care
(5) Long-stay hospital care.

15.2.2 The assessment procedure

Your local authority should publish guidelines of the criteria it uses for eligibility for assistance and the way it carries out assessments. It should also publish details of the needs for which it accepts responsibility, the type of service available and its charging policy.

The claimant or his representative should always be involved in the assessment, though the local authority cannot insist on this. The 'assessment decision' is usually given in writing and always defines the individual's needs in relation to community care services regardless of whether those services are available. The 'service provision decision' follows on from the assessment decision by stating what services the local authority will provide in meeting the assessed needs, either in whole or in part.

There is an appeals/complaints procedure for contested assessments.

15.3 FINANCIAL ASPECTS OF COMMUNITY CARE

15.3.1 Local authority assessments

An essential aspect of the 1990 Act is that services have to be provided in a cost-effective manner. Government policy is that care should be provided to people in their existing homes as far as possible where this is their preference, but only where it is cost-effective. The cost of services may also be recoverable in whole or in part from the person receiving the service.

If the service required is residential care of some kind, the local authority is obliged to charge for the accommodation and the charge must be the exact cost of providing that accommodation. The actual payment made by the resident towards the cost of the accommodation depends on his means; the social services department looks at the resident's total income (including any social security benefits) and also the total amount of the resident's capital. There is then an assessment of how much the resident can afford to pay towards the total cost of the accommodation, subject to his being left with a weekly amount of at least the 'personal expense allowance' (which, in April 1999, is £14.75).

If the resident's capital (which may include the value of his home) exceeds £16,000, it is assumed that the resident is able to meet the full cost.

The guidelines followed by local authorities in assessing residents' ability to pay for residential care are those introduced by the Department of Health in the *Charging for Residential Accommodation Guide* (CRAG for short).

Income

All income is taken into account so, for retired people, that would include all pensions income. The local authority is entitled to take into account any income that the resident has deprived himself of in order to reduce his liability to pay for accommodation, together with certain notional income that would be available to the resident if it were claimed.

For many couples, their main income is the husband's occupational pension. The effect of this means-testing could be that the entire pension could be assessed as his with no allowance for the fact that his wife may also depend on it. This is a perfectly legal interpretation of the regulations although local authorities do have the discretion to increase the amount of the personal expense allowance. This would allow the husband to support his wife while he was living in residential or nursing accommodation.

Any payments made to a resident by his wife or former wife are also treated as the resident's income regardless of whether they are regular or one-off payments.

Capital

If you have over £16,000 in assets you will receive no help towards residential care. There is a sliding scale of benefits if you have between £10,000 and £16,000 and where your assets fall below £10,000 you qualify for the full assistance available. This will vary from area to area.

Any income earned by the capital (eg interest on a deposit account) is treated as capital from the date it is due.

One of the issues which causes considerable anxiety is whether the individual's home must be taken into account and, possibly, sold to pay the bills. If an individual going into care owns his own home, its value is assessed as capital. A local authority cannot force the sale of the house, but it can have a legal charge put on it. Consequently, when the house is eventually sold, it is in a position to claim some or all of the proceeds.

According to the CRAG guidelines, the value of the house has to be disregarded if a relative either aged over 60 or incapacitated lives in the property. Some local authorities nevertheless include the value of the house in the assessment but this is quite incorrect. Local authorities also have the discretion to disregard the value of the property if it is the sole residence of someone who has given up his own home to look after the individual.

It would be unwise for an elderly person to transfer ownership of his home to his children, so that its value cannot be eroded by care fees. If a local authority suspects that any assets have been disposed of with the intention of avoiding charges (and the general rule would be to include in this any assets disposed of up to six months before taking up residence), it can regard the disposal as never having taken place and claim some form of compensation both from the person who disposed of the assets and the people who received them.

15.3.2 The financial resources of relatives

A spouse with separately owned assets and savings could be asked to agree to contribute towards the cost of residential care or nursing home fees. He is entitled to refuse but could be taken to court by the local authority to see what a reasonable contribution would be. The local authority is not entitled *automatically* to include the assets and savings of the spouse in the assessment.

Under most normal circumstances, other relatives should not be in any fear that their own savings or assets can be taken into account when assessing the needs of an elderly relative. However, although they are not obliged to contribute towards residential home fees (even if the elderly person is currently living with them), the final decision on what is best for the elderly person lies with the local authority. If the local authority decides that he is best left where he is (ie living with his relatives) then this decision is taken on the basis of what is best for the elderly person; the wishes of his relatives may not carry much weight. They have no choice other than to accept the decision; if they feel that they cannot cope with the situation then the only option they have is to pay the full fees of private residential accommodation.

15.4 SHELTERED HOUSING

Sheltered housing used to be the sole preserve of local authority housing departments and housing associations. The objective was to provide low-cost accommodation for rent to those people who could not afford their own homes, but who needed an element of care. This area of provision still exists but the majority of sheltered housing is now provided by private builders. Much of this housing is now owner-occupied.

The usual format is grouped housing for elderly people who, while living their own independent lives in a self-contained home, may be vulnerable because of their age and require some degree of care supplied by a warden. Although the main appeal is to the older-retired, there are increasing numbers of younger-retired (ie age 55+).

Sheltered housing schemes are not regulated or controlled in any way; they cater exclusively for people who expect to be fairly independent and getting on with their lives. The warden is there to help, but often plays a part in the scheme's general administration, and may even be referred to as the administrator or secretary. In some cases the warden has disappeared altogether and has been replaced by a continuously monitored alarm system.

15.4.1 The safeguards

Although there are no statutory safeguards surrounding sheltered housing as such, a number of the builders who specialise in this area do follow various guidelines laid down by their trade or marketing bodies. For example, builders and developers registered with the National House Building Council are expected to follow the NHBC Sheltered Housing Code (though this applies only to sheltered housing in England and Wales). Their definition of sheltered housing is accommodation that is exclusively for elderly people and which forms part of a scheme of grouped, self-contained accommodation provided with a package of estate management services. Under the NHBC rules, every first purchaser of a house has to be given an information pack giving full details of the commitment he is entering into and the services he is entitled to expect and the managing organisation of the scheme must enter into a management agreement which protects the rights of purchasers in the future.

As with any other form of voluntary code of practice, there is no guarantee that membership of a particular trade body or trade organisation means that you will have a trouble-free purchase. Some builders and developers decline to belong to any of these associations on the basis that their own individual standards more than meet the standards required by the trade organisations. When all is said and done, your assessment of a particular retirement housing development can only be by going and seeing for yourself, asking existing residents what they think about it and getting full details of the agreements you are expected to enter into.

15.4.2 The standards of management

The provision of shared amenities is usually paid for through a management fee. This clearly varies from development to development and like any other service can only be assessed in terms of value for money. The most important aspects to be clear about (once you have decided that a particular scheme is suitable in all other respects) are to what extent you will be liable for charges (and how they will increase in the future) and to what extent you are restricted in the reselling of your property. All of this will be contained in the lease and the management agreement.

An organisation which is very active in the area of the management of sheltered schemes is the Association of Retirement Housing Managers. Members of the ARHM now manage the bulk of private sheltered housing. They subscribe to a framework of practice and plans are well advanced to produce an ARHM Code of Practice. Also extremely helpful is AIMS, the Advice, Information and Mediation Service for Retirement Housing (part of Age Concern), which can help with any legal problems in the private and, from 1998, the rented sector.

15.4.3 The problems of leasehold

One of the problems for many people with sheltered housing is that it brings with it (at least in England and Wales) the concept of leasehold property. After possibly many years of owning the freehold of their property (or of paying relatively small ground rents under a leasehold arrangement), they have become used to doing largely what they want with their property (when to paint it, how much to spend on the garden and so on). Moving into sheltered accommodation often means coping with a lease for the first time and this can occasionally cause problems for retired people who now find that, as far as their home is concerned, they are no longer free to make their own decisions. Despite the fact that they may have paid a capital sum for their property, they may find themselves having to pay quite high ground rents as well.

There are occasional stories of unscrupulous managing agents who can, and do, exact quite extortionate increases in service charges and management fees with little or no explanation for the increase. Clearly, it is absolutely vital that you get a legal opinion on the terms and conditions of your lease and that you are fully aware of the costs you will be liable for both now and in the future.

Statutory rights

The statutory rights of leaseholders are contained in a series of Rent Acts, Housing Acts, Landlord and Tenant Acts and, most recently, in the Leasehold Reform, Housing and Urban Development Act of 1993. This legislation gives leaseholders and tenants the right to know who their landlord is, to be consulted about the appointment or employment of a managing agent and, in the event of bad management or actions in contravention of the terms of the lease, to request the courts to allow compulsory acquisition. Qualifying long leaseholders also have the right either to extend their lease or, under certain conditions, to buy it outright. Under the 1993 Act, leaseholders and tenants have a statutory right to information on the composition of service charges and a right to consultation on major expenditure. The new Act also gives the Department of the Environment powers to approve codes of practice for retirement housing management such as the ARHM code.

However, the right to take legal action over a breach of a lease, and the right to insist on their statutory rights when trying to prise information out of a reluctant landlord, are not what most people look for in sheltered housing. What they want is a relatively trouble-free life and what they hope is that the costs are fair now and that they will be kept fair in the future. In this area, the Sheltered Housing Advisory and Conciliation Service (SHACS) provides a meeting point for the resolution of problems between landlords (or managing agents) and tenants. There is no Ombudsman specifically for owner-occupied sheltered housing but there is an Ombudsman set up by the Housing Corporation for tenants of registered housing associations, some of which are covered by the Association of Retirement Housing Managers.

Also active in representing people in sheltered housing is the Federation of Residents Associations in Sheltered Housing (FRASH). This organisation acts as a representative body in trying to promote and protect the interests of its members and works closely with the Association of Retirement Housing Managers. FRASH is concerned with matters relating to retirement housing in England and Wales; the corresponding organisation in Scotland is the Sheltered Retirement Housing Owners Confederation (SRHOC) whose base is in Edinburgh.

All of this merely goes to show that sheltered housing is not automatically a way to a trouble-free existence. It is, of course, important to keep everything in perspective. Many sheltered housing schemes work extremely well with good relations between the residents and the managing agents. The most important steps to take are to decide whether the particular sheltered scheme suits you now and to get a full legal opinion on the terms of the lease and the management agreement to assess what changes could theoretically occur in the future.

15.5 RESIDENTIAL CARE HOMES AND NURSING HOMES

For the purposes of this chapter, residential care means managed accommodation providing a varying level of support for those people who are unable, or who no longer wish, to live independently.

Local authorities often run their own residential care homes with more and more running their own nursing homes. They are usually run by the local social services department (as distinct from locally supplied sheltered housing which is run by the housing department). Local authorities are also responsible for providing residential care for elderly people who, because of infirmity, are unable to live in their own homes. This is a requirement of Part III of the National Assistance Act 1948 and is referred to as Part III accommodation.

15.5.1 Private sector residential homes

The majority of available accommodation is run either privately or through voluntary agencies. The statutory safeguards to residential care are covered by the Registered Homes Act 1984. Any establishment which sets out to provide accommodation and personal care must be registered under the Act. The Act establishes standards of practice covering the care of people living in registered accommodation and also provides for the regular inspection of all registered homes. The responsibility for the implementation of the provisions of the Act lies with the local authorities (often at county level) and they usually issue their own guidelines to anybody wishing to set up a residential home.

Registration under the Act offers a number of safeguards but no guarantees that a home will be run to a particularly high standard. Many homes now belong to one of the three major professional organisations each with its own monitoring system. The National Care Homes Association, the British Federation of Care Home Proprietors and the Registered Nursing Homes Association all set out to ensure the maintenance of high standards of care.

Residential care homes

These are normally registered by the local social services department which is then required to carry out an inspection at least once every 12 months (and which may also carry out unannounced visits). There are minimum standards laid down by the local authority, and such homes are expected to provide the same level of personal help that would be provided by a caring relative. The basic level of care is assistance with toileting, feeding and dressing, together with three meals a day.

One weakness in the legislation surrounds those establishments which provide accommodation for less than four people. Although such establishments are now required to register under the Registered Homes (Amendment) Act 1991, the monitoring of them is entirely at the local authority's discretion. In addition, there is no requirement for such establishments to meet either fire regulations or the requirements of the environmental health officer (both of which are mandatory for larger retirement care homes).

Nursing homes

Nursing homes have to be registered under the 1984 Act but are also registered and inspected by the district health authority. Nursing homes have to provide the same general level of service as a residential care home but must also provide the services of a qualified registered general nurse 24 hours a day.

Dual registered homes

These are homes which provide the concept of continuous care, providing the requirements of residential care for people who are not suffering from any sickness, illness or infirmity but also providing nursing home facilities for those who are. Increasing frailty, therefore, need not mean a move to a different home.

Dual registered homes tend to be few and far between. They have to be registered by both the local social services department and the district health authority which is perhaps an indication that we have some way to go in providing an all-embracing framework of legislation covering the standards of care in residential accommodation.

The work of the local authority

The local authority has the responsibility of ensuring that all residential care homes and nursing homes in its area are registered under the

Residential Homes Act and regularly inspected. It will enter into contracts with those homes where it intends to place people assessed by them as being in need of residential care.

Residential homes do not necessarily have to restrict their contracts to their own local authority; they are perfectly entitled to contract with any local authority in the United Kingdom. There is nothing unusual in an individual of limited means, having been assessed as in need of residential care by his local authority, moving to another part of the country (perhaps to be near relatives) and going into suitable local residential accommodation, with the bills being paid by his original local authority. Provided the residential home can agree contractual terms with the original local authority, the system works perfectly well (and it may often be the new local authority that handles the regular paperwork).

15.5.2 The choice of residential care

The choice of both residential care homes and nursing homes is very wide and, if the fees are being paid for out of private funds, you can go where you please. All three of the organisations referred to above offer advice on the kind of topics to be considered when selecting a home, but the ultimate choice depends on the prospective resident's current state of health, his personal preference and, of course, the financial resources available.

Personal preference generally means proximity to friends or relatives, peace and quiet (or, alternatively, proximity to shops and other centres of activity) and so on. However, the most common source of dissatisfaction among people in residential care is the loss of privacy and independence.

This aspect should, perhaps, be given quite a high priority when it comes to considering the final choice. Of course, privacy and independence will disappear with increasing frailty but there are degrees to which it has to be sacrificed.

If the local authority has carried out an assessment and decided that the individual should go into residential care, the local social services department normally recommends a home – or a number of homes – which suit the individual. There is no need to accept one of these; even if the local authority is meeting the full costs, the individual is free (indeed, he has the right) to go to any home that meets his needs subject, of course, to the approval of the social services department. If the alternative home is more expensive, the difference has to be paid for by a third party or out of the individual's own remaining resources.

There is, of course, nothing to stop any individual entering a residential care or nursing home whenever he wishes. However, this will be as a private cost; if any help is required from the local authority, it must first assess the individual and decide what is the most appropriate solution for that individual (which may not necessarily involve residential care).

15.6 LONG-TERM CARE INSURANCE

Following a year of discussions with Government agencies, charities and insurance companies, in May 1996 the previous Government published a consultation paper in which it proposed several options to encourage people to insure and/or invest to cover long-term care. These were mainly aimed at asset protection – for example a US-style 'partnership' scheme where you are encouraged to insure a certain amount, say £30,000, and after this is exhausted the state steps in. Your assets up to a prescribed limit are not used to pay for care.

Some proposals build on existing products such as equity release schemes or home income plans (see 6.6.2), and 'impaired life annuities' (see 5.6). However, few changes, if any, are expected to be implemented until after the Labour Government has undertaken further consultation with consumer groups and insurance companies.

In the meantime an estimated 200,000 people a year enter care. For these people and their relatives any future partnership schemes will come too late. Besides, critics argue that the partnership concept will only help those with an asset base of less than £100,000, including the family home.

If you are interested in long-term care insurance, do seek the help of a specialist independent adviser. Most of these plans are complicated, expensive and they are not governed by the strict financial services regulatory system. You should also seek legal advice. If you want to act on behalf of an elderly parent, for example, you must have enduring power of attorney in order to appoint a professional adviser to help manage your relative's affairs.

Before considering a dedicated long-term care policy, check if you are covered under other protection insurance plans. Some critical illness policies pay a cash lump sum if you suffer 'loss of independence'.

There are two ways to insure the cost of long-term care. With a 'pre-funded' plan you pay regular premiums or a lump sum ahead of the time when you may need to claim. If you are elderly and not insured, an 'immediate care' plan would guarantee a regular income to pay the nursing home fees but for this you would need to invest a substantial sum.

15.6.1 Pre-funding plans

Several insurance companies sell pre-funded plans. The policies pay the benefit to your nursing home or, in some cases, to your carer. You may also qualify for help towards the cost of home alterations where this would enable you to stay put. Annual benefit, which is tax free, usually is limited to about £25,000. However, most people can insure for much less than this if they have other sources of income from pensions and investments.

To qualify for benefit you must fail two or three 'activities of daily living' (ADLs). ADL tests – also used by social services for those who qualify for state help – include washing, dressing, feeding, continence and mobility. Good plans also include cognitive impairment given the rapid increase in the number of sufferers of Alzheimer's Disease and similar conditions.

As with income protection you can reduce premiums if you opt for a long 'deferment period' before receiving the first payment. This can be anything from four weeks to two years. You can also reduce premiums if you restrict cover to a limited payment period – for example two to three years. However, whether you would enjoy peace of mind with this type of policy is questionable. Conditions that involve cognitive impairment can result in a lengthy stay in care.

Premiums vary but as a guide a man aged 65 who wants to insure annual benefit of £12,000 would pay monthly premiums of about £70 or a single premium of £9,500.

15.6.2 Immediate care annuities

If a relative needs to go into a home you might consider an immediate care annuity, although to fund this you may need to sell his house. Where the elderly person could stay at home, provided certain care was available and alterations were carried out, a home income plan might be more appropriate (see 6.6.2).

An annuity provides a regular income for life in return for your lump sum investment. One option for this age group is an 'impaired life annuity' as this offers a higher income if you have an illness which is likely to reduce your life expectancy.

The impairment must adversely affect life expectation and not just impact on the quality of life. Qualifying impairments include Aids, Alzheimer's, cancer, cirrhosis, coronary disease, diabetes and stroke. Depending on your impairment you could secure an income up to 30 per cent higher than that offered by a standard plan. If you are interested do go to an annuity specialist who will select the best terms for your particular circumstances.

Unlike pre-funded plans, the annuity payments are not tax free. Part of the income is treated as a return of capital so this is not taxed. The interest element is taxed but this reduces with age.

15.6.3 Long-term care investment alternatives

For many people the main drawback with long-term care is that it is an insurance product, not an investment. Insurance relies on the pooling of risk so the benefits of those who need to claim are paid for by the premiums of those who do not. This may be a price worth paying for peace of mind but some investors regard it as money down the drain.

There is an alternative which combines investment and insurance, but it is relatively new and untested. Only a handful of companies offer this type of product. Under a long-term care investment plan, you pay a lump sum into a fund from which the insurance company deducts monthly premiums to cover the risk. The products currently available use funds which, for one reason or another, can offer gross roll-up (that is, the fund does not pay income and capital gains tax). This means that if your fund does well and the investment growth covers the cost of the monthly insurance, your premiums effectively are tax free.

If you need to claim, initially you draw your agreed annual benefit from your fund and when this is exhausted the insurer picks up the tab for as long as you remain in care. In some cases, for an extra cost, you may be able to protect part or all of your fund so that the insurance covers the benefit payments from the outset. However, if you remain healthy to the end and do not make a claim, you can pass your investment on to your dependants.

15.7 STATE BENEFITS AND RESIDENTIAL CARE

15.7.1 Income support

People living in residential care, and of limited means, are entitled to claim income support in the usual way. However, the calculation of the resident's 'applicable amount' (ie his weekly assessed needs – see 14.1.4) depends on whether he first went into residential care before 1 April 1993 or on or after 1 April 1993.

Before 1 April 1993

Up until 1 April 1993, the applicable amount (see 14.1.4) for people living in a residential care or nursing home was a weekly accommodation allowance (and the cost of meals if charged separately) plus the weekly personal expense allowance. In 1996 local authorities which followed Government guidelines paid a maximum of £346 per week towards a London private nursing home and £303 outside London. The allowance also depends on the extent of physical disability suffered by the individual.

Individuals who were living in a residential care home or nursing home on 31 March 1993 come under the 'preserved rights' rules. Under these rules, the maximum benefits continue to be either the fees charged by the home or the higher amount of income support described above (whichever is the lower).

It is possible for the resident to move to a different residential care home or nursing home and still qualify for preserved rights.

On or after 1 April 1993

Under the community care rules, the accommodation fees are paid for by the local authority. These fees are then reclaimable, either in whole or in part, from the resident. If the individual is of limited means, he qualifies for income support in the usual way (ie as though he were living at home) but the applicable amount also includes a 'residential allowance'. This is a standard weekly allowance throughout the country (set at £54 in April 1997) although there is an additional £6 paid for accommodation in the Greater London area.

15.7.2 Housing benefit

Individuals living in a residential care home or nursing home cannot normally claim housing benefit (see 14.3.1), although there are two circumstances when it can be paid:

(1) If the resident was living in registered accommodation on 31 March 1993 and was obtaining housing benefit to meet the cost of fees, housing benefit continues to be paid unless the resident moves to a different residential care or nursing home.
(2) If the resident was living in registered accommodation on 29 October 1990 and was receiving housing benefit to help meet the fees, housing benefit continues to be paid provided the resident is not receiving income support.

15.7.3 Disability living allowance

Residents living in registered residential care homes or nursing homes always continue to be eligible for the mobility component of disability living allowance (see 14.5.1). If they qualify for the care component, this is generally withdrawn 28 days after they move into residential accommodation. However, residents may continue to be eligible for continued payments provided they live in private accommodation paid for out of their own resources and are not receiving income support, housing benefit or any help from the local authority.

15.7.4 Attendance allowance

Attendance allowance (see 14.5.2) is generally withdrawn 28 days after the claimant moves into residential accommodation. However, the resident continues to be eligible for attendance allowance provided he is living in private accommodation paid for out of his own resources and not receiving any form of financial support from the state or the local authority.

15.8 SOURCES OF HELP

The National House Building Council can give you details of sheltered housing in your area, as can the Association of Retirement Housing Managers. Your local authority also has details of sheltered housing schemes in the locality.

You will find that your local authority can give you details of the registered care homes and nursing homes in the area. The Citizens Advice Bureaux is a useful source of help.

In addition, there are a number of other organisations up and down the country which may offer you assistance in your search for suitable accommodation.

Abbeyfield is a registered charity and is the name given to around 600 voluntary organisations throughout the United Kingdom to provide assisted living for older people. The aim is to provide a balance of privacy and caring support for those older people who would prefer not to live alone but who still retain a good deal of independence.

Each house is financially self-supporting with the cost being met by the charges paid by residents. For residents of limited means, help may be available from the local authority but only within the normal requirements of the Community Care Act.

The basic Abbeyfield house is not a residential care home as such, ie it is not registered under the Registered Homes Act. This is because the level of care required by residents is not as high as that required by a resident of a registered home. This sort of half-way house is called 'very sheltered' housing and, in Abbeyfield's case, it usually means live-in staff, an alarm system and two cooked meals a day. The absence of registration is no barrier to its availability to the local authorities. If very sheltered housing is appropriate to the needs of the individual, then local authorities may regard such homes as available resources under the provisions of the Residential Care (Accommodation) Act 1992.

For those residents who need a higher level of care, Abbeyfield has a number of 'extra care' homes which *are* registered and which provide 24-hour residential care. They also have a small number of nursing homes.

Age Concern is probably the best known of the organisations representing the interests of elderly people. It is a widely spread national organisation with branches throughout the United Kingdom. It offers not only practical help on an individual basis but has also established a formidable library of books, booklets and factsheets on many of the topics of relevance to older people, including 'A Buyer's Guide to Retirement Housing'. These are all available from their Information and Policy Department in London.

Information on the law and service provision in Scotland is available from Age Concern Scotland.

Counsel and Care is a registered charity which operates a free advice and information service on residential care in the Greater London area. It visits registered residential care and nursing homes on a regular basis and can suggest homes to people wishing to move into residential care and can also advise people on the suitability of homes after they have been assessed as requiring residential care.

For people outside the Greater London area, advice is available on appropriate sources of local information and what to look for when choosing a home.

Counsel and Care also undertakes studies into the general provision of care for older people; copies of its reports are available from its London office.

The **Elderly Accommodation Counsel** is a charity which, in conjunction with the British Medical Association and the British Geriatric Society, has established a database of over 12,000 residential care and nursing homes throughout the United Kingdom. Information is held on the type of accommodation, the services offered, the level of fees etc and this forms the basis of a search facility available to the general public. By feeding in the parameters of the accommodation you are looking for, the

Counsel can offer you a list of names and addresses. There is normally a fee for this service but it could help you to narrow your search for a residential home to those in your area that meet your needs.

The Counsel also maintains a database of sheltered housing for rent or for sale and is also building up a database of the services offered by various local authorities.

The National Care Homes Association is a national organisation of residential care home owners often with local ancillary associations. It advises its members on all aspects of retirement care and issues a code of practice which its members are expected to follow.

The Registered Nursing Homes Association deals specifically with the standards of care in nursing homes. Those who pass the initial inspection become one of the so-called 'Blue Cross' nursing homes and agree to maintain a high standard of care for their residents. Homes are inspected once every two years and the Association helps its members to maintain standards through advice and education.

The Relatives Association is a registered charity established by and for relatives and friends of older people in residential care, nursing homes and long-stay hospitals. Such people often face problems in coming to terms with this situation and the Association provides a forum for discussion and a centre of advice for helping relatives and friends make sure the quality of care in a residential home is as good as it can be. The Association is a relatively new organisation having been set up in 1992 under the auspices of Counsel and Care. It publishes its own Newsletter and provides a telephone advice line. Local branches are being formed in different parts of the country; the central office can put you in touch.

The Shaftesbury Housing Association was founded in 1970 and provides sheltered housing for the elderly. The Association operates mainly in the South and South-East of England and the majority of accommodation is for the frail elderly with full warden support.

Further information

Community Care Assessments by Richard Gordon (published by Longman) gives a good understanding of the legal framework behind assessments and explains the basis of means testing.

The **Centre for Policy on Ageing** publishes a number of booklets on residential care and other issues facing the elderly.

Social Security leaflet IS 50 (Income support) explains how the payment of certain state benefits is affected by a move into residential accommodation.

Appendix 1

BLUFFERS' GUIDE TO JARGON

Accrual rate The rate at which a pension scheme member's pension rights build up. In a '60ths' scheme your pension would build up at a rate of $^{1}/_{60}$ of your final salary for each year of service. In this case it would take 40 years to build up the maximum pension allowed by the Inland Revenue of $^{40}/_{60}$ or two-thirds of final salary (subject to restrictions in the case of some higher earners – see **earnings cap**).

Accumulation unit Units in a unit trust where the income generated is reinvested automatically, increasing the unit price. The alternative is **income units** where the income is distributed to the unitholders.

Active investment management Active managers use in-house and external research, together with their own detailed knowledge of companies and their management teams, in order to actively select the stocks. See **passive investment management**.

Added years Where the pension is expressed as a proportion of final salary, typically it builds up at the rate of $^{1}/_{60}$ of final salary for each year of service.

Additional voluntary contributions (AVCs) Extra pension contributions to a separate fund paid by the member in addition to the main scheme contributions. Total employee contributions to the main scheme and AVCs combined must not exceed 15 per cent of annual earnings. AVCs are normally run by insurance companies, building societies and, occasionally, unit trust groups. (See also **free standing additional voluntary contributions**.)

ADL Activities of daily living, used to assess an elderly person's residential or nursing home needs, among other benefits.

Advisory management An advisory investment management service means that you may discuss investment opportunities with your manager but no action can be taken without your prior approval.

AFPC Advanced Financial Planning Certificate – a higher level qualification in financial services, examined by the Chartered Insurance Institute.

Annual charge The annual management charge made by your investment manager.

Annuity An annuity provides a guaranteed income, usually for life, in return for a lump sum investment.

Appointed representative Companies that have a contract with a life office to sell one or more of its products on an exclusive basis in return for a commission payment.

Appropriate personal pension Introduced in 1988, the appropriate personal pension allows employees who are not members of a 'contracted out' company pension scheme to contract out of **SERPS** on an individual basis in return for a rebate of national insurance contributions which are invested in your chosen plan.

Assets A catch-all phrase which refers to the sectors in which funds invest, for example, UK equities, EU equities and fixed interest securities (bonds). Also possessions, such as property.

Association of Investment Trust Companies (AITC) The main trade body for investment trusts.

Association of Unit Trust and Investment Companies (AUTIF) The main trade body for unit trusts and open ended investment companies.

Authorised unit trust Unit trusts sold to the public must be authorised by the Securities and Investments Board, the chief regulator for financial services in the United Kingdom.

Band earnings National insurance for employees is levied on what are known as 'band earnings', that is earnings between lower and upper limits (known as the lower earnings limit or LEL and the upper earnings limit or UEL). These are £66 and £500 per week for the 1999–2000 tax year.

Basic state pension The basic or 'old age' pension is a flat rate benefit paid to individuals who reach state pension age and have paid or been credited with sufficient national insurance contributions during their working life.

Bed and breakfast At the end of the tax year it is common practice to sell shares and repurchase them later in order to crystallise a capital gain or loss to use in conjunction with the annual capital gains tax exemption (£7,100 for 1999–2000).

Beneficiaries Literally, those who benefit from a trust. With a unit trust, the trustees run the fund on behalf of the beneficiaries – in this case the unitholders. With a pension fund the beneficiaries are the scheme members and their dependants.

Bid/offer spread The full initial cost of your investment in a fund. This includes administration, sales commission if applicable, dealing costs and stamp duty among other items. Typically the spread is about 5–6 per cent but where the initial charge is reduced or abolished it could be as low as 0.5 per cent.

Bid price The price at which you sell units in a unit trust back to the investment manager. You purchase at the 'offer' price.

Bonds UK bonds are issued by borrowers – for example the Government and companies – which undertake to repay the principal sum on a specified date, rather like an IOU. During the time the bond is outstanding a fixed rate of interest is paid to the lender. Not to be confused with insurance bonds which are collective investments sold by insurance companies.

Capital gains tax The tax on the increase in the value of an asset when it is sold, compared with its value at the time of purchase.

Capital growth An increase in the value of shares or assets in a fund.

Carry forward/carry back A special provision exists for employees and the self-employed who have unused tax relief in previous years and want to make a substantial personal pension payment. Through the Inland Revenue's carry back and carry forward rules it is possible to 'mop up' unused tax relief for up to seven previous tax years by treating a payment this year as though it had been made in a previous tax year.

CFP Certified Financial Planner – a higher level qualification for financial planners run by the Institute of Financial Planning. The qualification is recognised in many countries around the world.

Commission 1. On the sale of an investment or insurance product a management company may pay a financial adviser a commission. 2. The fee that a stockbroker may charge clients for dealing on their behalf.

Commutation See **tax free cash**.

Company representative Also known as a direct salesman and a tied agent. Company representatives are employed directly by the life office and work solely for that company.

Contracted out/contracted in Most company pension schemes in the United Kingdom are 'contracted out' of the state earnings related pension scheme (**SERPS**) and pay a reduced rate of employee and employer national insurance contribution. The difference between the full and reduced rate contribution is invested to provide a level of pension which broadly matches what members would have got under SERPS.

Contribution limits The Inland Revenue sets out maximum contributions that an individual can pay each year. In a company scheme employees can pay up to 15 per cent of 'pensionable pay' while in a personal pension the limit is between 17.5–40 per cent of 'net relevant earnings' depending on age. The employer's contributions are not restricted under a company scheme but are included under the personal pension limits.

Controlling director Special benefit restrictions apply to certain directors who are members of pension schemes and who own 20 per cent or more of the voting rights of the company.

Convertibles Fixed interest securities which may be converted to equities at some future date.

Corporate bond An IOU issued by a public company. See **bonds**.

Coupon The rate of interest paid by a bond or gilt.

Custodian Usually a bank, whose primary function is to look after the trust's assets.

Death in retirement benefits The pension and lump sum paid to the deceased member's spouse and/or other dependants where death occurs in retirement.

Death in service benefits The pension and lump sum paid to the deceased member's spouse and/or other dependants where death occurs while still employed.

Debentures bonds Issued by UK companies which are secured on the company's underlying assets – for example property. Unsecured bonds are known as loan stocks.

Deferred pensioner A scheme member who changes employment and leaves behind his or her pension benefits. The benefits are known as a deferred pension because the pension is held by the scheme until retirement age.

Deficit In pension fund terms a deficit is identified when the fund cannot meet its liabilities in terms of the guaranteed benefits it must pay. See **surplus**.

Defined benefit A US term for **final salary schemes**. These are pension schemes which link your pension to your salary – usually at or just before retirement. Usually there is no direct link between what you pay in and the emerging pension.

Defined contribution This refers to money purchase pensions, where there is no direct link between the pension and your salary at retirement.

Dependants In the context of a pension scheme, the members' or beneficiaries' dependants are usually limited to the spouse and children under age 18.

Derivatives Financial instruments are referred to as derivative securities when their value is dependent on the value of some other underlying asset. In other words, the value of the derivative security is *derived* from the value of the underlying security. See **futures**, **options** and **warrants**.

Discount If the share price of an investment trust is lower than the value per share of the underlying assets the difference is known as the discount. If it is higher the difference is known as the premium. As a general rule a share trading at a discount represents good value.

Discretionary benefits Non-guaranteed benefits, although in some cases they can become an expectation – typically where pension increases above the guaranteed minimum are paid on a regular basis. Discretionary payments are paid at the 'discretion' of the trustees. The trust deed and rules, for example, may include a 'discretion' to allow trustees to pay death benefits and spouse's pensions to common law partners.

Discretionary management An investment service where you give your manager total control over the day-to-day running of your portfolio or units. The manager makes all the investment decisions.

Distributions Income paid out from an equity or bond fund.

Dividend The owner of shares is entitled to dividends – the annual or six-monthly distribution to shareholders of part of the company's profits.

Dividend yield See **gross yield**.

Earnings cap Introduced in the 1989 Budget, the cap restricts the amount of salary on which pension contributions and benefits are based. For the 1999–2000 tax year the earnings cap is £90,600.

Enterprise investment schemes (EIS) Available by direct subscription. EISs offer a range of tax reliefs if you invest in the shares of mainly unquoted trading companies.

Enterprise zones trusts (EZTs) Available by direct subscription. EZTs are designated areas where tax reliefs and reduced administrative controls are used to attract new business, providing investment in property with income tax relief on most of the cost.

Equities The ordinary share capital of a company.

Execution only With this type of service, the investment manager/stockbroker simply buys and sells at your request without offering any advice.

Exit charges A charge deducted from certain funds if you pull out early – usually within the first five years.

Fee based adviser Many firms of financial advisers do not accept sales commission. Instead they charge a fee calculated on an hourly basis or occasionally on a per case basis. This means that the adviser's remuneration is not dependent on the sale of financial products.

Final salary scheme Final salary schemes (in the US known as 'defined benefit' schemes) link the value of the pension to earnings – usually in the few years leading to retirement. Typically the pension builds up at a rate of 1/60 of final salary for each year of service up to a maximum of 40/60 or two-thirds final salary (subject to restrictions in the case of certain higher earners – see **earnings cap**). See also **money purchase**.

Financial Services Act 1986 The Act which set up the system of self-regulation for financial services and a series of self-regulatory organisations (SROs) which regulate different types of financial institutions and the advisers and representatives who sell their products.

Fixed interest securities Another term for bonds. (See **bonds**, **corporate bonds**.)

Free-standing additional voluntary contributions (FSAVCs) If your company pension is likely to fall short of the maximum two-thirds final salary set by the Revenue, it is possible to pay voluntary top up contributions either to the company additional voluntary contribution (AVC) scheme or to an individual plan called a free-standing AVC (FSAVC).

FTSE-100 Index The index which covers the top 100 companies on the UK Stock Exchange measured by market capitalisation (the number of shares times the share value).

FTSE A All-Share Index The index which measures the bulk of the companies listed on the UK Stock Exchange – about 915 in total.

FTSE Mid-250 Index The index which measures the 250 companies below (by market capitalisation) the FTSE-100.

Funded and unfunded unapproved schemes These are pension schemes recognised by the Revenue but not approved for tax purposes. They are used to provide pension for employees caught by the **earnings cap**.

Fund of funds Unit trusts which can only invest in other authorised unit trusts.

Futures A type of **derivative**. A futures contract is a legally binding agreement to buy or sell an amount of shares (or other instruments) at a fixed date in the future at a fixed price.

Gearing The relationship between debt and assets. High gearing means that there is a large proportion of debt in relation to the assets held. Investment trusts can borrow to invest in assets; unit trusts can only do so to a limited extent.

Gilts The most secure type of **bonds** because they are issued by the UK Government.

Gross yield This is another method of assessing the income from an investment. It is the annual gross dividends expressed as a percentage of the current market price. This shows the rate of gross income return a shareholder would receive on an investment at the share price on the date specified – much as one might describe the interest received on a deposit account. The important point to note is that for equities, investment trusts and equity based unit trusts held within a PEP, the yield is quoted gross but paid net. The PEP manager reclaims the tax.

Group personal pension This is little more than a series of individual personal pension plans although if the employer sets up the group plan he is more likely to make a contribution and, perhaps, provide life assurance and other benefits on top. The GPP is not defined as an occupational scheme and so the same contribution and benefit limits as individual personal pensions apply.

Guaranteed equity funds Funds which limit your exposure to falls in the stock market and provide a percentage of the gains. They do this by investing mainly in gilts and cash and then buying **derivatives** to provide the guarantees. Guaranteed funds may be worth considering for **income drawdown** plans but otherwise it is not clear whether long-term equity investors get value for money given the cost of the guarantee. Some commentators regard guaranteed funds as the natural replacement for with-profits funds. But then nobody really understands how these work either.

Higher yield unit trusts A category of unit trusts which yields a minimum of 110 per cent of the FTSE A All-Share Index.

HRP Home Responsibilities Protection can be claimed if you are a carer for an older dependent relative. This helps build up your rights to a state pension even though you are not paying national insurance contributions.

Income drawdown Allows you to keep your personal pension fully invested in retirement up to age 75.

Independent financial adviser IFAs, as they are known in the trade, are not tied to any one life office but instead search the market to find the best product for your needs.

Index tracking With a tracker fund, the investment manager uses a computer model to select stocks to simulate the performance of a specific stock market index. Also known as passive management.

Inheritance tax A tax on wealth passed on at death. The nil rate band is £231,000. Anything over this is taxed at 40 per cent although gifts between husband and wife are exempt.

Initial charge A charge, typically 5 per cent, levied by the investment manager to cover administration and sales commission when you invest in a fund. However, the full upfront cost of your investment is shown in the **bid/offer spread** which includes additional charges such as stamp duty.

Integration Company pension schemes that are integrated with the basic state pension scheme do not provide a pension for the first slice of earnings up to the lower earnings limit (LEL) for **national insurance**.

Investment trust A UK company, listed on the stock exchange, which invests in the shares of other companies in the United Kingdom and overseas. Investment trust companies have a fixed number of shares which are subject to the usual market forces, so the share price does not necessarily reflect the underlying net asset value. See **discount** and **premium**.

Key features The (supposedly) simple summary of the product you receive before you sign up. The most important feature is the details on charges but it should also include details on the risk level of the investment and the pattern of contributions to which you are committed.

Life office A life assurance company authorised to sell life and pensions products. The term is also used to describe the life assurance arm of a composite insurer. Composites sell life and pensions products and also general insurance such as household and motor cover.

Loan stocks Unsecured bonds issued by UK companies. Bonds secured on a company's underlying assets (property, for example) are known as debentures (see **bonds**).

Lower earnings limit The threshold above which you pay national insurance contributions – up to the upper earnings limit. The lower limit is £66 per week and the upper limit is £500 per week.

Managed/mixed fund This is a broadly diversified fund which invests in a range of the manager's other main funds, usually including UK and overseas equities, gilts, bonds and, in some cases, property.

Market maker A dealer who can buy and sell shares.

Married woman's stamp More correctly, the 'reduced' rate of national insurance contribution women can still pay provided they were married or widowed before 5 April 1977. The reduced rate does not build up an entitlement to the basic state pension, among other benefits.

Money purchase Money purchase or **defined contribution** schemes do not guarantee a pension linked to the member's final salary. Instead contributions are invested to build up a fund which is used at retirement to buy an annuity from a life office. The annuity provides the guaranteed regular income until death. See **annuity**.

Mutual life office A mutual life office is effectively owned by its policyholders and, unlike a 'proprietary' company, it does not have shareholders.

National insurance A form of taxation (levied at 10 per cent in most cases) on 'band' earnings – that is earnings between the lower and upper earnings limits (LEL and UEL). These are £66 and £500 per week (£3,432 and £26,000 pa) for the 1999–2000 tax year.

National insurance rebate A partial return of national insurance contributions is rebated to individuals who contract out of the state earnings-related pension scheme (**SERPS**) with an **appropriate personal pension**.

National Savings Available direct from National Savings or via the Post Office. NS certificates offer a tax-free return.

Net asset value (NAV) The market value of an **investment trust's** underlying assets. This may be different from the share price since the latter is subject to market forces and supply and demand. See **discount** and **premium**.

Net relevant earnings Earnings on which personal pension contributions are based.

Net yield The return on an investment after tax has been deducted. See **gross yield**.

Non-qualifying funds Unit or investment trusts with more than 50 per cent of their assets invested outside of the EU.

Occupational pension scheme A scheme sponsored by an employer to provide relevant benefits to employees.

OEICs Open ended investment companies are a new type of investment fund. They are similar to unit trusts but have a corporate structure, rather than based on a trust, and they have a single price rather than a bid/offer spread.

Offer price The price at which you buy units from the unit trust manager. You sell back to the manager at the **bid price**.

Open market option Your right at retirement to take the proceeds of your personal pension (or similar) and buy your **annuity** elsewhere. Annuity rates (the income you buy with your pension fund) vary considerably so it is essential to shop around.

OPRA The Occupational Pension Regulatory Authority is a new regulator for company pensions, established under the Pensions Act 1995. It took over from the Occupational Pensions Board in April 1997.

Options A type of **derivative**. A call option gives the buyer the right (but not the obligation – hence *option*) to buy a commodity, stock, bond or currency in the future at a mutually agreed price struck on the date of the contract. Put options give you the right, but not the obligation, to sell.

Passive investment management Another term for **index tracking**.

Pension age The age at which you can draw your pension from the state scheme, your company scheme or your individual plan.

Pension forecast A useful service provided by the Department of Social Security which tells you what your state pension is worth.

Pensions Available from a range of financial institutions and also provided by many employers in the form of an occupational pension scheme. Pension schemes and plans approved by the Inland Revenue offer tax relief on contributions, tax-free growth of the fund and, in some cases, a tax-free lump sum at retirement. The pension income is taxed.

Pensions Ombudsman An independent arbitrator for pension disputes. The ombudsman has statutory power to enforce his decisions.

Performance measurement Used to check how well or badly the investment manager has done. There are usually two measurements; first against an industry average, and secondly against a specific benchmark or target set by the trustees of the fund.

Personal Investment Authority (PIA) Under the Financial Services Act 1986, the PIA is the regulator for companies which market and sell retail investments such as PEPs, pensions and life assurance savings plans.

Pooled funds Another term for collective or mutual funds which invest in a range of different shares and other instruments to achieve diversification and economies of scale for the smaller investor who buys units in these funds.

Potentially exempt transfer You can avoid inheritance tax if you live for seven years after giving away an asset. A sliding scale of tax applies if you die within the seven years.

Preference shares ('prefs') These are similar to **bonds** in that they pay a fixed rate of interest, although their payments depend on company profits. Preference shares are first in the pecking order of payouts when an investment trust is wound up. (See **stepped preference shares** and **zero dividend preference shares**).

Premium If the share price of an investment trust is higher than the value of the underlying assets the difference is known as the premium. Normally investors are advised not to buy under these circumstances. If the price is lower than the **net asset value** (NAV) the difference is known as the **discount**.

Price earnings ratio The market price of a share divided by the company's earnings (profits) per share in its latest 12-month trading period.

Property In the context of pension fund investment, property means the ownership of land and buildings that are used by businesses or other organisations which pay rent to the owner. Ownership is often on a collective basis.

Proprietary life office Proprietary life offices are quoted companies and have shareholders, unlike 'mutual' which are effectively owned by their policyholders.

Protected rights The fund which is built up from the rebates of national insurance contributions under a personal **pension** and other types of **money purchase** pensions.

Purchased life annuity (PLA) See **annuity**.

Qualifying year A complete tax year in which the full rate of national insurance contribution was paid or credited. Qualifying years count towards your basic state pension.

Redemption The date at which a **bond** becomes repayable.

Retirement annuity Retirement annuity contracts were the predecessor of personal pensions and were similar in most respects except that they did not allow individual employees to contract out of SERPS.

Return The amount by which your investment increases as a result of interest or dividend income and capital growth.

Risk A measure of the probability that the value of your savings and the income they generate will fall as well as rise.

Scrip issue/dividends A scrip issue is where a company turns part of its accumulated reserves into new shares.

Securities The general name for all stocks and shares. Broadly speaking stocks are fixed interest securities and shares are the rest. The four main types of securities listed and traded on the UK Stock Exchange are UK equities, overseas equities (ie issued by non-UK companies), UK gilts (bonds issued by the UK Government) and bonds/fixed interest stocks (issued by companies and local authorities).

Securities and Investments Board (SIB) The chief regulator for financial services in the United Kingdom. See **Financial Services Act 1986**.

Self-invested personal pensions (SIPPs) These are similar to personal pensions but allow the individual to separate the administration and investment and therefore allow the individual to exercise much greater freedom in the investment choice. Only viable for larger investments.

Self-select PEP A plan which does not restrict you to the funds of one PEP manager but instead allows you to hold the entire range of PEPable assets, including individual shares and bonds as well as unit and investment trusts.

SERPS The state earnings-related pension scheme was set up in 1978 to provide employees with a pension linked to average earnings between the lower and upper threshold for national insurance.

SOFA The Society of Financial Advisers is the financial services arm of the Chartered Insurance Institute.

Split capital trust An **investment trust** which has different types of shares – for example, some offer a high income but no capital growth and some offer pure capital growth but no income.

Stamp duty A tax on the purchase (but not the sale) of shares, currently 0.5 per cent.

Stepped preference shares Shares in a **split capital trust** which pay dividends that rise at a predetermined rate and have a fixed redemption value, paid when the trust is wound up.

Stock market indices An index is a specified basket or portfolio of shares and shows how these share prices are moving in order to give an indication of market trends. Every major world stock market is represented by at least one index. The **FTSE-100 Index**, for example, reflects the movements of the share prices of the United Kingdom's largest 100 quoted companies by market capitalisation.

Tax-free cash Under Inland Revenue rules it is possible to take part of your pension benefits at retirement in the form of tax-free cash. This process is known as 'commutation'.

Tax year Tax and investment allowances apply to the 12 months from 6 April to the following 5 April.

Tracker funds See **index tracking**.

Transfer value The amount you take out of a pension scheme if you leave employment and want to transfer your pension benefits into the new employer's scheme or into an individual pension plan.

Trust deed The legal document on which a pension scheme unit trust is based. The use of a trust separates the fund from the employer's or investment management company's assets. The trustees manage the fund on behalf of the beneficiaries.

Trustee You cannot have a trust without a trustee who, as legal owner of the fund, looks after the assets on behalf of the beneficiaries.

UCITS (Undertaking for Collective Investments in Transferable Securities) An EU term for a collective fund, such as a unit trust or OEIC which can be marketed in all the Union's markets.

Unapproved pension schemes Schemes that are recognised by the Revenue but are not approved for tax purposes. Used mainly to top up benefits for employees caught by the **earnings cap**. See **funded and unfunded schemes**.

Upper earnings limit See **national insurance**.

Venture capital trusts (VCTs) Available from a range of financial institutions and by direct subscription. VCTs allow you to participate in **EIS**-type investments on a collective basis.

Waiver of premium With a regular premium pension plan if you have this feature the pension company credits your fund with contributions under certain circumstances – for example if you are too ill to work.

Warrants Risky and volatile investments which give the holder the right but not the obligation to buy investment trust shares at a predetermined price within a specified period. This type of share has no voting rights and holders do not normally receive dividends.

Winding-up The term used to explain the legal termination of a pension scheme. Details on how the scheme should be wound up are set out in the trust deed and rules.

With-profits/unitised with-profits pension funds With-profits funds are invested in UK and overseas equities, gilts, bonds and property. Under a with-profits contract the life office provides a guaranteed minimum sum at maturity to which it adds annual or 'reversionary' bonuses which, once allocated, cannot be taken away. The annual bonuses are 'smoothed' to avoid volatility. On top of this there is a discretionary (not guaranteed) final 'terminal' bonus which reflects recent performance of the with-profits fund.

Yield The annual dividend or income on an investment expressed as a percentage of the purchase price. See **gross yield**.

Zero dividend preference shares ('zeroes') A lower risk and predetermined investment. It offers a fixed capital return in the form of a redemption value which is paid when the trust is wound up. These shares are not entitled to income and therefore there is no income tax liability.

This is reproduced from the *Investors Chronicle Personal Financial Planner* by Debbie Harrison, published by Pitman. Some of the definitions were drawn from other publications written by Debbie Harrison and reproduced by kind permission of the publisher, including *Investors Chronicle Good PEPs Guide*, also published by Pitman; *Pensions Power*, published by John Wiley & Sons; and *Unit Trust User's Handbook*, published by Pearson Professional.

Appendix 2

SOURCES OF INFORMATION

THE FINANCIAL SERVICES AUTHORITY (FSA)

Most regulation is carried out by specialist bodies recognised by the Financial Services Authority (FSA) (formerly the Securities Investment Board (SIB)). The FSA can be contacted at:

The Financial Services Authority, 25 The North Colonnade, Canary Wharf, London E14 5HS. Tel: (020) 7676 1000; Fax: (020) 7676 1099; Web: <www.fsa.gov.uk>; E-mail: <enquiries@sib.co.uk>.

The FSA recognises:

(1) three Recognised Self-Regulating Organisations (SROs) (two further SROs (FIMBRA and LAUTRO) have transferred their regulatory responsibilities to the Personal Investment Authority (PIA));
(2) nine Recognised Professional Bodies (RPBs);
(3) six Recognised Investment Exchanges (RIEs); and
(4) two Recognised Clearing Houses (RCHs).

Self-Regulating Organisations (SROs)

Most investment business is carried out by firms regulated by one of the three SROs. The SROs have the power to authorise firms to conduct investment business in the UK (and now under the Investment Services Directive, throughout the European Economic Area). The SROs' work comprises the following elements:

(1) examining firms for the purposes of authorisation, to ensure that they are honest, solvent and competent to conduct investment business;
(2) continuing supervision of firms, including monitoring the adequacy of their financial resources;
(3) overseeing firms' dealings with investors to ensure that information provided is clear and not misleading and that advice given is suitable;
(4) making arrangements for handling investors' complaints against

firms and for the resolution of disputes through Ombudsmen schemes; and

(5) disciplining those who have broken the rules by censuring them, fining them or excluding them.

All three SROs – The Investment Management Regulatory Authority (IMRO), The Securities and Futures Authority (SFA) and The Personal Investment Authority (PIA) – can be contacted at the following address:

25 The North Colonnade, Canary Wharf, London E14 5HS. Tel: (020) 7676 1000; Fax: (020) 7676 1099; Web: <www.fsa.gov.uk>;
E-mail: <enquiries@sib.co.uk>.

Other contacts at this address are The Building Societies Commission, The Friendly Societies Commission, The Insurance Directorate of HM Treasury and The Registry of Friendly Societies.

Recognised Professional Bodies (RPBs)

The Financial Services Act established a special regime for members of certain professions whose main activity is the practice of their profession but who have some involvement in investment business. These firms conduct investment business following certification by their professional body, which then regulates their main activity and their investment business.

The Association of Chartered Certified Accountants (ACCA), 29 Lincoln's Inn Fields, London WC2A 3EE. Tel: (020) 7242 6855;
Web: <www.acca.org.uk>; E-mail: <public.relations@acca.org.uk>.

The Institute of Actuaries (IoA), Staple Inn Hall, High Holborn, London WC1V 7QJ. Tel: (020) 7632 2100; E-mail: <institute@actuaries.co.uk>.

The Institute of Chartered Accountants in England and Wales (ICAEW), Silbury Court, 412–416 Silbury Boulevard, Milton Keynes MK9 2AF. Tel: (020) 7920 8100; Web: <www.icaew.co.uk>.

The Institute of Chartered Accountants in Scotland (ICAS), 27 Queen Street, Edinburgh EH2 1LA. Tel: 0131 247 4883; Fax: 0131 225 3813; Web: <www.icas.org.uk>; E-mail: <icas@icas.org.uk>.

The Institute of Chartered Accountants in Ireland (ICAI), Chartered Accountants House, 87–89 Pembroke Road, Dublin 4. Tel: 00 353 1 668 0040.

The Insurance Brokers Registration Council (IBRC), 63 St Mary Axe, London EC3A 8NB. Tel: (020) 7621 1061.

The Law Society, The Law Society's Hall, 113 Chancery Lane, London, WC2 1PL. Tel: (020) 7242 1222; Web: <www.lawsociety.org.uk>.

The Law Society of Northern Ireland (LSNI), Law Society House, 98 Victoria Street, Belfast, BT1 3JZ. Tel: (028) 9023 1614;
E-mail: <lawsoc-ni.org.uk>.

The Law Society of Scotland (LSS), The Law Society's Hall, 26 Drumsheugh Gardens, Edinburgh EH3 7YR. Tel: 0131 226 7411;
Web: <www.lawscot.org.uk>; E-mail: <lawscot@lawscot.org.uk>.

Recognised Investment Exchanges (RIEs)

The FSA supervises the six UK RIEs (ie organised markets on which member firms trade investments ranging from equities to financial and commodity derivatives). An RIE is responsible for ensuring that business on the exchange is conducted in an orderly manner and affording proper protection to investors.

The London Stock Exchange (LSE), Old Broad Street, London EC2N 1HP. Tel: (020) 7588 2355; Fax: (020) 7410 6842;
E-mail: <lse@dial.pipex.com>.

Tradepoint Stock Exchange, 35 King Street, Covent Garden, London WC2E 8JD. Tel: (020) 7240 8000; Fax: (020) 7240 1900;
E-mail: <enquiries@tradepoint.co.uk>.

The London International Financial Futures and Options Exhange (LIFFE), Cannon Bridge, London EC4R 3XX. Tel: (020) 7623 0444; Fax: (020) 7588 3624.

The London Securities and Derivatives Exchange Ltd, Milestone House, 107 Cannon Street, London EC4N 5AD. Tel: (020) 7283 0678; Fax: (020) 7815 8508.

The International Petroleum Exchange of London Ltd, International House, 1 St Katharine's Way, London E1 9UN. Tel: (020) 7265 3636; Fax: (020) 7481 8485; E-mail: <info@ipe.co.uk>.

The London Metal Exchange (LME), 56 Leadenhall Street, London EC3 2BJ. Tel: (020) 7264 5555; Fax: (020) 7680 0505.

Recognised Clearing Houses (RCHs)

The FSA supervises the two UK RCHs (which organise settlement of transactions on Recognised Investment Exchanges).

The London Clearing House (LCH), Aldgate House, 33 Aldgate High Street, London EC3N 1EA. Tel: (020) 7426 7000; Fax: (020) 7426 7001;
Web: <www.lch.co.uk>; E-mail: <elgoharyd@lch.co.uk>.

CrestCo Ltd, 10th Floor, Trinity Tower, 9 Thomas More Street, London E1 9YN. Tel: (020) 7849 0000; Fax: (020) 7849 0130; Web: <www.crestco.co.uk>.

INDEPENDENT FINANCIAL ADVISERS

Before you contact a firm you should check with the Financial Services Authority central register, tel: 08456 0612344 or Web: <www.fsa.gov.uk>.

Fees vary considerably from firm to firm, so if you have a tight budget you should ask about the hourly rate and get a rough idea of the total bill in advance. Other useful numbers are as follows:

Actuaries

The Association of Consulting Actuaries (ACA), Number 1, Wardrobe Place, London EC4V 5AH. Tel: (020) 7248 3163; Fax: (020) 7236 1889; Web: <www.aca.org.uk>; E-mail: <acahelp@aca.org.uk>.

Financial Planners and Advisers

The Institute of Financial Planning (IFP), Whitefriars Centre, Lewins Mead, Bristol BS1 2NT. Tel: 0117 930 4434; Fax: 0117 929 2214; Web: <www.financialplanning.org.uk>; E-mail: <enquiries@institutefinplan.demon.co.uk>.

The Society of Financial Advisers (SOFA), 20 Aldermanbury, London EC2V 7HY. Tel: (020) 7417 4419; Fax: (020) 7600 0766; Web: <www.sofa.org>; E-mail: <info@sofa.org>.

The Society of Pension Consultants (SPC), Ludgate House, Ludgate Circus, London EC4A 2AB. Tel: (020) 7353 1688; Fax: (020) 7353 9296; Web: <www.spc.uk.com>; E-mail: <eleen.damsel@spc.uk.com>

IFA Promotions (for list of three local IFAs), 17–19 Emery Road, Brislington, Bristol BS4 5PF. Tel: 0117 971 1177; Web: <www.ifap.org.uk>.

Matrix Data Services (for a list of six fee-based investment advisers), Freepost, Gossard House, 7–8 Saville Row, London W1X 1AF. Tel: 0870 0131 925

Solicitors

Solicitors for Independent Advice (SFIA), 10 East Street, Epsom, Surrey KT17 1HH. Tel: 01372 721172; Fax: 01372 745277;
Web: <www.sfia.co.uk>; E-mail: <sfia@sfia.co.uk>.

The Association of Solicitor Investment Managers (ASIM), Chiddingstone Causeway, Tonbridge, Kent TN11 8JX. Tel: 01892 870065; Fax: 01892 870160;
E-mail: <heather_martin@compuserve.com>.

The Association of Pension Lawyers (contact: Mrs Susan Andrews), Eversheds, Senator House, 85 Queen Victoria Street, London EC4V 4JL. Tel: (020) 7919 4500; Fax: (020) 7919 4919;
E-mail: <andrews@eversheds.co.uk>.

Stockbrokers

The Association of Private Client Investment Manaagers and Stockbrokers (APCIMS), 112 Middlesex Street, London E1 7HY. Tel: (020) 7247 7080; Fax: (020) 7377 0939;
Web: <www.apcims.co.uk>; E-mail: <info@apcims.co.uk>.

Taxation advisers

The Chartered Institute of Taxation (CIOT), 12 Upper Belgrave Street, London SW1X 8BB. Tel: (020) 7235 9381; Fax: (020) 7235 2562; Web: <www.tax.org.uk>; E-mail: <post@tax.org.uk>.

REGULATORS AND OMBUDSMEN

Most of these publish a consumer guide to complaints. For the professional bodies, approach the institutes and societies listed under 'Recognised Professional Bodies' above.

The PIA Ombudsman Bureau, Hertsmere House, Hertsmere Road, London E14 4AB. Tel: (020) 7216 0016; Fax: (020) 7712 8742.

The Insurance Ombudsman Bureau, 135 Park Street, London SE1 9EA. Tel: 0845 600 6666; Fax: (020) 7902 8197;
Web: <www.theiob.org.uk>; E-mail: <complaint@thiob.org.uk>.

The Office of the Investment Ombudsman, 6 Fredericks Place, London EC2R 8BT. Tel: (020) 7796 3065; Fax: (020) 7726 0574.

The Occupational Pensions Advisory Service (OPAS), 11 Belgrave Road, London SW1V 1RB. Tel: (020) 7233 8080; Fax: (020) 7233 8016; Web: <www.opas.org.uk>; E-mail: <opas@iclweb.com>.

The Pensions Ombudsman, 11 Belgrave Road, London SW1V 1RB. Tel: (020) 7834 9144; Fax: (020) 7821 0065;
E-mail: <pensions.ombudsman@iclweb.com>.

The Banking Ombudsman, 70 Gray's Inn Road, London WC1X 8NB. Tel: (020) 7404 9944; Fax: (020) 7405 5052;
Web: <www.obo.org.uk>;
E-mail: <banking.ombudsman@easynet.co.uk>.

The Building Societies Ombudsman, Millbank Tower, Millbank, London SW1P 4XF. Tel: (020) 7931 0044; Fax: (020) 7931 8485;
E-mail: <bldgsocombudsman@easynet.co.uk>.

See also:

Investors Compensation Scheme, Cotton's Centre, Cotton's Lane, London SE1 2QB. Tel: (020) 7367 6000; Fax: (020) 7367 6001.

Inland Revenue, Customs and Excise and Contributions Agency Adjudicator, 3rd Floor, Haymarket House, 28 Haymarket, London SW1Y 4SP. Tel: (020) 7930 2292; Fax: (020) 7930 2298;
Web: <www.open.gov.uk/adjoff>;
E-mail: <adjudicators@gtnet.gov.uk>.

OTHER USEFUL INVESTMENT ORGANISATIONS

The Association of Investment Trust Companies (AITC), Durrant House, 8–13 Chiswell Street, London EC1Y 4YY. Tel: (020) 7431 5222; Fax: (020) 7638 1803; Web: <www.aitc.co.uk>.

The Association of Unit Trusts and Investment Companies (AUTIF), 65 Kingsway, London WC2B 6TD. Tel: (020) 7831 0898; Fax: (020) 7831 9975; Web: <www.investmentfunds.org.uk>;
E-mail: <autif@investmentfunds.org.uk>.

The Stock Exchange, Old Broad Street, London EC2N 1HP. Tel: (020) 7797 1000; Web: <www.londonstockex.co.uk>

Contacts for experienced investors and DIY investment enthusiasts

ProShare, Library Chambers, 13–14 Basinghall Street, London EC2V 5BQ. Tel: (020) 7600 0984; Fax: (020) 7600 0947; Web: <www.proshare.org.uk>;

Charles Schwab Europe, Cannon House, 24 The Priory Queensway, Birmingham B4 6BS. Tel: 0121 200 2474; Fax: 0121 233 2789; Web: <www.schwab-worldwide.com\europe>.

USEFUL ORGANISATIONS

Abbeyfield Society, Abbeyfield House, 53 Victoria Street, St Albans, Herts AL1 3UW. Tel: 01727 857536; Fax: 01727 846168; Web: <www.vois.org.uk/abbeyfield>; E-mail: <abbeyf@geo2.poptel.org.uk>.

Age Concern England, Astral House, 1268 London Road, London SW16 4ER. Tel: (020) 8679 8000; Fax: (020) 8765 7211; Web: <www.ace.org.uk>.

Advice, Information and Mediation Service for Retirement Housing (AIMS), Walkden House, 3–10 Melton Street, London NW1 2EB. Tel: (020) 7383 2006; Fax: (020) 7383 3614; Web: <www.ace.org.uk>; E-mail: <aims@ace.org.uk>.

Age Concern Northern Ireland, 3 Lower Crescent, Belfast BT7 1NR. Tel: (028) 9024 5729.

Age Concern Cymru, 4th Floor, 1 Cathedral Road, Cardiff CF1 9SD. Tel: (029) 2037 1566; Fax: (029) 2039 9562; Web: <www.ace.org.uk/cymru>; E-mail: <contact@accymru.demon.uk>.

Age Concern Scotland, 113 Rose Street, Edinburgh EH2 3DT. Tel: 0131 220 3345; Fax: 0131 220 2779; Web: <www.ace.org.uk/scotland>.

Association of British Insurers, 51 Gresham Street, London EC2V 7HQ. Tel: (020) 7600 3333; Fax: (020) 7696 8999; Web: <www.abi.org.uk>; E-mail: <info@abi.org.uk>.

Association of Policy Marketmakers, Holywell Centre, 1 Phipp Street, London EC2A 4PS. Tel: (020) 7739 3949; Fax: (020) 7613 2990; Web: <www.moneyworld.co.uk/apmm>; E-mail: <apmm@dircon.co.uk>.

Carers National Association, Ruth Pitter House, 20–25 Glasshouse Yard, London EC1A 4JS. Tel: (020) 7490 8818; Carer's line: 0808 808 7777; Fax: (020) 7490 8824; Web: <www.carersuk.demon.co.uk>; E-mail: <internet@ukcarers.org>.

Help the Aged, 16–18 St James's Walk, Clerkenwell Green, London EC1R 0BE. Tel: (020) 7253 0253; Fax: (020) 7250 4474; Web: <www.helptheaged.org.uk>; E-mail: <info@helptheaged.org.uk>.

Pre-Retirement Association (PRA), 9 Chesham Road, Guildford, Surrey GU1 3LF. Tel: 01483 301170; Fax: 01483 300981; Web: <www.pra.uk.com>; E-mail: <info@pra.uk.com>.

Safe Home Income Plans (Hinton & Wild (Home Plans) Ltd, Tolworth Tower, Ewell Road, Surbiton, Surrey KT6 7EL. Tel: (020) 8390 8166; Fax: 0800 32 88 432; Web: <www.hinton-wild.co.uk>; E-mail: <hintonwild@btinternet.com>.

PUBLIC/GOVERNMENT AGENCIES

Department of Social Security (DSS), The Head Of Unit, Department of Social Security, HQ Correspondence Unit, Room 540, The Adelphi, 1–11 John Adam Street, London WC2N 6HT. Tel: (020) 7712 2171; Fax: (020) 7712 2386; Web: <www.dss.gov.uk>; E-mail: <peo@MS41.dss.gsi.gov.uk>.

The Government Actuary's Department (GAD), New Kings Beam House, 22 Upper Ground, London SE1 9RJ. Tel: (020) 7211 2600; Fax: (020) 7211 2630; E-mail: <enquiries@gad.gov.uk>

Inland Revenue (Savings and Investment Division), South West Wing, Bush House, London WC2B 4RD. Tel: (020) 7438 6622.

Occupational Pensions Regulatory Authority (OPRA), Invicta House, Trafalgar Place, Brighton, East Sussex BN1 4BY. Tel: 01273 627600; Fax: 01273 627688; Web: <www.opra.gov.uk>; E-mail: <helpdesk@opra.gov.uk>.

The Pension Schemes Registry, PO Box 1NN, Newcastle upon Tyne NE99 1NN. Tel: 0191 225 6393.

Pension Schemes Office (PSO), Yorke House, PO Box 62, Castle Meadow Road, Nottingham NG2 1BG. Tel: 0115 974 1600 (occupational)/0115 974 1777 (personal); Fax: 0115 974 1680; Web: <www.inlandrevenue.gov.uk/pso>.

GUIDE TO COMPLAINTS

If you think you have a complaint concerning your investments you first need to find out to whom you should complain. This might not be immediately obvious because different types of financial institutions and advisers are authorised by different regulatory bodies. However, details of the regulator should be shown in the letterhead of the company which sold you the investment. If you are in any doubt, contact the Financial Services Authority (FSA), which keeps on a central register the details of all the companies authorised under the Financial Services Act.

The main regulator for sales of retail investment products is the Personal Investment Authority (PIA), which has its own ombudsman. However, you may also come across the Securities and Futures Authority (SFA), the Investment Management Regulatory Organisation (IMRO) and the chief regulator, the FSA.

Most independent financial advisers are authorised by the PIA but if you were advised by a professional firm then you will deal with the appropriate 'recognised professional body' (RPB), for example the Institute of Chartered Accountants or the Law Society. Due to their complexity, pension complaints, particularly those which relate to company schemes, have their own system for complaints.

Not everything is regulated under the Financial Services Act. For example, most protection insurances, examined in Chapters 7–12 of this book, are classed as general insurance business and do not come under the aegis of the investment regulators, even if there is a significant element of investment within the policy, as is the case with some whole of life plans and long-term care policies (which cover nursing home fees for the very elderly).

In these cases if you have a problem you would probably contact the Insurance Ombudsman or even the Department of Trade (DTI) – but again, the company which sold you the policy is obliged to tell you which is the correct complaints channel.

Most of the regulators and ombudsmen publish a consumer guide to complaints which will help you prepare your case.

What to say

Different regulators have different rules but in most cases they expect you first to tackle the company which sold you the plan before taking your complaint further. Clearly, your complaint stands a much greater chance of being taken seriously if you prepare your case well. The regulators and ombudsmen recommend the following procedure:

- Write first to the compliance officer at the company which sold you the plan.
- State clearly the nature of the complaint.
- Give contact details, including your daytime telephone number.
- Provide the name of the plan, the date you invested, and the name of your contact – the salesman or adviser who dealt with your case.
- Quote all relevant plan details and reference numbers.
- Photocopy letters and supporting material.
- Set a sensible deadline for the reply. You should receive an acknowledgment of your letter within seven days but allow two months for the actual investigation before taking the case to the ombudsman or regulator.

Occupational pension schemes

The new Pensions Act (1995), which came into force in April 1997, requires trustees to establish a two-stage internal dispute resolution process for members who have a complaint. This system is the first port of call for any scheme member who has a problem or feels the scheme has in some way failed to provide the promised benefits.

If this fails to resolve your dispute you can go to the Occupational Pensions Advisory Service. OPAS is a grant aided, non-profit-making company limited by guarantee. It is an independent and voluntary organisation providing free help and advice to members of the public. As with other financial products discussed above, the first step is to contact the scheme authorities.

Only after you have attempted to resolve your problem this way will OPAS step in. The best way to approach OPAS is through your local Citizens Advice Bureau which puts you in touch with your nearest OPAS adviser. If there is no CAB locally then send a brief letter direct to OPAS, enclosing any relevant material.

While OPAS has an outstanding track record on settling disputes, nevertheless there will always be the stubborn cases where the scheme authorities refuse to budge even if it is clear that they are in the wrong. If OPAS fails to rectify the problem, you can turn to the Pensions Ombudsman.

The Pensions Ombudsman was appointed under the Social Security Act 1990 to deal with complaints against and disputes with occupational schemes and personal pensions. He is completely independent and acts as an impartial adjudicator. His services are free and he has statutory power to enforce his decisions.

Personal pension transfers

A new system to deal with complaints about the sale of personal pensions to employees in company schemes got under way in Spring 1997. This requires almost all of the 520,000 investors identified to date to complete a new questionnaire about their company scheme and personal pension. This is vitally important. Investors who do not respond will be struck off the list and will not qualify for compensation. If you are concerned about the progress of your case, contact the PIA pension helpline.

Personal pensions complaints cover a wide area and fall under the remit of both the PIA and the Pensions Ombudsman. If in doubt write to OPAS or the PIA, both of which act as an unofficial sorting office for pensions complaints and will make sure your details go to the right place.

STOCKBROKER SERVICES

APCIMS represents well over 90 per cent of private client stockbrokers as well as an increasing number of other investment managers. Members have direct access to the stockmarket for buying and selling shares.

The directory of stockbrokers published by APCIMS provides a brief guide to the services offered by each firm and an indication of the minimum size of portfolio considered acceptable by the firm. The symbols used in the directory relate to the following services.

Dealing or 'execution only'

This service is designed for investors who do not require advice but who do need a stockbroker to buy and sell shares for them. There is no advice or management in this service so the costs of transactions generally are lower than with other services. Some stockbrokers specialise in this low cost, no frills service so if this is what you are after, look them up in the APCIMS directory under 'E'.

Those who want help from a stockbroker have several options. In each case you should be offered an initial interview without obligation.

Advisory

As the name implies, with an advisory service, you take the decisions based on your own ideas and the advice of your manager. Almost all firms of stockbrokers offer an advisory service.

In practice there are different types of advisory service. For example you may want a more limited service where the manager advises on the purchase, sale or retention of individual stocks but you do not necessarily have to reveal full details of your investments. Alternatively, you may want a more comprehensive service and be prepared to give your manager full details of all your investments. This enables the stockbroker to give advice on individual stocks, capital gains tax and provide regular valuations on your entire portfolio.

Unlike the discretionary service described below, the advisory manager will not take any investment action without your authority.

Advisory services are indicated by an 'A' in the APCIMS directory.

Discretionary

If you want your investment manager to make all the decisions for you and to simply get on with it without checking with you before each transaction then you are looking for a discretionary investment management service.

You do not lose control entirely however, since you and your manager will spend some time at the outset discussing your financial circumstances, your requirements and your investment views. This gives your manager a clear framework within which he must work. You might, for example, state that certain stocks within your portfolio should not be sold or that for ethical reasons you do not wish to invest in certain types of companies.

You will also keep up to date with changes in your portfolio as the manager will send you a contract note every time a transaction takes place and will also send you regular valuations.

Discretionary or portfolio management services are indicated by a 'P' in the directory.

Comprehensive financial planning

In addition to the core investment management services many stockbrokers offer a broader financial planning service. This can cover PEPs, ISAs, pensions, mortgages, life assurance, school fees, inheritance tax, cash and deposits, and tax exempt special savings schemes, among others. Many stockbrokers run their own PEPs and ISAs although you should consider whether you will receive as good a service from a stockbroker as a large institutional manager, given the huge research resources available to the latter.

Comprehensive financial planning is indicated by a 'C' in the directory.

Appendix 3

WHAT GOES INTO A WILL

Every will has slightly different wording, depending on personal circumstances and, to some extent, the particular style of the person drafting it. The notes explain the contents clause by clause.

The example follows a fairly typical sequence. First are the introductory clauses dealing with the appointment of executors and trustees together with a clause dealing with funeral arrangements. Next are the main provisions dealing with who is to receive money and other property from the estate and who are to be the guardians of any children. Finally, there are some administrative provisions. At the end are the signatures of the testator and witnesses.

The will is based on English law but the basic contents would be found, in a different form, in a will written under the laws of Scotland.

LAST WILL AND TESTAMENT

1 Revocation

I James Rogers of 23 Acacia Villas Willstone Wiltshire revoke all former wills and testamentary dispositions and declare this to be my last Will ('my Will')

2 Appointment of Executors

(a) I appoint my wife Jennifer Rogers to be the Executor and Trustee of this my Will but if she shall be unable or unwilling to act for any reason then I appoint Malcolm Rogers of 17 High Street Willstone Wiltshire and William Smith of 23 The Street Upper Willstone Wiltshire to be the Executors and Trustees of my Will

(b) 'my Executors' shall mean the executors or executor of my Will whether original or substituted

3 Funeral Directions

I wish my body to be cremated and the ashes scattered in the grounds of the Willstone Crematorium

4 Definition of My Estate

In my Will where the context so admits 'my Estate' shall mean:

(a) all my property of every kind wherever situate and

(b) all property of every kind wherever situate over which I have a general power of appointment and

(c) the money investments and property from time to time representing all such property

5 Administration of My Estate

My Executors shall hold my Estate upon trust

(a) as to investments or property other than money in their absolute discretion to sell call in or convert all or any such investments or property into money with power to postpone such sale calling in and conversion and to permit the same to remain as invested and upon trust as to money with a like discretion to invest the same in their names or under their control in any of the investments authorised by my Will or by law with power at the like discretion from time to time to vary or transpose any such investments for others so authorised

(b) to pay my debts funeral testamentary and administration expenses

(c) to give effect to legacies

6 Pecuniary Legacy

I give free of inheritance tax One Hundred Pounds (£100.00) to each of my Executors provided that they accept their appointment as Executors

7 Appointment of Guardians

I APPOINT Malcolm Rogers and Sarah Rogers both of 17 High Street, Willstone, Wiltshire to be the guardians of my minor children

8 Gifts of Residue

SUBJECT as above my Executors shall hold my Estate

(a) for my wife Jennifer Rogers absolutely if she shall survive me by twenty eight days but if this residuary gift shall fail for any reason then

(b) for such of my children as shall survive me and attain the age of twenty one years and if more than one in equal shares absolutely provided that

(c) if any child shall fail to attain a vested interest leaving issue who shall survive me and attain the age of twenty one years then such issue shall take the share of my Estate which such child would otherwise have taken

(d) if there shall be more than one of such issue they shall take in equal shares per stirpes but so that no one shall take a share if their parent is alive and takes a share

9 Executor's Powers

MY Executors shall in addition and without prejudice to all statutory powers have the powers and immunities set out in the Schedule provided that they shall not exercise any of their powers so as to conflict with the beneficial provisions of my Will

Testimonium and Attestation

SIGNED by me on the day of 19 as and for my last will and testament comprising 3 pages

____

Signature of testator

SIGNED by the testator in our presence and then by us all in his

	Witness 1	Witness 2
Signature:		
Full name:		
Address:		
Occupation:		

NOTES

Clause 1 This ensures that any earlier wills are revoked. Whilst the will says that it is the 'last Will' this does not mean that it cannot be revoked at a later date.

Clause 2 This appoints the executors and the trustees. The executrix in this case is Jennifer, James Rogers' wife, but if she is dead or incapable of acting as executrix for some reason the executors will be his brother and a close friend.

Clause 3 This sets out James's wishes for his funeral.

Clauses 4 and 5 These are administrative clauses. Clause 4 states that the will is to apply to all of James Rogers' property. Clause 5 sets out the Executors' duties to gather in all the assets, pay all the debts and expenses and distribute the balance in accordance with the will.

Clause 6 This clause makes a token gift called a 'pecuniary legacy' to the executors, if they accept their appointment.

Clause 7 This appoints the children's guardians. They are James's brother and sister-in-law. It is important to note that James has chosen people of near his own age to act rather than the grandparents. Also there is an independent joint trustee, William Smith, appointed under Clause 2, who is there to help James's brother look after the money matters. This is a useful safeguard to ensure that the children's interests are fully protected.

Clause 8 This is probably the most important clause in the will as it deals with the bulk of James's assets, ie the residue of the estate after the gift to the executors. In the first instance the residue will pass to Jennifer but the gift is conditional on her surviving for 28 days. Making the gift conditional in this way can have inheritance tax advantages, particularly if one spouse dies shortly after the other, perhaps as a result of the same accident. The 28-day period could be extended up to a maximum of six months but 28 days is long enough to cope with most situations without being so long that there is an undue delay in the administration of the estate.

The remainder of the clause deals with what happens in the event of Jennifer not surviving the 28-day period. If this does happen the estate will be held in trust for Jane and Michael, James's two children, until they attain the age of 21. In the event that either Jane or Michael dies before they reach 21, the result will depend on whether they have any children living at their death. If they have a living child at that time (ie if there are any grandchildren), that child will take the share that his parent would have received had he or she attained the age of 21 (this is what 'per stirpes' means, ie the share passes down through one branch of the family tree). If there are no grandchildren, the half share in the estate will pass to whichever of Jane and Michael survives the other.

Clause 9 Clause 9 gives the Executors some additional powers to enable them to administer the estate more easily and to ensure that the children are adequately provided for. For convenience these are contained in a separate schedule (not reproduced).

For the most part these clauses are standard and would include as a minimum:

(a) a power of investment so that the Executors are able to take advantage of the wide range of investment opportunities that exist.

(b) a power of 'maintenance and advancement' which allows the executors to pay out money to look after the children before they attain the age of 21, at which point they become entitled to the money absolutely. This is needed to ensure that, for example, the children's school fees can continue to be paid. There would also be other powers depending on the complexity of the will.

Attestation Clause This is the part of the will where James and the two witnesses have signed. The rules for witnessing wills are quite complicated and must be rigidly adhered to for the will to be valid. This is covered in more detail in 10.5.4.

INDEX

(All references are to paragraph number.)